THE FORTY-FIVE

T0382039

PRINCE CHARLES EDWARD

THE FORTY-FIVE

A NARRATIVE OF THE LAST
JACOBITE RISING

BY SEVERAL CONTEMPORARY HANDS

EDITED BY

CHARLES SANFORD TERRY
LITT.D. CANTAB.

BURNETT-FLETCHER PROFESSOR OF HISTORY
IN THE UNIVERSITY OF ABERDEEN

CAMBRIDGE
AT THE UNIVERSITY PRESS
1922

CAMBRIDGE
UNIVERSITY PRESS

University Printing House, Cambridge CB2 8BS, United Kingdom

Published in the United States of America by Cambridge University Press, New York

Cambridge University Press is part of the University of Cambridge.

It furthers the University's mission by disseminating knowledge in the pursuit of
education, learning and research at the highest international levels of excellence.

www.cambridge.org
Information on this title: www.cambridge.org/9781107425903

© Cambridge University Press 1922

This publication is in copyright. Subject to statutory exception
and to the provisions of relevant collective licensing agreements,
no reproduction of any part may take place without the written
permission of Cambridge University Press.

First published 1922
First paperback edition 2014

A catalogue record for this publication is available from the British Library

ISBN 978-1-107-42590-3 Paperback

Cambridge University Press has no responsibility for the persistence or accuracy of
URLs for external or third-party internet websites referred to in this publication,
and does not guarantee that any content on such websites is, or will remain, accurate
or appropriate.

PREFACE

MORE than twenty years ago, on the invitation of the late Professor York Powell, I contributed to the Series issued under the title of 'Scottish History from Contemporary Writers' a volume entitled *The Rising of* 1745: *With a Bibliography of Jacobite History* 1689–1788 (David Nutt: 1900). A second edition, with an enlarged Bibliography, was called for in 1903. The book has long been out of print and is now unobtainable, except through second-hand booksellers.

The present volume does not reprint the Bibliography, nor is it a reissue of its predecessor. In the interval between them the literature of the Forty-Five has been enriched by valuable contributions, in particular, Lord Elcho's Journal, the Woodhouselee MS, Dr Walter Biggar Blaikie's *Origins of the Forty-Five*, the Walsh MSS (including the log of the *Du Teillay*), Captain Colin's exhaustive monograph on the French preparations in 1744–5, and my own *Albemarle Papers*. I have reconstructed the narrative of the Rising in order to incorporate these new materials.

At the same time I have set myself to piece together these contemporary materials in such a manner that the narrative, uninterrupted by explanatory notes and paragraphs, reads connectedly, as though it were the work of a single pen. I venture to think it a reliable historical document of quite vivid reality.

PREFACE

At the beginning and end of the volume are provided a List of Authorities and a Table of Persons engaged in the Rising. This method appeared to be preferable to the employment of recurring footnotes.

I am indebted to Dr W. B. Blaikie for his Map of the Clans and for Sir Robert Strange's contemporary engraving of Prince Charles in 1745, and to the Hon. Evan Charteris for permission to reproduce Elcho's plans of the march to Derby and of Culloden.

C. S. T.

KING'S COLLEGE,
　　OLD ABERDEEN

CONTENTS

ILLUSTRATIONS

LIST OF AUTHORITIES

AND THE ABBREVIATIONS BY WHICH THEY ARE INDICATED

A. H. P.   *Historical Papers relating to the Jacobite Period,* 1699–1750. Edited by Colonel James Allardyce. 2 vols. Aberdeen: New Spalding Club. 1895, 96.

A. P.   *The Albemarle Papers. Being the Correspondence of William Anne, Second Earl of Albemarle, Commander-in-Chief in Scotland,* 1746–7. *With an Appendix of Letters from Andrew Fletcher, Lord Justice-Clerk, to the Duke of Newcastle,* 1746–8. Edited by Charles Sanford Terry. 2 vols. Aberdeen: New Spalding Club. 1902.

> The second Earl of Albemarle (1702–54) was present at Culloden and on August 23, 1746, was gazetted Commander-in-Chief in Scotland in Cumberland's room. He vacated it in March, 1747, and died suddenly at Paris in 1754. The volumes illuminate the civil and military administration of Scotland after Culloden.

B. I.   *Itinerary of Prince Charles Edward Stuart from his landing in Scotland July* 1745 *to his departure in September* 1746. *Compiled from* The Lyon in Mourning: *supplemented and corrected from other contemporary sources* by Walter Biggar Blaikie. Edinburgh: Scottish History Society. 1897.

> An exhaustive diary of the movements of the Prince, his army and his opponents in 1745–6. Contains valuable Appendices.

B. O.   *Origins of the 'Forty-Five and other papers relating to that Rising.* Edited by Walter Biggar Blaikie. Edinburgh: Scottish History Society. 1916.

> Contains John Murray of Broughton's account of the preliminaries (1742–4) of the Rising; Alexander Macbean's 'Memorial concerning the Highlands' (the author was minister of Inverness in 1745–6); Memoirs of the Rising as it affected Aberdeenshire and Banffshire; Captain Daniel's narrative of his service under Prince Charles in 1745–6; Neil Maceachain's narrative of the Prince's Highland wanderings; a short narrative of Ludovick Grant of Grant's conduct in the Rising; papers relating to proceedings in Urquhart; the accounts, letters, and orders of Walter Grossett, Collector of Customs at Alloa; narratives of the battles of Prestonpans, Falkirk, and Culloden, by Andrew Lumisden, Prince Charles' Private Secretary; and an account of proceedings in Ross and Sutherland.
> Captain Daniel, whose narrative is quoted in these pages, joined the Prince's

army in Lancashire and served throughout the Rising in Lord Balmerino's troop of Life Guards, of which Lord Elcho was colonel. His animus against Lord George Murray is evident, and probably arose from the fact that he enjoyed the patronage and friendship of the Duke of Perth, Lord George's less competent colleague. Of Daniel nothing is known beyond what he writes of himself.

C. *Louis XV et les Jacobites: le projet de débarquement en Angleterre de 1743–4.* By J. Colin. Paris: 1901.

C. P. *Culloden Papers: comprising an extensive and interesting correspondence from the year 1625 to 1748.* London: 1815.

    Mainly the correspondence of Lord President Duncan Forbes during the period of the two Risings.

E. J. *A short Account of the Affairs of Scotland in the years 1744, 1745, 1746, by David, Lord Elcho. Printed from the Original Manuscript at Gosford. With a Memoir and Annotations* by the Hon. Evan Charteris. Edinburgh: 1907.

    Lord Elcho, the eldest son of the 4th Earl of Wemyss, joined Charles at Gray's Mill, near Edinburgh, on September 16, 1745, served throughout the campaign, and escaped to France after Culloden. His narrative is tinged with strong bias against Charles and his Irish advisers. He died at Paris in 1787.

H. H. *The History of the Rebellion in the year 1745.* By John Home. London: 1802.

    John Home (1722–1808), author of *Douglas*, was educated at Edinburgh University and joined the volunteers called out to resist Charles' advance on Edinburgh in 1745. He was made prisoner at Falkirk and published his History of the Rebellion six years before his death. An Appendix contains documents of importance.

J. *Memoirs of the Rebellion in 1745 and 1746.* By the Chevalier de Johnstone. Translated from a French MS originally deposited in the Scots College at Paris. London: 1820.

    James Johnstone (1719–1800?) was the only son of an Edinburgh merchant. Educated in Jacobite principles, and by his sister's marriage allied to Lord Rollo, he joined Prince Charles at Perth in September, 1745, and was appointed aide-de-camp to Lord George Murray and subsequently assistant aide-de-camp to Prince Charles. He escaped to England after Culloden, and later to the Continent, and entered French service. His Memoirs were written, probably, between 1760 and 1770.

J. M. *Jacobite Memoirs of the Rebellion of 1745. Edited from the Manuscripts of the late Right Rev. Robert Forbes, Bishop of the Scottish Episcopal Church,* by Robert Chambers. Edinburgh: 1834.

The Bishop's MSS have been more thoroughly explored in the *Lyon in Mourning* (*infra*). The 1834 volume contains Lord George Murray's narrative of the Rising, with particular reference to his own actions in it.

L. M. *The Lyon in Mourning, or, A collection of speeches, letters, journals, etc., relative to the affairs of Prince Charles Edward Stuart by the Rev. Robert Forbes, A.M., Bishop of Ross and Caithness 1746–75.* Edited by Henry Paton. 3 vols. Edinburgh: Scottish History Society. 1895, 1895, 1896.

Robert Forbes (1708–75), the son of an Aberdeenshire schoolmaster, settled at Leith as an Episcopal minister in 1735. He was arrested on his way to join Prince Charles on September 7, 1745. Released in 1746, he was elected to the See of Ross and Caithness in 1762 and to that of Aberdeen five years later, though the Episcopal Synod disallowed the latter election. His collections, contained in ten MS volumes, were purchased by Robert Chambers, who bequeathed them to the Edinburgh Faculty of Advocates. The volumes are bound in sombre black leather: a deep black border surrounds each title-page, and the edges are blackened.

L. P. *The Lockhart Papers: containing Memoirs and Commentaries upon the Affairs of Scotland from 1702 to 1715, by George Lockhart, Esq., of Carnwath, his secret correspondence with the son of King James the Second from 1718 to 1728, and his other political writings; also Journals and Memoirs of the Young Pretender's Expedition in 1745, by Highland Officers in his Army.* 2 vols. London: 1817.

George Lockhart (1673–1731) was arrested during the '15 and in 1718 became the Chevalier de St George's confidential agent in Scotland.

M. B. M. *Memorials of John Murray of Broughton, sometime Secretary to Prince Charles Edward 1740–7.* Edited by Robert Fitzroy Bell. Edinburgh: Scottish History Society. 1898.

Born in 1715, John Murray acted from about 1740 as the official correspondent between the Scottish Jacobites and their titular sovereign at Rome. The first part of his Memorials details minutely their arrangements for Charles' descent in 1745. Part ii narrates the events of the Rising down to the retreat from Derby. Part iii describes Murray's movements after Culloden. Part iv consists of two letters dealing with the conduct of the Earl of Traquair in the Rising. Murray was not present at Culloden owing to illness and did not accompany Charles upon his flight. He set out to join him in Uist, however, but again fell ill and on June 27, 1746, was made prisoner at his sister's house in Peebleshire. He furnished evidence against Lord Lovat on the latter's trial in March, 1747, and, as 'Mr Evidence Murray,' was execrated by those he had till then zealously served. Pardoned in 1748, his Memorials were written as a vindication of his conduct about 1757. He died in 1777.

M. C. *Carlisle in* 1745: *authentic account of the occupation of Carlisle in* 1745. By George G. Mounsey. London and Carlisle: 1846.

M. K. *Narrative of Charles Prince of Wales' Expedition to Scotland in the year* 1745. By James Maxwell of Kirkconnell. Edinburgh: Maitland Club. 1841.

> The author was born in 1708 (?) and joined Prince Charles after the latter's occupation of Edinburgh. He served as Major of Elcho's troop of Life Guards and escaped with him to France after Culloden. There he wrote his Narrative. Returning to Scotland before 1755, he died at Kirkconnel in 1762. Apart from its prejudice regarding Murray of Broughton, the narrative exhibits a cautious reticence prompted by an evident intention to publish the MS.

R. *A compleat History of the Rebellion, from its first Rise, in* MDCCXLV, *To its total Suppression at the glorious Battle of Culloden, in April,* 1746. By James Ray. Bristol: 1750.

> Ray describes himself as a native of Whitehaven and a volunteer under the Duke of Cumberland, whom he joined at Stafford on December 5, 1745.

S. H. *A complete history of England, to the Treaty of Aix-la-Chapelle.* 11 vols. By Tobias George Smollett. London: 1758–60.

> Smollett, a grandson of the Whig provost of Dumbarton, and educated at Glasgow University, was twenty-four in the year of the Rising. He died in 1771.

S. M. *The Scots Magazine.* Vols. vii and viii. Edinburgh: 1745, '46.

> Follows the contemporary Rising in great detail, month by month, and has special articles upon its chief incidents.

W. M. *The Woodhouselee MS. A narrative of events in Edinburgh and district during the Jacobite occupation, September to November* 1745. Edited by A. Francis Steuart. London and Edinburgh: 1907.

> The author, a keen Whig and pious Presbyterian, is conjectured to have been Patrick Crichton, of Woodhouselee, a successful Edinburgh burgess about fifty-five years of age in 1745. He died in 1760.

W. P. *A Royalist Family, Irish and French* (1689–1789), *and Prince Charles Edward.* Translated by A. G. Murray Macgregor. Edinburgh: 1904.

> A translation of the Duc de Trémoille's *Une Famille Royaliste Irlandaise et Ecossaise et le Prince Charles Edouard* (1901). The book contains the Prince's correspondence with Anthony Walsh and the log of the *Du Teillay*.

CHAPTER I

THE HIGHLANDS

That[1] the story may be understood without the help of digressions, to explain and illustrate some circumstances concerning the Highlanders, which are not generally known, I shall introduce the subject by describing the country of the Highlands, and the manners of the Highlanders, who, when Charles Stuart landed amongst them, were essentially different from the other inhabitants of Britain....

A winding line from Dunbarton, upon the river Clyde, to Duninstra, upon the frith of Dornoch, separates the Highlands from the Lowlands. This line, beginning at Dunbarton, goes on by Crief and Dunkeld to Blairgowrie in Perthshire, from which it runs directly north to the forest of Morven, in the heights of Aberdeenshire: at Morven it proceeds still northwards to Carron in Banff-shire; from Carron it takes its course due west, by Tarnoway [Darnaway] in the shire of Murray, to the town of Nairne (in the small shire of that name); from Nairne the line is continued by Inverness to Conton [Contin], a few miles to the west of Dingwall in Rossshire: at Conton it turns again to the north-east, and goes on to Duninstra, upon the south side of the frith of Dornoch, where the line of separation ends, for the country to the north of the frith of Dornoch (that runs up between Rossshire and Sutherland) is altogether Highland, except a narrow stripe of land, between the hills and the German Ocean, which washes the east coast of Sutherland and Caithness. To the west of this line lie the Highlands and Islands, which make nearly one half of Scotland, but do not contain one eighth part of the inhabitants of that kingdom. The face of the country is wild, rugged, and desolate, as is well expressed by the epithets given to the mountains, which are called the grey, the red, the black, and the yellow mountains, from the

[1] *H. H.* 3.

colour of the stones of which in some places they seem to be wholly composed, or from the colour of the moss, which, in other places, covers them like a mantle.

In almost every strath, valley, glen, or bottom, glitters a stream or a lake; and numberless friths, or arms of the sea, indent themselves into the land. There are also many tracts of no small extent (which cannot properly be called either mountains or valleys) where the soil is extremely poor and barren, producing short heath, or coarse sour grass, which grows among the stones that abound every where in this rough country. Nor is the climate more benign than the soil: for the Highlands in general lying to the west, the humid atmosphere of that side of the island, and the height of the hills in such a northern latitude, occasion excessive rains, with fierce and frequent storms, which render the Highlands for a great part of the year a disagreeable abode to any man, unless it be his native country.

The[1] inhabitants of the lands adjoining to the mountains...in the shires of Perth, Forfar, Kincardine, Aberdeen, Banff, and Murray, where some sort of Industry has prevailed, and where the soil is tolerable, have for many years left off the Highland dress, have lost the Irish language, and have discontinued the use of Weapons; the consequence whereof is, that they cannot be considered as dangerous to the Public peace, and that the laws have their course amongst them.

The inhabitants of the mountains, unacquainted with industry and the fruits of it, and united in some degree by the singularity of dress and language, stick close to their antient idle way of life; retain their barbarous customs and maxims; depend generally on their Chiefs, as their sovereign Lords and masters; and being accustomed to the use of Arms, and inured to hard living, are dangerous to the public peace; and must continue to be so, untill, being deprived of Arms for some years, they forget the use of them.

From Perth to Inverness, which is above 100 measured miles, and from thence to the Western Sea, including the Western

[1] *C. P.* 298. From a Memorandum by Lord President Duncan Forbes, written perhaps in 1746.

Islands, there is no Town or Village, of any consequence, that could be the Seat of any Court of Justice the least considerable, except Dunkeld, which is within 10 computed miles of Perth; neither is there any sort of Inn or Accommodation for travellers, excepting a few that have been built on the King's Roads made by Marshall Wade. Of this large tract of land, no part is in any degree cultivated, except some spots here and there in Straths or Glens, by the sides of Rivers, brooks, or lakes, and on the Sea Coast and Western Islands. The Grounds that are cultivated yield small quantities of mean Corns, not sufficient to feed the Inhabitants, who depend for their nourishment on milk, butter, cheese, &c., the product of their Cattle. Their constant residence during the harvest, winter, and spring, is at their small farms, in houses made of turf; the roof, which is thatched, supported by timber. In the summer season, they drive their flocks and herds many miles higher amongst the mountains, where they have large ranges of coarse pasture. The whole family follow the Cattle; the men to guard them, and to prevent their straying; the women to milk them, and to look after the butter and cheese, &c. The places in which they reside when thus employed they call sheolings, and their habitations are the most miserable huts that ever were seen.

A Highland Clan is a set of men all bearing the same sirname, and believing themselves to be related the one to the other, and to be descended from the same common Stock. In each Clan, there are several subaltern tribes, who own their dependance on their own immediate Chief; but all agree in owing allegiance to the Supreme Chief of the Clan or Kindred, and look upon it to be their duty to support him at all adventures....

As those Clans or Kindreds live by themselves, and possess different Straths, Glens, or districts, without any considerable mixture of Strangers, it has been for a great many years impracticable (and hardly thought safe to try it) to give the Law its course amongst the mountains. It required no small degree of Courage, and a greater degree of power than men are generally possessed of, to arrest an offender or a debtor in the midst of his Clan. And for this reason it was, that the Crown, in former times, was obliged to put Sheriffships, and other Jurisdictions, in the hands of powerful families in the Highlands, who by their respective Clans and followings could give execution to the Laws within their several territories, and frequently did so at the expence of considerable bloodshed....

The description of the Highlands already given shows why, whilst the rest of the Country is generally improving, they continue the prey of their accustomed sloth and barbarity. The Want of Roads, excepting the King's Roads already mentioned, the Want of Accommodation, the supposed ferocity of the inhabitants, and the difference of language, have proved hitherto a bar to all free intercourse between the high and the low lands, and have left the Highlanders in possession of their own idle customs and extravagant maxims, absolute strangers to the advantages that must accrue from Industry, and to the blessing of having those advantages protected by Laws.

I[1] now proceed to Narrate the Highland followings and dependances, beginning in the South at Argyll-Shire.

CAMPBELLS. The Duke of Argyll is their Chieften, and...can raise out of his own property, Small Vassals, and Kinsmen Lands, 3000 Men, The Earl of Broadalbine more than 1000, and the many Great Barrons, Such as Auchinbreck, Ardkindloss, Lochnell, &c., &c., at least Another 1000. So that that Clan Could bring to the field above 5000 Men, besides a Vast many Barrons and Gentlemen, not only out of Argyll, but out of Dumbarton, Streoling [Stirling], and Perth Shires, and are at present the Richest and Most Numerous Clan in Scotland....

MACKLEANS. Sir Hector Macklean is their Chieften, and... [his] was a verry potent Clan About 200 years Agone, and Could have raised above 800 men, but now that the familie of Argyll are possessed of their Chieften's Estate, they will hardly make 500, and even Many of these brought out of the Duke's Lands.

MACKLACHLEN. The Laird of Macklachlen is the Chief [and] can raise 200 Men.

---

[1] *A. H. P.* i, 167. From a 'Memoriall anent the true state of the Highlands,' ascribed to Lord President Duncan Forbes.

STEWART OF APPIN. The Laird of Appin is the Chief; he holds his Lands of the Crown, and can raise 300 Men.

McDOUGALS OF LORN. Their Chieften [is] the Laird of Mackdougall, and...was a more potent familie of old, but now much Diminished by the Campbells, and Can (I believe) Still bring out 200 Men.

Proceeding Northward by the Coast and Isles.

MACKDONALD OF SLATE. Sir Alexander Mackdonald is their Chief....He has a very Considerable Estate which holds all of the Crown, and lyes in the Isles of Sky and Uist and can bring out 700 Men.

MACKDONALD OF CLANRONALD. The Chieften is Called...in English, Captain of Clanronald; he has a Very handsome estate; holds most of it of the Crown, which lyes in Moidart and Arisack [Arisaig] on the Continent, and in the Isles of Uist, Benbecula, Can[n]a, Rum, &c. He brings out 700 Men.

MACKDONALD OF GLENGARY. The Laird of Glengary is their Chief, who...has a pretty good estate all holden of the Crown, which lyes in the Countreys of Glengary and Knoidart, both on the Continent, and Can bring out 500 Men.

MACKDONALD OF KEPOCH. Kepoch is their Chieften...[but] is not so much as a Propriatar of one furr of Land, but only Tacksmen and tennants...in the most part of their possessions to the Laird of Mackintosh, and the remaining part to the Duke of Gordon, All lying in Lochaber. He can raise and bring out 150 men.

MACKDONALD OF GLENCO. The Laird of Glenco is their Chief...but a very small propriatar. He holds his lands of Stewart of Apin, and Can raise 150 Men....

CAMERONS. A very potent Clan in Lochaber. The Laird of Lochiel is their Chief, who...has a good Competent estate, but none of it holden of the Crown. The most of it is of the Duke of Argyll, and the remainder of the Duke of Gordon. He can bring out 800 Men....

MACKLEODS. Were Two distinct and both very potent families of Old, Viz. Mackleod of Lew[i]s and Mackleod of Harris; both thought to be of Danish Extraction, But the former is Utterly Extinct, and their Lands purchased and possessed by the

THE HIGHLANDS

Mackenzies. The now only Laird of Mackleod is their Chieften and...has a very Considerable Fortune all holden of the Crown, lying in Glenelg on the Continent, and in the Isles of Sky and Harris, &c., &c. He can raise and bring out 700 Men.

MACKINNONS. The Laird of Mackinnon is their Chief, who ...holds his Lands of the Crown both in the Isles of Sky and Mull, and Can raise 200 Men.

I pass now again to the South to give Account of the Inland Chieftens, beginning again at Argyle Shire, and from thence proceeding Northward.

There are Severalls of Qualitie...who have the Command of Severall Highlanders in the Countreys of Argyll, Monteith, Dumbarton, Streoling, and Perth Shires...whom I freely pass over, Since for Some Considerable time they have given No disturbance by Armaments or Convocations.

DUKE OF PERTH. Is no Claned familie, although the head of a Considerable Number of Barrons and Gentlemen of the Name of Drummond in the Low Countreys. He is brought in here Allennarly Upon account of his command of about 300 Highlanders in Glenertonie [Glenartney] and Neighbourhood.

ROBERTSONS. The Laird of Strowan [Struan] is their Chief.... His Lands holds of the Crown and lye in Roinach [Rannoch] and Brae of Atholl. He can raise on his own Estate about 200 Men. There are near 500 More Robertsons in Atholl who Seldom or Never follow their Said Chief, being a part of the following of the Duke of Atholl after Named.

MENZIESE'S. Sir Robert Menzies of Weem is the Chieften, and ...has a very handsome Estate all holden of the Crown, Lying in Apenedull [Strath Appin] and Roinach, and can raise 300 Men.

STEWART OF CAIRNTULLIE [Grantully]. Is no Chieften, but has an handsome Estate in Strathbran and Strathtey, all holden of the Crown, out of which he can raise 200 Men.

CLAN GREGORE. Are a people very Remarkable for wicked Achievements....So that they are at present Disguised Under the Severall Names[1] of Campbells, Graham, Murray, and Drummond, &c., and Dispersed thorrow Dumbarton, Streoling, and

[1] The prohibition of their name dated from 1603.

Perthshires. They...can raise among them 500 Men, and Are rarely Absent from any Great Convocation, whatever the Quarrell may be, Since plunder and Booty is their Bussiness.

DUKE OF ATHOLL. He is no Claned familie...but is deservedly placed here upon the Account of his extensive following of About 3000 Highlanders, a Good Many of them out of his own property, but most of them Upon the Account of Vast Superiorities in Glenamond, Glenlyon, Balquhidder, Strathtay, Atholl, Bishopruk of Dunkeld, Strathardel, and Glenshee.

Crossing the Grampians we come to Marr.

FARQUHARSONS. The only Claned familie in Marr, or Aberdeenshire, Are the Farquharsons....They Can bring out 500 Men. The Laird of Invercald is their Chief....

DUKE OF GORDON. Is no Claned familie, Although a Chieften of a Very Considerable and powerfull Name in the Low countries....His extensive Superiorities and Jurisdictions in the Highlands, Viz. in Badenoch and Lochaber, does not yield him Any followers....

GRANTS. A Considerable Name and familie in Strathspey. The Laird of Grant is their Chief....He can raise out of Strathspey 700 Men, and out of Urquhart 150....

MCINTOSHES. This was one of the most potent Clans in Scotland...but the Cammerons having purchased most of Said estate has much Diminished their power. The Laird of Mackintosh is their Chief...[and] he can bring out 800 Men, Including the Small Neighbouring familis of Mackgillivray, Mackqueen, Mackbain, &c., &c., who all own themselves his Kinsmen. His Countreys are Brae Lochabar, Badenoch, Strathern, and Strathnern....

MCPHERSONS. Their Chief is the Laird of Clunie. He can bring out 300 Men. His whole Lands, and all his Kinsmens lands, are holden of the Duke of Gordon and lye in Badenoch.

FRAZERS. Are a Considerable Clan in the Countreys of Aird and Stratharrigg [Stratherrick]. Their Chieften is Lord Lovat ...[who] has a very Considerable estate all holden of the Crown, and Can raise 700 Men. He has a good Number of Barrons of his Name, All in Inverness Shire.

GLENMORISTON GRANT. Is no Chieften, neither does he ever

follow any. He brings out 100 Men. His lands are holden of the
Crown, and does frequently in Armaments Join with McDonald
of Glengary.

CHISOLMS. Their Chieften is Chisholm of Straglass...[who]
holds his Land of the Crown and Can bring out 200 Men.

McKENZIES. One of the Most Considerable Clans Under one
head (next to the Campbells) in the Nation. The Earl of Seaforth
was, and Now Lord Fortrose is their Chief....He out of his
Countreys of Kintaile, Lochelsh [Loch Alsh], Lochbroon [Loch
Broom], and Lochcaron [Loch Carron] on the Continent, and
in the Isles of Lew[i]s, &c., Can raise 1000 Men, which is all
he can Command. The Earl of Cromartie, with 8 or 9 Barrons
of the Name and an Number of Smaller Gentlemen, can amongst
them raise 1000 More, but are not Much Inclined to follow
their Chief. Neither are they in Use or Very Apt to Armaments
in that Countrey of Ross, &c., [and] of late they are much come
in to Independancy.

MONROES. Sir Hary Monroe of Foules is their Chief. His
lands are holden of the Crown, and Can raise 300 Men.

ROSSES. Lord Ross is their Chief. His Lands hold of the
Crown, and Can raise 300 Men.

SUTHERLANDS. The Earl of Sutherland is their Chief. Can
raise 700 Men.

MACKAYS. The Lord Rae is their Chief. His Estate lyes in
Strathnaver, and he can raise 500 Men.

SINKLAIRS. The Earl of Cait[h]ness is their chief and Could
raise 500 Men, but his Estate being Mostly gone, both it and the
followings are now in the hands of Sincklairs of Dunbeth and
Ulpster, &c....

Ye have Now all the power of the Armed Highlanders att one
View, which ye may perceive to be above 20 Thousand, A
Sufficient force to have Conquered All the rest of the Scottish
Nation, if they had a mind, and Could but have agreed how to
Divide the Booty, and Consequently a force that was Capable,
when United, to Disturb the peace of the whole United Island
at their pleasure, and Might at last, with but a small Conjunction
of foreigners, have endangered the totall overthrow of our Happy
Constitution.

All[1] kinds of fire-arms are directly at variance with the natural disposition of the Highlanders, who are quick, ardent, and impetuous in their attack. The sword is the weapon which suits them best. When they are kept passive they lose their ardour.... Their manner of fighting is adapted for brave, but undisciplined men. They advance with rapidity, discharge their pieces when within musket-length of the enemy, and then, throwing them down, draw their swords, and holding a dirk in their left hand with their target, they dart with fury on the enemy, through the smoke of their fire. When within reach of the enemy's bayonets, bending their left knee, they, by their attitude, cover their bodies with their targets, that receive the thrusts of the bayonets, which they contrive to parry, while at the same time they raise their sword-arm, and strike their adversary. Having once got within the bayonets, and into the ranks of the enemy, the soldiers have no longer any means of defending themselves, the fate of the battle is decided in an instant, and the carnage follows; the Highlanders bringing down two men at a time, one with their dirk in the left hand, and another with the sword.

The reason assigned by the Highlanders for their custom of throwing their muskets on the ground is not without its force. They say, they embarrass them in their operations, even when slung behind them, and, on gaining a battle, they can pick them up again along with the arms of their enemies; but, if they should be beaten, they have no occasion for muskets. They proved that bravery may supply the place of discipline at times, as discipline supplies the place of bravery. Their attack is so terrible, that the best troops in Europe would with difficulty sustain the first shock of it; and if the swords of the Highlanders once come in contact with them, their defeat is inevitable[2].

Troublesome[3] neighbours, no doubt, [the Highlanders] were ...but not at all formidable enemies to the government of Scotland, as long as England and Scotland were separate kingdoms, and under different sovereigns; for...the Lowlanders...accustomed to contend with the English, and armed and appointed like

[1] *J.* 85.
[2] Cf. an army order in Scott, *Tales of a Grandfather*, chap. lxxxi.
[3] *H. H.* 12.

warriors against whom they fought, were...superior to the Highlanders....But when James the Sixth succeeded to the crown of
England [1603]...the English and the Scots (that is, the Lowlanders of Scotland) at once laid down their arms....The untasted
pleasures of peace were delicious to both nations....The militia
was totally neglected....

Meanwhile the Highlanders continued to be the same sort of
people that they had been in former times: Clanship flourished,
depredation and petty war never ceased: then it was that the
Highlanders became superior to the Lowlanders in arms.

The alteration of circumstances, which produced so great a
change, does not seem to have been much attended to, nor its
effects foreseen, but by the Marquis of Montrose, who...made
his way through the Low Country of Scotland to the Highlands,
where he erected the king's standard [1644]....

The victories of Montrose raised the reputation of the Highlanders, and fixed them in the interest of the family of Stuart, to
which they were naturally well inclined; for, ignorant and care-
less of the disputes, civil and religious, which occasioned the war,
Charles the First appeared to them in the light of an injured
chief.

At the Restoration [1660], the Highlanders, who had given
such proofs of their loyalty to Charles the First, were in great
favour with his sons Charles and James the Second, who looked
upon them as the firmest friends of monarchy, and confided in
them so much, that...Highlanders were...employed as a body of
troops [1678] to enforce the laws against the Covenanters.

Soon after the Revolution [1689], the Highlanders took arms
against the government of King William. They were commanded by the Viscount Dundee; and, at the battle of Killie-
crankie, defeated the king's army, which was greatly superior to
them in number....

From the year 1689, the Highlanders kept a constant correspondence with James the Second as long as he lived, entreating
him to procure from the king of France a body of troops to
invade Britain; and engaging to support the invasion by an
insurrection.

After the death of James [1701], they continued their correspondence with his son[1] at St Germain's, at Avignon, at Rome, or wherever he was....

At the accession of the family of Hanover [1714], the Highlanders took arms against the parliamentary settlement of the crown, though no French troops came to their assistance.

Louis the Fourteenth was dead [1715] before the Earl of Mar erected his standard in the Highlands; and the Duke of Orleans, regent of France, never intended to do any thing in favour of the Pretender's cause.

Notwithstanding these disappointments, the Earl of Mar was joined by so many fighting men, that the army he commanded at the battle of Sheriffmuir [1715] was greatly superior to the royal army; but the...battle of Sheriffmuir was a drawn battle, for the number of the slain was nearly equal on both sides; and both generals claimed the victory.

This rebellion...was very soon followed by another, which was part of a plan to restore the family of Stuart, formed by Cardinal Alberoni, minister of Spain. In the year 1719, the king of Spain...equipped a fleet....While this armament (destined to invade England under the command of the Duke of Ormond) was preparing at Cadiz, the Marquis of Tullibardin[2], the Earls of Seaforth and Mareschal...landed in the island of Lewes... [with] 300 Spanish soldiers, some ammunition, arms, and a sum of money. The Marquis of Tullibardin and his associates remained at the island of Lewes, corresponding with the disaffected chiefs in the Highlands, and engaging them to take arms when the Duke of Ormond with his troops should land in England. But the Duke of Ormond never did land in England; for the Spanish fleet, having sailed from Cadiz, met with a violent storm off Cape Finisterre, which dispersed them completely. Meanwhile, the Marquis of Tullibardin...left the Island of Lewes with the 300 Spaniards, and came over to the main land of Scotland; but...General Wightman (commander in chief for Scotland)...coming up with the enemy at Glenshiel (between Fort Augustus and Bernera), he attacked them immediately. The

[1] James Francis Edward Stewart, Chevalier de St George.
[2] The Jacobite Duke of Atholl of the '45.

engagement, if it may be called so, was a very short one. The Highlanders, favoured by the ground, withdrew to the Hills, without having suffered much. The Spaniards laid down their arms, and were made prisoners.

Such had been the state of the Highlands, and the attachment of the greater and more warlike part of the Highlanders to the family of Stuart, from the reign of Charles the First, to that of George the Second.

CHAPTER II

GLENFINNAN

War[1] having been declared against Spain, in the year 1739, some of the most zealous Jacobites met at Edinburgh, in the beginning of the year 1740; and, concluding that the Spanish war would certainly bring on a war with France, they framed an Association, engaging themselves to take arms, and venture their lives and fortunes to restore the family of Stuart, provided that the king of France would send over a body of troops to their assistance. This Association...was delivered to [William] Drummond [or Macgregor] of Bochaldy [Balhaldie]...to be carried to the [Old] Pretender at Rome, whom they entreated to procure assistance from France. Besides the Association, Drummond carried with him a list of those chiefs and chieftains, who, the subscribers thought, were willing and ready to join them, if a body of French troops should land in Britain.

With these papers Drummond went to Rome, where the Pretender lived; for by an article of the Treaty of peace made at Utrecht [1713], he had been obliged to quit the dominions of France; and, leaving St Germain's, went to Bar in Lorraine, from that to Avignon, and at last to Rome. The Pretender, having examined the papers, thought the project practicable and well-timed; for the clamour against the government of George the Second, conducted by Sir Robert Walpole, resounded through Europe, and foreigners mistook the outcry of faction and party rage for the voice of disaffection and revolt. To the Pretender and his adherents at Rome, who were very willing to believe what they wished, Britain seemed ripe for another revolution; and the papers brought from Scotland by Drummond were immediately forwarded by the same messenger to Cardinal Fleury at Paris, with the Pretender's approbation of the plan, and a

[1] *H. H.* 24.

request that his Eminence would grant the assistance required. The French minister thought it sufficient to promise that the assistance required should be granted as soon as the undertakers for an insurrection could show a reasonable prospect of success.

During this correspondence, before any thing was settled with Cardinal Fleury, a general war broke out in Europe at the death [in 1740] of Charles the Sixth, Emperor of Germany, the last of the male line of the House of Austria....The House of Austria, divested of the imperial dignity, was attacked in every part of her hereditary dominions by a powerful combination of princes, which she could not have resisted long, if Great Britain, at war with Spain, and upon very ambiguous terms with France, had not interposed in this great quarrel with her money and her arms. The British subsidies had begun to operate with effect in Germany; the British troops were preparing to embark for the Continent, and some foreign troops in British pay had marched to join the Austrian army, when the minister of France, finding that the designs of his court were counteracted every where by this zealous ally of the House of Austria, resolved to call the attention of George the Second and his ministers to their own affairs, by reviving the pretensions of the Stuart family to the crown of Britain.

In the beginning of the month of February, 1742, Drummond of Bochaldy, formerly mentioned, came privately to Edinburgh, where he...assured the members of the concert, that he had been exceedingly well received by Cardinal Fleury, who expressed much satisfaction with the contents of the papers from Scotland, and had the Pretender's interest so much at heart that, provided he had the same assurances from the friends of the Stuart family in England, he would send over an army of 13,000 men, of whom 1500 were to be landed in the West Highlands of Scotland, near Fort William, and 1500 on the East coast at Inverness; while the main body, consisting of 10,000 men, under the command of Marshal Saxe, should land with Charles Stuart, the Pretender's eldest son, as near London as possible....

To be certain how matters stood, [John] Murray of Broughton, a member of the concert, was prevailed upon to go to Paris, and learn from the cardinal himself, what he really intended, and what the friends of the Stuart family were to expect from the court of France.

In the beginning of the month of January [1743], Murray left Edinburgh, and on his way to Paris heard that Cardinal Fleury was dead [January, 1743]. This piece of intelligence, he thought, made it still more necessary for him to proceed.

When Murray arrived at Paris, he had an audience of Monsieur Amelot, secretary for foreign affairs, who told him that Cardinal Fleury had delivered to him all the papers relating to the Pretender's business, and had recommended to his successor, Cardinal de Tencin, the execution of his design to restore the family of Stuart: that the king of France...had the interest of the Stuart family as much at heart as any of those gentlemen who had signed the Association; and, as soon as an opportunity offered, would certainly put the scheme in execution.

Murray returned immediately to Scotland, and gave his friends an account of the conversation which he had with Monsieur Amelot, whose assurances of the king of France's intention to execute the plan of invasion proved very soon to be true.

James Francis Stewart to Louis XV

De[1] Rome, ce 23 décembre
1743

Monsieur mon frère et cousin,

Le sieur Mac Gregor [Balhaldie] est arrivé ici mardi passé [December 17] et m'a communiqué les résolutions et les intentions de Votre Majesté selon qu'il en était chargé, et dont le récit m'a pénétré de si vifs sentiments de reconnaissance et d'attachement envers Elle, que les paroles ne sauraient jamais lui en faire connaître toute l'etendue. J'avoue ingénuement à Votre Majesté que mon premier mouvement était de différer le départ de mon fils jusqu'à ce que j'aie pu recevoir des ordres et des instructions plus précis de sa part, puis, en faisant réflexion sur la probité de M. Mac Gregor et aux éminentes vertus de Votre Majesté, j'ai cru que je pouvais, en cette occasion, passer par-dessus les règles ordinaires sans risquer sa désapprobation en aucun cas qui pourrait arriver dans sa suite, de sorte qu'à la fin je me suis déterminé de ne pas contraindre l'ardeur et la vivacité de mon fils pour aller où

[1] *C.* 36.

son devoir, son honneur, et Votre Majesté l'appellent....Il partira donc, en conformité de ce que M. Mac Gregor a rapporté, vers le 12 du mois prochain, et, en attendant, ce dernier part demain avec les manifestes et les autres papiers nécessaires, pour les remettre entre les mains de M. d'Amelot.

In[1] [January 1744] the Chevaliers Eldest son left Rome incognito and came to Genova [Genoa]. From thence he embark'd aboard of a filucque for Antibes, and...came to Paris, & Lodged at Lord Semples, in the month of January 1744. He was a fortnight at Lord Semples before it was known. At the end of that time Lord Semple Came & invited the Earl Marischall & Lord Elcho, who were then at Paris, to Come and see him. They went seperately. He told them that the King of France was to send him over to England from Dunkirk at the head of 12,000 men, that there was to be a fleet to Sail from Brest to support that Embarkation, and that he was to land in the river Thames as near London as they Could....He desired the Earl Marischall and Lord Elcho to get ready and told them that he was to sett out for the sea coast in a Short time....

The Prince left Paris in the Beginning of Febrewary 1744 and went to Graveline, where he remained incognito with his secretary Bakaldie untill the Embarkation was laid aside. About the End of the same month the troops who were to Embark assembled at Dunkirk, and the Comte de Saxe, who was to Command them, arrived with the General officers under his Command. There were large Ships gott together in the road into which the troops were to be putt, by means of Bilanders which lay in the harbour. About the Beginning of March they Embarked the Duke D'Antin and the Prince of Monaco with their Regiments. Mons[r] de Roqufeuille, who Commanded the Brest Squadron, Came into the Channel & sent Mons[r] de Barailh with four men of war to protect the Embarkation, and Sir John Norris Came with a large English Squadron into the downs.

The Embarkation went on but Slowly upon account of the distance of the Ships from the harbour; and when their was about

[1] E. J. 229.

6000 men embark'd, their came on a violent Storm which putt a stop to the Embarkation, and as the Storm continued for 15 days it drove most of the Ships with the troops Ashoare and a great Many men were drownded. During the Storm Monsieur de Rocquefeuille came into Dungeness Bay: Sir John Norris Stood into the Bay to him, but the Badness of the weather prevented their engadging, and Seperated them. Monsr de Rocquefieulle died in Dungeness Bay of an Apoplecthick fitt, & his Squadron returned to Brest. Sir John Norris return'd to the Downs, and the French gave up their Embarkation....

So soon as the Embarkation was over, the French declared War Against The King of England, Elector of Hanover (as they termed it)...in the End of March 1744.

In[1] the beginning of June [1744]...being very uneasy to think we had received no accounts from Abroad, I said if I could afford the expence I would go over on pretence of seeing the Army in flanders and so see the Prince myself and learn distinctly what situation things were in....About this time came a letter from Lord Semple to Lord T[ra]q[uai]r by way of an account of their procedure in the Spring which...was so little to our satisfaction that my Lord still thought my going over more necessary than before.

On[2] the 7th of July, 1744, [Murray] sat out for London... and proceeded to Paris....Upon his arrival at Paris, [he] went to [Æneas] M^cdonald's, a Banker, where the Pretender then was; the next day [he] was introduced to the Pretender by Sempil and Drummond [of Balhaldie], and told him the occasion of his being sent to France. The Pretender assured him that the French had been serious in the Invasion, which had been disappointed by the Weather and other accidents; that he, the Pretender, had the strongest assurances from the French King and his Ministers that it would be put into execution that Harvest.

Having desired to see the Pretender alone...[Murray] represented to him that his Friends in Scotland were dissatisfied with

[1] B. O. 53. From Murray of Broughton's narrative of the preliminaries of the '45.

[2] M. B. M. 426. From Murray's statement, August 13, 1746, made while a prisoner in the Tower.

the Letters sent from Drummond and Sempil, and doubted whether the French were in earnest to support him. To which the Pretender answered that he was well assured of their good Intentions...[and] was determined to come over into this Kingdom if he brought only a single Footman...[He] asked [Murray] how many men...might join him. To which [Murray] said that at the most he thought there would not be above 4 or 5000, even if all those who were looked upon to be the most attached to his Family should appear for him.

Mr Murray[1] returned from France in October 1744, and gave out, in all the meetings he had with the Princes friends, that the Prince told him he would certainly be in Scotland next Summer whether the King of France assisted him or not. Most of the Gentlemen of that party look'd upon it as a mad project and were utterly against it....There were likewise some gentlemen, who were against his Coming, used in their Conversations to Say that they would do all they could to prevent his Coming, but if he did come & persisted in Staying, they believed they could not hinder themselves from joining in his fortune....

In the Beginning of this year [1745] the Prince sent several Commissions to Mr Murray to be distributed amongst his friends in Scotland, which were all signed by himself, as his Father had made him Regent of the three Kingdoms; and in June Sir Hector Maclean [of Duart] arrived with letters from the Prince, wherein he told he would be in Scotland in June. He beg'd his friends in the Highlands to be in readyness to receive him, & desired if possible all the Castles & fortresses's in Scotland might be taken before his arrival. Every body was vastly alarm'd at this news, & were determined when he came to endeavour all in their power to prevail upon him to go back; and the Gentlemen of the party then at Edinburgh sent Mr Murray to the Highlands to lett the Prince know their sentiments, but upon his not Coming all the month of June, Mr Murray return'd to the Lowlands[2].

In the Month of June 1745 The Prince Sett out from [the

[1] E. J. 234.

[2] In his *Memorials*, 137, Murray declares that he went to encourage the Highlands, whom the arrest of Sir Hector Maclean on his arrival in Scotland might discourage.

Château de] Navare, a Country house of [his cousin] the Duc de Bullions [Bouillon], Attended by the Duke of Athole [William Murray, Marquess of Tullibardine], Sir Thomas Sheridan, his old Governor, Sir John Macdonald, a Captain in the Carabineers, M^r O'Sulivan, who was Marèchal Maillebois's aid du camp in the wars of Corsica, M^r [George] Kelly, [a Nonjuror] who had been a prisoner in the tower of London, M^r [Francis] Strickland, who had been about his Father, M^r [Æneas] Macdonald, Banker at Paris[1], & Mr Buchanan[2], that came with him from Rome. From Navare he went to Nantes, where he met with M^r [Anthony] Welch [Walsh], a rich Irish merchant, who had prepared a little vessell[3] of 14 Guns for him, & aboard of which the Prince embark'd [June 21] at a Villadge call'd la Vraix Croix, a little below Pleinbeuf at the Embouchure of The Loire....The Prince had on board with him 4000 Lewis d'ors, 1000 Guns[4], and Eighteen hundred broadswords, which he had bought with his own money. He was detained by Contrary winds a week at Bell'isle, where he was join'd by the *Elizabeth*, a 60 gun Ship Commanded by Captain d'O & fitted out for a Cruize by M^r [Walter] Rutlidge, an Irish Merchant at Dunkirk, who had given the Captain orders to Escort the Prince to Scotland. They Sail'd from Bellisle the [4] of July[5].

They[6] had not been above five or six days at sea, till one evening the *Lyon* ship of war appeared, and came pretty near them, and then disappeared. Next morning she came again in view and disappeared. She continued to do so three or four times, and the last time of her appearing she came within a mile of so of them.

[1] These are the 'Seven Men of Moidart.'
[2] He lived in Æneas Macdonald's house and was employed as a Jacobite messenger between England and France.
[3] The vessel was named the *Du Teillay* after the Commissary of Marine of that name at Nantes. The name is also spelled *Dutillet* and *Doutelle*.
[4] Charles himself calls them 'fusees,' i.e. muskets.
[5] July 15 New Style.
[6] *L. M.* i, 202. From a journal chiefly based on conversations with Duncan Cameron, of Barra.

We[1] perceived that they were pursuing us, and coming obliquely upon us. Seeing the said ships nearing us, we spoke M. Dau [d'O], commander of the *Elizabeth*, and prepared for battle at noon [on July 9]. The said vessel was to the E. at a distance of a league and a half, with all sails set to overtake us. We recognised it as a ship with two and a half batteries, suspected to be English. Being prepared for battle, and the Chaplain having given absolution, Monsieur d'O and I approached to speak to each other. M. d'O told me he was going to furl his lower sails. Monsieur [Anthony] Walsh, in agreement with the Prince, told me to wait an hour and continue our route. In which M. d'O acquiesced, and we agreed with the said d'O that if we were obliged to fight, as soon as he had fired his first round, we should board [the *Elizabeth*], and as soon as he was in grips with the English ship, to board it also and put fifty men on board. This is what we agreed upon at 2 o'clock in the afternoon.

Seeing that the English ship was always drawing nearer, M. d'O furled his lower sails, put his long boat to sea, and lay to. We saw that [the enemy] only wanted to make us to lose way, to give time for the [other] ships we had seen in the morning to come up. We agreed to hoist sail and to continue our route, which we did. The English ship, seeing this, and sailing always better than we, hoisted sail also and sent his long boat out to gain greater advantage over us, and have more room on deck. At half past 5 in the evening the English ship was on the beam of the *Elizabeth*. We all furled our lower sails. The English commander fired from his port guns. M. d'O answered with all his starboard guns. The Englishman, being to windward of the *Elizabeth*, hauled down his mizzen and hoisted his jib. The *Elizabeth* having delayed a little in executing the same manoeuvre, the Englishman had time to pass forward, and contrived so well that he fired all his port volley, which raked the *Elizabeth* fore and aft, and must have killed many and done her great damage, so that the Englishman got between our two ships, and fired from his starboard guns three shots, which passed between my masts; my sails were riddled with his small shot, so much so that we did

[1] *W. P.* 19. From the captain of the *Du Teillay's* log-book.

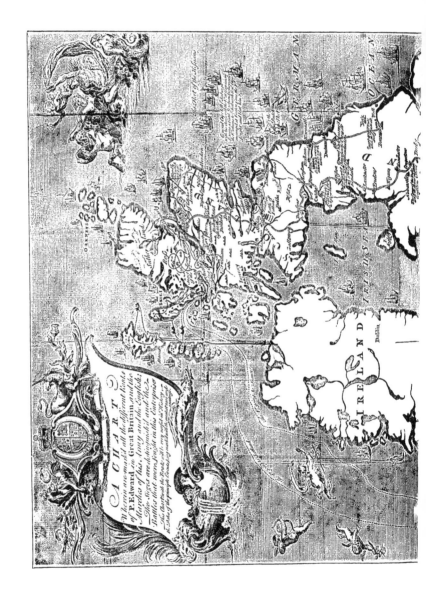

A CHART
Wherein are marked all the different kinds of P. Edward to Great Britain, the Marches of this Army and the English, the Sieges are also taken of, and the Battles that were fought in this Enterprise.

GRAMPIAN

OCEAN

IRISH SEA

IRELAND
Dublin

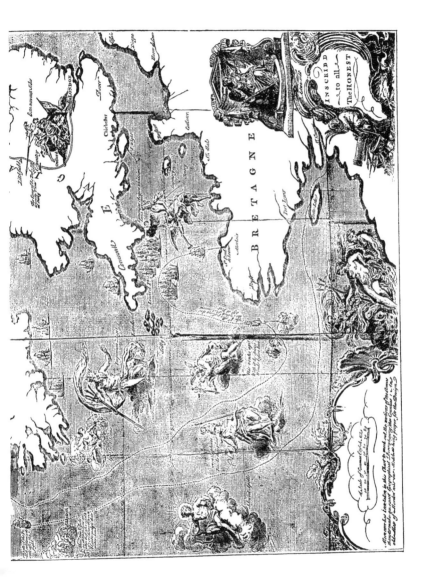

INSCRIBD to all THeHONEST

BRETAGNE

Cornwall

Chichester

Dover

Bulloign

Dieppe

S. Malo

Alderne

Brest

Port Lovis

not fire, being out of range to reach him with our small guns. The [other] two ships changed places and steered S.E., crossing each other, so that the Englishman fired his starboard and the *Elizabeth* her port volley. We waited to board the *Elizabeth* as had been agreed. We followed her close to be able to put some men on board in case of her being boarded, not being able to give her any other help, because the English guns, which were 33 pounders, did not permit us to approach her. We were much afraid that in making the course S.E. we might meet the vessels seen in the morning. We still followed the *Elizabeth* closely to be able to help her in case of her being boarded. At 10 in the evening the firing ceased on both sides, and we went to speak the *Elizabeth*. M. Bar, flag captain of the said ship, told us that M. d'O was dangerously wounded, and that his ship was more damaged than he could say, and begged me to let down a small boat and send him some men to fit up again. I said I would do this, and keep my boat outside. I told him to lie to, that I might be able to send it; he said he could not do it, and that I must follow him. As we feared to fall in with the vessels we had seen in the morning, we held council till it was resolved to find out if the *Elizabeth* was in a condition to put to sea, in which case we would have followed her. I inquired as to this from M. Bar, who told me it was not [fit] and that he must absolutely put into Brest. Seeing this, as we did not want to put into port, we decided by the Prince's order to continue our course to Scotland, which we did after wishing *bon voyage* to M. Bar.

[The[1] *Du Teillay*] had not been long parted from the *Elizabeth* till the crew descried two ships of war at some distance, which they could not have well got off from, but that a mist luckily interveened, and brought them out of sight.

Two or three hours before landing, an eagle came hovering over the frigate....Before dinner the Duke of Athol had spied the eagle [and]...could not help remarking it to the Prince and his small retinue, which they looked upon with pleasure. His grace, turning to the Prince, said, 'Sir, I hope this is an excellent omen, and promises good things to us. The king of birds is

[1] *L. M.* i, 204. See note *supra*, p. 19.

come to welcome your royal highness upon your arrival in Scotland.'

When they were near the shore of the Long Isle, Duncan Cameron was set out in the long boat to fetch them a proper pilot. When he landed he accidentally met with Barra's piper, who was his old acquaintance, and brought him on board. The piper piloted them safely into Erisca....

When they landed in Eriska [July 23], they could not find a grain of meal or one inch of bread. But they catched some flounders, which they roasted upon the bare coals in a mean, low hut they had gone into near the shore, and Duncan Cameron stood cook. The Prince sat at the cheek of the little ingle, upon a fail sunk [heap of peats], and laughed heartily at Duncan's cookery, for he himself owned he played his part awkwardly enough.

The[1] very first night they landed [July 23][2] happened to prove violently stormy and wet, and they were obliged to lodge in one of the little country houses, wherein there were already many others that were weatherbound.

Here they were all refreshed as well as the place could afford, and they had some beds, but not sufficient for the whole company, on which account the Prince, being less fatigued than the others, insisted upon such to go to bed as most wanted it. Particularly he took care of Sir Thomas Sheridan, and went to examine his bed, and to see that the sheets were well aired. The landlord, observing him to search the bed so narrowly, and at the same time hearing him declare he would sit up all night, called out to him, and said that it was so good a bed, and the sheets were so good, that a prince need not be ashamed to lie in them.

The Prince, not being accustomed to such fires in the middle of the room, and there being no other chimney than a hole in the roof, was almost choaked, and was obliged to go often to the door for fresh air. This at last made the landlord, Angus MacDonald, call out, 'What a plague is the matter with that fellow, that he can neither sit nor stand still, and neither keep within nor without doors?'

[1] *L. M.* i, 288. From Æneas Macdonald's Journal.
[2] Cf. *B. I.* 2.

Next[1] day [July 24] the Prince sent for young Clanranald's uncle (Alexander MacDonald of Boisdale), who lived in South Uist, and discovered himself to him. This gentleman spoke in a very discouraging manner to the Prince, and advised him to return home. To which it is said the Prince replied, 'I am come home, sir, and I will entertain no notion at all of returning to that place from whence I came; for that I am persuaded my faithful Highlanders will stand by me.' Mr MacDonald told him he was afraid he would find the contrary. The Prince condescended upon Sir Alexander MacDonald [of Sleat] and the Laird of MacLeod as persons he might confide in. Mr Mac-Donald begged leave to tell him that he had pitched upon the wrong persons; for…on the contrary, they might chance to act an opposite part. And seeing the Prince had been pleased to mention Sir Alexander MacDonald's name, Boisdale desired he might run off an express to him, and let his return be the test of what he had advanced….

According to this advice the Prince did send a message to Sir Alexander MacDonald, intimating his arrival, and demanding assistance. Before the messenger could return, Æneas Mac-Donald (anxious to have the honour of seeing the Prince in the house of his brother, the Laird of Kinlochmoidart) prevailed upon the Prince to set out for the continent [mainland], and they arrived at Boradale in Moidart, or rather Arisaig, upon July 25th, St James's day, 1745. When the messenger returned to the Prince he brought no answer with him, for Sir Alexander refused to give any.

Mr[2] Hugh MacDonald, brother to the Laird of Morar… happened to meet with MacDonald of Kenlochmoydart crossing the water of Lochy, who asked him, 'What news?' 'No news at all have I,' said Mr Hugh. 'Then,' said Kenlochmoydart, 'I'll give you news. You'll see the Prince this night at my house.' 'What Prince do you mean?' said Mr Hugh. 'Prince Charles,' said Kenlochmoydart. 'You are certainly joking,' said

[1] *L.M.* i, 205. From a Journal chiefly based on Duncan Cameron, of Barra's, information.

[2] *Ibid.* iii, 50. From the record of a conversation with Hugh Macdonald, Morar's brother.

Mr Hugh, 'I cannot believe you.' Upon this Kenlochmoydart assured him of the truth of it. 'Then,' said Mr Hugh, 'what number of men has he brought along with him?' 'Only seven,' said Kenlochmoydart. 'What stock of money and arms has he brought with him then?' said Mr Hugh. 'A very small stock of either,' said Kenlochmoydart. 'What generals or officers fitt for commanding are with him?' said Mr Hugh. 'None at all,' replied Kenlochmoydart. Mr Hugh said he did not like the expedition at all, and was afraid of the consequences. 'I cannot help it,' said Kenlochmoydart. 'If the matter go wrong, then I'll certainly be hanged, for I am engaged already....'

Next day, [Æneas] and Mr Hugh Macdonalds went on board the vessel in Lochnannuagh when the Prince happened to be above deck, to whom Mr Hugh made up, saluting him as an abbee[1], welcoming him to Scotland, asking how he liked the country, etc. The Prince soon learning what Mr Hugh was[2], went to the cabin, desiring Mr Hugh to be brought to him and discovered himself to him, informing him upon what design he had come. Upon this Mr Hugh paid his respects to him as to a prince, and begged he would be exceedingly cautious and keep himself very private, as the garrison at Inverlochie was not far off, and the Campbells in the neighbourhood...would be too ready to take him, and give him up to his enemies, etc. 'I have no fear about that at all,' said the Prince.

July[3] [26]th ane express was dispatch'd for young [Ranald Macdonald of] Clanronald, and next day, being the [27]th, Clanronald, Alexander McDonald of Glenaladale, Æneas McDonald of Dalily, and I[4], came to Forsy, a small village opposite to the road where the Prince's vessel lay. We called for the ships boat and were immediatly carryed on board, and our hearts were overjoyed to find ourselves so near our long wished for P—ce. We found a large tent erected with poles on the ships deck, covered and well furnished with variety of wines and

1 Charles passed as 'M. l'Abbé.'
2 See biographical note *infra*, p. 195.   3 *L. P.* ii, 479.
4 The writer of this 'Journall and Memoirs' declares himself a Highland officer in the Prince's army. I have emended his dates. They are exactly a week behind the correct ones.

spirits. As we enter'd this pavilion we were most chearfully wel-
com'd by the Duke of Athole, to whom some of us had been
known in the year 1715. While the Duke was talking with us,
Clanronald was a-missing, and had, as we understood, been called
into the P——ce's cabin, nor did we look for the honour of seeing
His R.H. at least for that night. After being 3 hours with the
P., Clanronald returned to us, and in about half ane hour after
there entered the tent a tall youth of a most agreeable aspect, in
a plain black coat, with a plain shirt, not very clean, and a cam-
brick stock fixed with a plain silver buckle, a fair round wig out
of the buckle, a plain hatt with a canvas string haveing one end
fixed to one of his coat buttons; he had black stockins and brass
buckles in his shoes; at his first appearance I found my heart
swell to my very throat. We were immediatly told by one
Obrian, a churchman, that this youth was also ane English
clergyman who had long been possess'd with a desire to see and
converse with Highlanders.

When this youth entered, Obrian forbid any of those who
were sitting to rise; he saluted none of us, and we only made a
low bow at a distance. I chanced to be one of those who were
standing when he came in, and he took his seat near me, but
immediatly started up again and caused me sitt down by him
upon a chest. I, at this time taking him to be only a passenger
or some clergyman, presumed to speak to him with too much
familiarity, yet still retained some suspicion he might be one of
more note than he was said to be. He asked me if I was not cold
in that habite (viz. the highland garb). I answered, I was so
habituated to it that I should rather be so if I was to change my
dress for any other. At this he laugh'd heartily, and next enquired
how I lay with it at night, which I explaind to him; he said
that by wraping myself so closs in my plaid I would be unpre-
pared for any sudden defence in the case of a surprise. I answered,
that in such times of danger, or during a war, we had a different
method of useing the plaid, that with one spring I could start to
my feet with drawn sword and cock'd pistol in my hand without
being in the least incumber'd with my bedcloaths. Severall such
questions he put to me; then rising quickly from his seat he calls
for a dram, when the same person whisper'd me a second time,

to pledge the stranger but not to drink to him, by which season-
able hint I was confirm'd in my suspicion who he was. Having
taken a glass of wine in his hand, he drank to us all round, and
soon after left us....

On [July] the [29th], Clanronald and Allan McDonald,
younger brother to Kinlochmoydart, were sent to Sir Alexander
McDonald of Slate and the Laird of M^cloed [Macleod] to
induce them to join His R.H. according to duty and promise;
Glenalad[ale], another gentleman and I being likewise sent to
conveen Clanronald's men and to get some of the best of them
for the P——'s guard in the mean time, and others to be employed in unloading the ship of the arms and amunition. This
was our whole business till Clanronald's return from the Isle of
Sky, whose errand was in vain, those gentlemen alledging, that
the P. comeing without some regular troops, more arms and
money, they were under no engagement to concurr in the enterprize. Donald McDonald of Scotos came also on board as Glen-
garies representative, as likewise Cameron of Lochiel, M'Donald
of Keppoch, and M'Donald of Glenco, who having concerted
measures with His R.H. in behalf of their king and country,
repaired immediatly to their respective homes with orders to conveen all their followers....These chieftains carried with them some
arms and amunition for the use of such of their people as wanted.

Donald[1] Cameron, called by the Highlanders Young Locheil,
(for his father was still alive, but attainted and in exile,) had
succeeded, in the year 1719, to his grandfather Sir Ewen
Cameron (of whom so many marvellous stories are told by his
countrymen at this day)....He was one of the seven who, in the
year 1740, signed the Association which Drummond of Bohaldy
carried to the Old Pretender at Rome; and when the court of
France, after the disaster at Dunkirk, withheld their aid, he was
one of those who sent over Murray to dissuade Charles from
ccming to Scotland without a body of foreign troops; and he
was not a little troubled when he received a letter from Charles,
acquainting him that he was come to the Highlands, and desired
to see him immediately. Locheil complied....He was no sooner

[1] *H. H.* 41.

arrived at Boradale, than Charles and he retired by themselves....
Locheil acknowledged the engagements of the chiefs, but observed that they were no ways binding, as he had come over
without the stipulated [French] aid; and therefore, as there was
not the least prospect of success, he advised his Royal Highness
to return to France....Charles refused to follow Locheil's advice.
...'In a few days' (said he), 'with the few friends that I have,
I will erect the royal standard, and proclaim to the people of
Britain, that Charles Stuart is come over to claim the crown of
his ancestors, to win it, or to perish in the attempt: Locheil, who,
my father has often told me, was our firmest friend, may stay at
home, and learn from the newspapers the fate of his prince.'
'No,' said Locheil, 'I'll share the fate of my prince; and so shall
every man over whom nature or fortune hath given me any
power[1].' Such was the singular conversation, on the result of
which depended peace or war. For it is a point agreed among the
Highlanders, that if Locheil had persisted in his refusal to take
arms, the other chiefs would not have joined the standard without
him, and the spark of rebellion must have instantly expired.

About[2] the 2 of August they gott notice at Edinburg from
fort William of the Princes being Landed, and Lt Gen: Sir John
Cope, who at that time commanded the Forces in Scotland,
order'd away arms and amunition to all the forts and Castles
in Scotland, put in two Companys of Lascelles regiment into the
Castle of Edinburgh and Stored it with provisions....About the
8 of August a Camp was form'd at Stirling, Consisting of
Lascelles's [47th] Regiment 8 Companys 560, Murrays [46th]
Regiment Compleat 700, 5 Companies of Lee's [44th] 350, one
Company of the old highland regiment 70 men, Gardners
Dragoons [13th Hussars] 300 men, and Hamiltons [14th
Hussars] 300, in all 1680 foot and 600 Dragoons, with some
field pieces of Cannon and some Coehorns.

Captain[3] Walsh...took his leave of the P[rince][4] on the [5th
of August], which day His R.H., the Duke of Athole, Clan-

[1] Cf. *H. H.* 44.   [2] *E. J.* 241.
[3] L.P. ii, 482. See note on p. 24 *supra*.
[4] Charles's letters to his father and the King of France are in Mahon,
The Forty-Five, 151; *M. B. M.* 507.

ronald, &c., came on shore and landed at the little village of
Borradel, in the country of Arisaig, belonging to Clanronald,
and here H.R.H. first sett foot on Scotish ground, excepting one
night that he tarried in the house of Angus McDonald, at a place
called Eriskay in the isle of Wist [Uist]....We there did our best
to give him a most hearty welcome to our country, the P. and
all his company with a guard of about 100 men being all entertained in the house, &c., of Angus McDonald of Borradel in
Arisaig, in as hospitable a manner as the place could aford.
H.R.H. being seated in a proper place had a full view of all our
company, the whole nighbourhood without distinction of age or
sex crouding in upon us to see the P. After we had all eaten
plentifully and drunk chearfully, H.R.H. drunk the grace drink
in English, which most of us understood; when it came to my
turn I presumed to distinguish myself by saying audibly in Erse
(or highland language), *Deochs laint-an Reogh*; H.R.H., under-
standing that I had drunk the Kings health, made me speak the
words again in Erse, and said he could drink the Kings health
likewise in that language, repeating my words; and the company
mentioning my skill in the highland language, H.R.H. said I
should be his master for that language.

Had[1] the Chevalier seemed in the least daunted by the
apparent caution of his friends, or agreed to their not raising in
arms for some time, and keep'd the ship hovering of the coast
for a retreat, it is more than probable that the interest L[ord]
L[ovat], S^r A[lexander] McDonald with M^cC[leod] had with
the others, together with the many dangers that would have
occurred to them every day, would have obligded him att last to
return after a fruitless attempt, and if not rendered him despicable
in the Eyes of foreigners, would att least have enduced them to
believe that he had no friends....This slip made Locheil, with
McDonald of Keppoch, Clanronald, Stewart of Ardsheil, with
principal gentlemen of Glengarys familly, to agree to have their
people in arms in two weeks after, and the Rendezvous was
appointed att Glenphinnen [Glenfinnan], a small place att the
head of Locheil, upon the [19th] day of [August].

[1] *M. B. M.* 154.

[Meanwhile][1] the governor of Fort Augustus, concluding from the reports which he heard, that the Highlanders were hatching some mischief, sent, upon the 16th of August, two additional companies of the first [Royal Scots] regiment of foot, to reinforce the garrison of Fort William....Within eight miles of Fort William stands High Bridge, built over the river Spean, a torrent...extremely difficult to pass but by the bridge. Captain John Scott...who commanded the two companies...was near High Bridge, when he heard a bagpipe, and saw some Highlanders on the other side of the bridge skipping and leaping about with swords and firelocks in their hands. The captain ordered his men to halt, and sent a serjeant with his own servant, to learn who these people were. When the messengers came near the bridge, two nimble Highlanders darted out, seized them both, and carried them to the party at the bridge. Captain Scott, ignorant of the number of his enemies...ordered his men to face about, and march back again. The Highlanders who had taken post at the bridge were not above eleven or twelve men, assembled and commanded by Macdonald of Tierndreich [Tiendrish], who had...sent expresses to Locheil and Keppoch to demand assistance. When the soldiers...had passed the west end of Loch Lochie, and were got a little way upon the narrow road between the lake and the mountain, the Highlanders...ascending the hill ...began to fire at the soldiers....The number of the Highlanders encreased every moment; for the report of the pieces was heard far and wide....Captain Scott, having reached the east end of Loch Lochie, descried some Highlanders on a hill at the west end of Loch Oich, and not liking their appearance, crossed the isthmus between the lakes, intending to take possession of Invergary, a place of some strength, which belonged to Macdonald of Glengary. He had not marched far, when he saw another body of Highlanders (who were the Macdonalds of Glengary) coming down the hill to oppose him. Captain Scott formed the hollow square and marched on. The pursuers, joined by Macdonald of Keppoch, and a party of his men, came up very fast. Keppoch advanced alone, and called out to the troops to surrender, offering them good quarter....The soldiers, surrounded on every side,

[1] *H. H.* 46.

laid down their arms. The affair was scarcely over, when Locheil, with a body of his Camerons, arrived, took charge of the prisoners, and carried them to his house at Achnacarie. In this scuffle one or two of the soldiers were killed, and Captain Scott himself was wounded.

The Highlanders did not lose a single man; and their success in this first essay had no small effect in raising their spirits, and encouraging them to rebel.

The[1] Chevalier had been all this time [at Kinlochmoidart[2]] busied in incitting his friends to gett their people together, and to have his arms and ammunition, &c., convey'd from the place where they were landed to his own quarters, which notwith-standing his own continual care and industry, was a great whille of being accomplished, so superiorly indolent and Idle are the people of that part of the Country. Mr Walsh, the gentleman who commanded the Frigate, had met with two ships loadened with oat meal off the Island of Skey, which he sent in to the Bay from whence he saild, to provide the Chevaliers army, but notwith-standing the absolute unpossibility there was to procure bread for the men in that season of the year, and the easy access there was from the place of landing to the [appointed rendezvous at Glenfinnan on] Loch of Sheil, he could not procure one Boll of it to be carried to the place of Rendezvous, so that in spite of all the care he could take, of two ship loads of oat meal and flouer, infinitely more than his army could have destroyed during their stay in the Highlands, there were only about Sixty Bolls ever went out of Clanronalds Country....

The Chevalier, very much taken up in writting of letters and sending expresses to hasten the march of his friends to the Rendezvous...at Glenphinan the [19] of Agust, accordingly arrived there the [19]th in the evening with only three Com-panys of Clanronalds followers.

Glenfinn[a]n[3] is a narrow vale, in which the river Finnin runs between high and craggy mountains, not to be surmounted but by travellers on foot. At each end of the glen is a lake about twelve miles in length; and behind the mountains on both sides

[1] *M. B. M.* 162.

[2] Murray of Broughton joined Charles here on August 18 and was made his Secretary.   [3] *H. H.* 49.

of the glen are other two lakes, nearly of the same length. When
Charles landed in the glen, Locheil and his Camerons were not
to be seen. Anxious for the arrival of this great auxiliary, Charles
entered one of the hovels, which still stand there, and waited for
about two hours. At last Locheil with his men appeared on the
top of the hill.

The Camerons advanced in two lines (each of them three
men deep). Between the lines were the soldiers taken on the 16th,
marching as prisoners without their arms. Charles, elevated with
the sight of such a clan (for the Camerons are said to have been
700 or 800 men that day, many of them without arms), proceeded immediately to erect the standard.

The Marquis of Tullibardine [Duke of Atholl] unfurled the
standard; and, supported by a man on each side, held the staff till
the manifest and commission of regency were read, both dated
at Rome, December 1743.

In an hour or two after this solemnity, Macdonald of Keppoch
arrived with about 300 men. In the evening of the same day,
some gentlemen of the name of Macleod came to Glenfinnin,
who disclaimed their chief, and offered themselves to return to
the Isles, and raise all the men they could for the service of their
Prince.

[When][1] the Royal Standart [was] display'd by the D. of
A[tholl] the Chevalier made them a short but very Pathetick
speech. Importing that it would be no purpose to declaim upon
the justice of his Father's tittle to the Throne to people who,
had they not been convinced of it, would not have appeared in
his behalf, but that he esteemed it as much his duty to endeavour
to procure their welfare and happyness as they did to assert his
right; that it was cheifly with that view that he had landed in a
part of the Island where he knew he should find a number of
brave gentlemen fired with the 'noble example of their prede-
cessors, and jealous of their own and their Country's honour, to
join with him in so glorious an enterprise, with whose assistance,
and the protection of a just God who never fails to avenge the
cause of the injured, he did not doubt of bringing the affair to a
happy issue.'

[1] *M. B. M.* 168.

CHAPTER III

TO HOLYROOD

From[1] the beginning of summer there had been a report flying through the Highlands, that Prince Charles intended to come over that season; but the King's servants at Edinburgh heard nothing of it till the 2d of July, when the President of the Court of Session [Duncan Forbes of Culloden] came to Sir John Cope, and shewed him a letter from a gentleman of consideration in the Highlands, acquainting him with a report current there, that the Pretender's eldest son was to land some where in the Highlands that summer, in order to attempt an insurrection.... The President assured Sir John Cope, that he...held the report to be groundless, but thought it necessary to let the Commander in Chief know that there was such a report....

However, their Lordships began very soon to apprehend there was some danger; for on the 30th of July the Marquis of Tweedale [Secretary of State] wrote to Sir John Cope, and acquainted him, that several informations had been laid before the Lords Justices[2], importing, that the French Court was meditating an invasion of His Majesty's dominions; that the Pretender's eldest son had sailed from Nantz in a French man of war, and was actually landed in Scotland....Letters of the same date were written to Lord Milton, the Justice Clerk, and to the King's Advocate, communicating to them the same intelligence, and enjoining his Majesty's servants to consult and concert together, what was best to be done, to make the strictest enquiry into the subject matter of this intelligence, and to transmit to the Marquis constant accounts of any discovery they should make.

Without waiting an answer from Scotland to these letters (which had been sent by express to Edinburgh, and arrived there on the 3d of August), the Lords Justices published a proclamation in the *London Gazette*, August 6th, offering a reward of thirty

---

[1] *H. H.* 51.   [2] Regents in the King's absence.

thousand pounds to any person or persons that should seize and secure the Pretender's eldest son, who, as their Lordships were informed, had embarked for Britain. Before the proclamation reached Edinburgh it was known there that the Pretender's son had landed in the Highlands. For on the 8th of August, an express came from the Lord Justice Clerk at Roseneath to the Commander in Chief at Edinburgh, with intelligence that the Young Pretender was landed in Arisaig; that part of the Clan Macdonald were already in arms, and that other Highlanders were preparing to join them....

Such was the state of intelligence (communicated only to His Majesty's principal servants, civil and military) when the *Gazette* with the proclamation arrived. From that moment every body spake of nothing but the young Pretender, though very few people knew what to believe about him....

Sir John Cope, Commander in Chief during these alarms, was one of those ordinary men who are fitter for any thing than the chief command in war, especially when opposed, as he was, to a new and uncommon enemy; and, like every man of that character, extremely solicitous that nothing might be laid to his charge, he resolved to propose the most vigorous measures. Accordingly, in his letters to the Secretary of State (dated the 9th and 10th of August), he proposed to march his troops into the Highlands, to seek out the rebels, and try to check their progress....

The King's army in Scotland...consisted of three battalions and a half of infantry, and two regiments of cavalry, both horse and foot (one old corps excepted[1]) the youngest regiments of the British army. Besides these forces there were in Scotland nine additional companies, that had been lately raised there for the

[1] 'The old regiment was Guise's, No. 6, raised in the year 1673, which was dispersed among the forts and barracks in the north. The three young regiments were, Lee's, the 44th, of which five companies were in Berwick, and five in Scotland; Murray's, the 46th; and Lascelles's, the 47th; all of them raised in the year 1741. The two regiments of dragoons were Gard[i]ner's and Hamilton's, the 13th and 14th, both raised in the year 1715, but had never seen any service.'— Home's note.

national regiments serving abroad: there were also several companies almost complete of Lord Loudon's Highland regiment, for which the levies were carrying on all over the North. Of the nine additional companies, two had fallen into the hands of the rebels [August 16], as has been mentioned; most of the other companies had been draughted, and were so weak, as not to exceed twenty-five men a company. Lord Loudon's men were scattered about in different parts of the North Country, and had not received their arms.

Sir John Cope, arriving at Stirling on the 19th of August, next day began his march to the North, and proceeded by Crieff and Tay Bridge[1], along the Highland road towards Fort Augustus. ...The troops, with which the General undertook this expedition, consisted altogether of infantry, for cavalry being judged unserviceable in so rough a country, where it was not easy to subsist them, one of the regiments of dragoons [Hamilton's] was left at Leith, and the other [Gardiner's] at Stirling. With twenty-five companies of foot, whose number did not exceed 1400 men[2], with four field-pieces (one and a half pounders), as many cohorns, with a great number of carts and horses, carrying provisions, baggage, and 300 stand of arms, the General arrived at Dalnacardoch on the 25th of August. At Dalnacardoch he was informed that the rebels intended to meet him at Corryarrak, in his way to Fort Augustus. The person who brought him this intelligence was Captain Sweetnam of Guise's regiment, who... was taken prisoner by the rebels on the 14th, at a place called Letter Finlay...[and] was carried to Glenfinnin, where he saw the standard erected on the 19th; and giving his parole, was dismissed on the 21st.....From Dalnacardoch Sir John Cope with his army advanced to Dalwhinnie, where he arrived on the 26th....

At Dalwhinnie, surrounded with hills, from which Corryarrak may be seen, a Council of War was called....The Council ...were unanimously of opinion that the march to Fort Augustus,

[1] ? Wade's bridge at Aberfeldy.

[2] The foot included five companies of Lee's [44th], two companies of Lord John Murray's Highlanders [42nd], and Murray's [46th] regiment. Eight companies of Lascelles's [47th] regiment joined Cope at Crieff.—*Report on General Cope's Conduct,* 16.

by Corryarrak, was impracticable; and...that it was more expedient...to march to Inverness....

Sir John Cope, acquiescing in the opinion of the Council of
War...marched his army on the 27th towards Garv[e]more; but
when the Van reached Blarigg Beg, and the Rear was at Catlaig,
where the road to Inverness turns off from the military road to
Fort Augustus, the troops were ordered to halt, to face about,
and take the road to Inverness by Ruthven, [where they arrived
on the 29th of August].

I[1] shall now return to the Chevalier[2], who, quite surprised
with the unexpected retreat of his Enemy, immediatly called a
Council to consult of what was the most proper course for him
to take, and soon determined to march south[3] and make the
most of the advantages given him [by Cope's retreat]....He then
proceeded on his march and encamped [on August 29th] att a
place called Dalnacardoch, about six miles from Blair Castle,
and sent letters to some of the gentlemen of Atholl, to whom the
D[uke] write att the same time desiring they would meet him
the second day after att his house of Blair, where the Chevalier
marched next morning [August 30]....His troops were here very
commodiously quartered, there being a number of small villages
in that part of the Country, and here was the first time that the
men could properly be said to have had bread from the time of
their rendezvous att Glenfinnan, having eat nothing but beef
roasted on the heath, without even bread or salt, durring their
march thither[4].

September[5] 2d. He left Blair and went to the house of Lude,
where he was very chearful and took his share in several dances,
such as minuets, Highland reels (the first reel the Prince called

[1] *M. B. M.* 183.
[2] Charles's force, over 2000 strong, was on August 27 advancing
from Glen Garry towards Fort Augustus, purposing to cut off Cope
before he reached that position.
[3] He had already rejected Lord Lovat's suggestion that he should
rally the northern clans. Cf. *L. P.* ii, 442.
[4] An unsuccessful attempt on the barracks at Ruthven on August 28
had been partly undertaken in the hope of obtaining oatmeal.
[5] *L. M.* i, 208.

for was, 'This is not mine ain house,' etc.), and a Strathspey minuet.

September 3d. He was at Dunkeld, and next day he dined at Nairn house [in Strathord], where some of the company happening to observe what a thoughtful state his father would now be in...and that upon this account he was much to be pitied...the Prince replied that he did not half so much pity his father as his brother. 'For,' said he, 'the king has been inured to disappointments and distresses, and has learnt to bear up easily under the misfortunes of life. But poor Harry! his young and tender years make him much to be pitied, for few brothers love as we do.'

September 4th. In the evening he made his entrance into Perth upon the horse that Major MacDonell [of Tiendrish] had presented him with[1].

The[2] Prince sent a party from Perth to proclaim his Father at Dundee. Both at Perth and Dundee the Manifesto's which he had brought with him were read: one of them was a Commission of Regency appointing the Prince Regent of The three Kingdoms until the arrival of his Father; the others were declaring that both the father and son were willing in a free parliament to Grant the Nations all the Securities they Should demand for their rights and privileges & for the Churches at that time Established by Law. Their was a pardon Granted for all past Offences to all those that would accept of it, and the Union was declared Nul, as having been made to prevent the house of Stuart from their right to the Crown.

[Perth][3] being the most centrical place in the Country, [the Prince] determined to fix his residence there till such time as he should learn the motions and designs of his Enemy. For this purpose he dispatchd expresses to the north, to be acquainted with S[r] J[ohn] C[ope's] motions, to Edinburgh, to know what was passing there, and to know their sentiments, and likewise to his freinds in England. From thence he was informed that the enemy were amarching towards Aberdeen, and from Edinburgh, that associations were carrying on against him, and mighty pre-

---

[1] It had been captured in the skirmish on August 16.
[2] *E. J.* 251.   [3] *M. B. M.* 187.

parations making for the defence of that Capital, which was
treated by his freinds with that contempt and disdain which so
Idle and foolish a design deserved, and the Authoris of it
rediculed, as by their future conduct they demonstrated that they
had justly merited.

Parties were sent to Dundee, and some other adjacent places,
to seise upon what arms and ammunition could be found, which
was executed with the outmost order and discreation....All the
wrights then in the town were ordered to make Targets, for
which they were paid, and passes and protections granted indis-
criminatly to all that asked them.

Here[1] [at Perth the Prince] was join'd by [James Drummond]
the Duke of Perth with 200 men, & Ld George Murray.
(There had been a Warrant out to Seise his Grace some weeks
before this, and he narowly Escaped being taken at his own
house by a Party and had been oblidged to keep private always
untill he joined the Prince.) Both the Duke and Lord George
were made Lieutenant Generals....

There happen'd a Circumstance here at Perth that was ever
after very detrimental to the Princes affairs and was the chief
means of breading any jealousies that happen'd afterwards in that
army. Mr Murray of Broughton, who the Prince had made his
Secretary, had gott a Great deal of his masters Ear, and it was
Suppos'd he aim'd at having the chief direction of all that concerned Military affairs as well, as he had already the administra-
tion of all moneys belonging to the Prince and every thing that
concerned private Correspondence. To Effectuate this Scheme
it was necessary to remove a great obstacle, which was to deprive
Lord George Murray of the Princes favour....To bring this
about he told the Prince that Lord George had taken the oaths
to the Government, and that he had been looked upon for some
time past as no friend to the Cause[2], and in Short his Opinion
was, that he had join'd only out of an intent to Betray the Affair.
What Mr Murray said to the Prince upon this Subject had such

[1] *E. J.* 248.
[2] Lord George admittedly had been in touch with Cope and the
Lord Advocate immediately before his arrival at Perth. Murray himself
was in a similar predicament.

weight that he ever afterwards suspected Lord George, which did his Affairs great harm, as Lord George by his behaviour gained the Esteem and Confidence of the whole Army[1].

Lord[2] George Murray...possessed a natural genius for military operations; and was indeed a man of surprising talents, which, had they been cultivated by the study of military tactics, would unquestionably have rendered him one of the greatest generals of the age. He was tall and robust, and brave in the highest degree; conducting the Highlanders in the most heroic manner, and always the first to rush sword in hand into the midst of the enemy. He used to say, when we advanced to the charge, 'I do not ask you, my lads, to go before, but merely to follow me': a very energetic harangue, admirably calculated to excite the ardour of the Highlanders; but which would sometimes have had a better effect in the mouth of the Prince. He slept little, was continually occupied with all manner of details, and was altogether most indefatigable, combining and directing alone all our operations: in a word, he was the only person capable of conducting our army....However, with an infinity of good qualities, he was not without his defects: proud, haughty, blunt, and imperious, he wished to have the exclusive ordering of every thing; and, feeling his superiority, he would listen to no advice.

The[3] Chevalier having certain intelligence that Capt Rogers had been sent south by G^{ll} C[ope] to provide ships att Leith to transport him to the firth of Forth, and that these transports were actually providing for him, called a Councill of War to consult of what was proper to be done upon that occasion. He urged... that in case the Enemy gott south, it was not impossible but they might be joind by some of the troops ordered from Flanders[4] before he could bring them to an action...and that upon this account it seemd necessary for him to have matters ordered so as to be able to give them a meetting immediatly upon their landing, before they could be reinforced. The uncertainty of the place where they might debark appeared to some of the Council

[1] Lord George came to stand for every interest opposed to the incompetence that surrounded the Prince.

[2] *J.* 19.   [3] *M. B. M.* 189.

[4] They did not arrive until October.

a difficulty not easily to be surmounted....To prevent this difficulty, and to procure the immediate rising of their freinds in the north, it was proposed to march north from Perth, and attack S^r J[ohn] on his road to Aberdeen. Tho the Chevalier seemd of opinion that he might by forced marches gett to Aberdeen before him, and that his army would be augmented on his march, yett he was too quick sighted not to discover the ruin he might bring upon his affairs by that step; for so soon as the Enemy discovered his intentions, they had only to post themselves on the side of the River Spey att Gordon Castle till they had drawn him within a day's march, and if they than did not care to risque a battle, they had it in their power to retire again under the cannon of Inverness, whille the two Regements of Dragoons then att Stirling would have marchd to harrase his rear, so that he must thereby have very much fatigued his troops, and losed a great deal of time, w^tout any probability of success. Having thus...demonstrated the advantages of marching south to waite for the Enemy there, and of what consequence it would be to render himself Master of the Capital before it was possible for the Enemy to come to its relief, [he] therefor gave orders for the march of the army to Dumblain [Dunblane] against Thursday the 11th of Sept^r [1].

On[2] the 13th we marched from Dumblane through Down, and crossed the water of Teath [Teith] at the bridge there. The P. stoped at a gentlemans house near Down, of the name of E[dmonsto]n[e], and drunk a glass of wine on horseback, where the ladys, &c., of the country were assembled to see him. We passed the river Forth that day at the ford of Frew, about 6 miles above Stirling, expecting to have been opposed there by Colonell Gardners dragoons, who encamped in the park of Stirling, and who we heard had threatned to cut us to pieces if we attempted to cross the water. The dragoons, however, upon our approach galloped away in a great hurry and lay that night at Falkirk.

The P. in crossing Forth may be said to have passed the

---

[1] Cluny Macpherson here consented to raise his Clan. *M. B. M.* 191.
[2] *L. P.* ii, 486. From the Journal of a Highland officer.

Rubicon; he had now no rough ground for a retreat in case of
any disaster, and being entered into the low country must fairly
meet his fate. He and his little army halted, soon after passing
Forth, and dined at the house of Leckie, belonging to a gentleman of the name of [George] Moir, who had the night before
been seized in his bed by a party of dragoons and carried prisoner
to Stirling Castle, upon intelligence that he was preparing to
receive and intertain the P. and his followers, which indeed we
were in a most hospitable manner, as well as many other of our
freinds who followed soon after. This night we lay at Touch.

From[1] Touch [we] marchd by the Town of St Ninians, and
as [we] passed, some few shott was fired from Stirling Castle,
but tho the balls fell very nigh [the Prince], they hurt nobody.
The army made a halt of some hours near to Bannockburn, and
had provisions brought them from Stirling and the Places about,
whille the Chevalier dined att S^r H[ugh] P[aterson's], and gott
intelligence that the dragoons had retired to Linlithgow, and
were encampd betwixt the Town and the Bridge, about half a
mille to the westward. So soon as the Army had refreshed themselves he continued his march, and encamped about a mille and
a half east of Falkirk upon the high road to Edn^r, and took up
his quarters att the [Earl of Kilmarnock's] House of Kallender.
The Earl of Kilmarnock, haveing dined that day in the Enemy's
Camp...and all the Country about agreeing that [the dragoons]
were still there, the Chevalier determined to attack them before
day, and with that view, provided himself with guides, and
ordered a detachment of five hundred men to be ready on a
minutes warning. Having supped, he retired as if going to bed,
to prevent any intelligence being given of his designe, and went
privately to the camp, where he put himself at the head of the
detachment, and marched with a view to pass the river of [Avon]
att a foord half a mille above the bridge and attack the dragoons
in flank; but before he had marched above half way, he gott
intelligence of the Enemys having retired towards Ed^r and encamped att Kirkliston Water upon the accounts of his aproach,
so that he took possession of the Town of Linlithgow about six

[1] *M. B. M.* 191.

in the morning the 15th, where the rest of the army joined him
about noon. It happening to be of a Sunday, the Chevalier...
encampd his army to the eastward of The Town, and discharged any of the men from entering save a very small guard
he keept with himself in the Palace, ordered the bells to be rung,
the church doors to be open'd, and gave orders to assure the
magestrates in his name that they should not be disturbed in their
worship; notwithstanding of which, the Minister either left the
Town, or declined preaching, to enduce the ignorant vulgar to
believe that if he had, he would have been insulted and persecuted.
In the Evening [the Prince] encamped about three milles from
the Town, and sleepd himself in a small farm house in the rear
of his army, having ordered the whole to be under arms next
morning by five a clock.

How soon all was ready in the morning [September 16], the
Chevalier drew up his army six in front...and advanced in the
greatest order, not a man offering to quite his Ranks, being
ready to receive the Dragoons in case they should venture to
attack them. He continued his march in this manner till he came
to Todshall [Foxhall], a gentleman's (Mr Horn) seat upon
Newliston River, where he made a halt for two hours and sent
out parties to reconnoitre the Enemy, who retired to the Colt
Bridge[1], about a mille from Edin[r]. About two in the afternoon
he advanced to Corsterphan [Corstorphine], three milles from
the Capital, where were numbers of people mett him from thence,
chiefly from curiosity, and then filled of to the right and encamped at Gray's Milles, 2 milles distant from the Citty to the
south west, having sent a summons to the Provost and Majestrates
[in the following terms], requiring them to open their gates and
receive him into the Town:

Being[2] now in a condition to make our way into this capital of his
Majesty's ancient kingdom of Scotland, we hereby summon you to
receive us, as you are in duty bound to do. And in order to it, we hereby
require you upon receipt of this to summon the Town Council and take

[1] Thence—in the 'canter of Colt-Brig'—they fled again, and joined
Cope upon his landing at Dunbar.
[2] *L. M.* i, 249.

proper measures in it for securing the peace and quiet of the city, which we are very desirous to protect. But if you suffer any of the Usurper's troops to enter the town, or any of the canon, arms, or amunition now in it, whether belonging to the publick or to private persons, to be carried off, we shall take it as a breach of your duty and a heinous offence against the king and us, and shall resent it accordingly. We promise to preserve all the rights and liberties of the city, and the particular property of every one of his Majesty's subjects. But if any opposition be made to us we cannot answer for the consequences, being firmly resolved at any rate to enter the city, and in that case, if any of the inhabitants are found in arms against us, they must not expect to be treated as prisoners of war.

(Signed)   CHARLES, PRINCE REGENT.

From our Camp, 16th September 1745.

Edinburgh[1] had never been fortified; the castle, and a wall of unequal height, from ten or twelve to eighteen or twenty feet high, shut in the city on three sides, and excluded the smugglers. On the north side there was no wall: the lake called the North Loch came up to the foot of the rock on which the castle stands, and was the only defence on that side of the city. The town wall in some places was strengthened with bastions and provided with embrazures, but there were no cannon mounted upon it; and for a considerable part of the circuit it was no better than a garden wall, or park wall of unusual height. In several places it had been built upon, so that dwelling houses made part of the wall, and some of these houses were commanded by higher houses, opposite to them, and without the city: of such houses there was one continued row from the Cowgate port to the Nether Bow port. Such was the condition of the walls of the city of Edinburgh; and the condition of the men who might be called upon to defend them was pretty similar to that of the walls.

Edinburgh[2] [however] had a good dale of zeale and spirit. There had been 800 volenteers raised. There was the King's signe manuall for a 1000 men lately come down, the walls were put in better order, and barricads of turfe at the gaites, and some canon planted. Generall Ghest [Guest] [commanding the Castle] had given the King's armes to those volunteers, [and] the town

    [1] *H. H.* 65.   [2] *W. M.* 14.

c *College kirk.*   d *The Calton.*   e *Holy Rood Houſe.*   f *Toll*
of which is the poultry market.   k *Weſt Bow.*   l *Parliament*
p *Weſt port.*   q *Magdalen chappel.*   r *The Society.*   s *Soc*
suburbs.   x *Potter's Row suburbs.*   y *The Pleaſants.*   z *Wh*
Note.—*The Weſt kirk lies behind the caſtle, and therefore does not appe*
A *Lady Yeſter's kirk.*   B *The Cannon Gate kirk.*   C *The*
GGG *Gardens.*   II *Street call'd Canongait.*   † *Grey Fryers* K

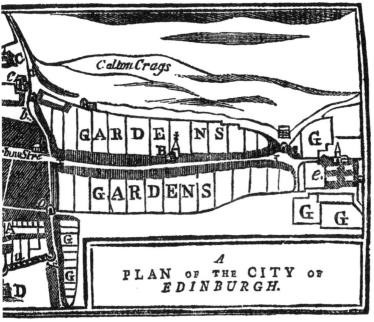

A
PLAN of the CITY of
EDINBURGH.

ooth. g *St. Giles's.* h *The Cross.* i *Tron kirk, at the back*
ouse. m *Meal-market.* n *Fiss market.* o *Cowgate port.*
ty port. t *Potter Row port.* uuu *Town wall.* w *Society*
ighouse.
ar in this plan.
Orphan hospital. D *The Infirmary.* E *The Flesh market.*
rk.

gaird was full. All these with the 2 Regs. of Dragoons might
have resisted and probable defeat fowr thousand or a few more
ill armed, ill accowtered, fatigued Highlanders. But this wanted a
cheife magistrat to conduct the numbers and there spirit, and the
Lord Provost [Archibald Stewart] was justly suspected of corresponding with the rebells by means of his cowsin Sir James
Stewart of Goodtrees and, by sevral, John Stewart, professor of
naturall phylosophie. It was said that of the train band captains
12 of 15 were Jacobit, and the Commandant a Jacobit...
[It] being now harvest, the Heighlanders of there partie, man
and weeman, had been sent up a good number under pretext
of harvest work. But the Provost's conduct cast a damp upon
all, he was so slow in his deliberations, bacward in executing
things agreed. He fixed upon a dismall signall—the ringing the
alarmer or fyer bell—to call the volonters or the burgers, and
this was a publick intimation to the rebell freinds within and
withowt the city. The volunteers had old crassey officers, [and]
the provost named there captains...Of these George Drummond
had some resolution, [and] Sir George Preston was hearty when
the call was [given] by the alarem bell to march to Grasmarket
in order to march to Corstorphin. Only Drummond and Prestons
companies marched down, and of these many looked as going to
execution (for this is the place of hanging)....All was confusion,
and they were not knitt by disiplin and awthority and were raw
men. They were betrayed, betrayed by the King's liftenent, the
cheif magistrat[1]. So they returned.

   [The[2] Prince's] summons being read, it was agreed upon by
the Provost and Majestrates to depute some of their number to
the Chevalier to know what terms were required of them, and
to gain a little time to see how matters would turn out. Accordingly Baily [Gavin] Hamilton, etc., came to Bells milns about
[eight o'clock] att night [September 16]. After notice had been
given of their arrival, and that they were brought into the
Chevalier's quarters, he order Mr M[urray] to go to them and
know their errand. They told him that they was deputed by the

---

[1] The Provost was tried and acquitted of treason.
[2] *M. B. M.* 193.

Majestracy and Town Council to the Prince to know what was expected from them; to which he answered, that his Master required no further than that they should open their gates to his army and delivre up the arms of the Town and garrison, with the ammunition and Military Stores than in the Town, in which case the liberties of the Citty should be preserved, and all necessary protection given them. They answered, that in regard to the arms of the militia they could not take upon them to be responsible, as they were not in their power, having received them from the Castle, but upon the whole desired time to return and consult with their breth[re]n. After Mr M[urray] had made his report to the Chevalier, he aggreed that they should have two or three hours to bring back an answer, but [would] grant them no further respite.

Soon[1] after the deputies were sent out [from Edinburgh], intelligence came to the Provost and Magistrates (assembled in the Council Chamber) that the transports with General Cope's army were off Dunbar; and as the wind was unfavourable for bringing them up the Frith, that the general intended to land his troops at Dunbar and march them to the relief of the city.

This piece of intelligence changed the face of affairs....Various proposals were then made in the Council, to beat to arms, to ring the alarm-bell, and re-assemble the volunteers. To these proposals it was objected, that most of the volunteers had left the town when they laid down their arms; that...the deputies were now in the power of the rebels, who, when they heard the alarm-bell, would probably hang the deputies.

About ten o'clock at night, the deputies returned, and brought a letter in answer to the message sent by them:

His Royal Highness the Prince Regent thinks his Manifesto, and the King his father's declaration already published, a sufficient capitulation for all His Majesty's subjects to accept of with joy. His present demands are, to be received into the city as the son and representative of the King his father, and obeyed as such when there. His Royal Highness supposes, that since the receipt of his letter to the Provost, no arms or ammunition have been suffered to be carried off or concealed, and will expect a particular account of all things of that nature. Lastly, he expects a

[1] *H. H.* 93.

positive answer, before two o'clock in the morning, otherwise he will think himself obliged to take measures conform.

At Gray's Mill, 16th September, 1745. By his Highness's command.

(Signed) J MURRAY.

...After long deliberation it was determined to send out deputies once more, to beg a suspension of hostilities till nine o'clock in the morning....The deputies were also instructed to require an explanation of what was meant by receiving Charles as Prince Regent.

About two o'clock in the morning [September 17] the deputies set out in a hackney coach for Gray's Mill; when they arrived there they prevailed upon Lord George Murray to second their application for a delay; but Charles refused to grant it; and the deputies were ordered in his name to get them gone.

The coach brought them back to Edinburgh, set them down in the High-Street, and then drove towards the Cannongate. When the Netherbow Bow port was opened to let out the coach, 800 Highlanders, led by Cameron of Locheil, rushed in and took possession of the city.

[For,]¹ the deputies had no sooner [obtained] liberty to return [to Edinburgh], than the Chevalier, sensible that they meditated to gain time and tire him out by a trifling treaty...proposed to send a Detachment to render themselves Masters of [Edinburgh] by force, in case the deputies did not return at the time appointed with a resolution to surrender. With this view he ordered Locheil to putt his people under arms...and ordered Mr M[urray] to be their guide...giving strickt orders to behave with all moderation to the Inhabitants, and that the sogers should not be allowed to taste spirits, and to pay for whatever they got, promising them two shillings each so soon as they rendered themselves Masters of the place. The detachment had immediately orders to march, and was commanded by Lochiel and Col¹ O'Sulivan, taking the road by Merkistown [Merchiston] and Hopes Park, where they passed without being observed by the garrison in the Castle, tho so near as to hear them distinctly call their rounds, and arrived at the nether bow Port without meetting any body on their way,

¹ *M. B. M.* 194.

and found the wall of the Town which flanks the Pleasants and St Marys wind mounted with cannon, but no person appeared. Locheil ordered one of his people in a great coat and hunting cape to go and demand entrance att the gate, whille he was ready to have followed him in case he had obtained admittance, but the fellow being refused access, and it now being clear daylight, Mr M. proposed to retire to a place call'd St Leonards hills, and after securing themselves from the cannon of the Castle, to waite for orders from the Chevalier where to attack the town....This retreat being thus agreed to, Mr M. went to the rear of the detachment to make them march and guide them to the place proposed, but before he had time to get so far, the Coach which had returned with the deputies came down the High Street, and oblidged the Guard to open the Port, upon which Locheil took the advantage and rushed in, the guard immediately dispersing. Thus did the Chevalier render himself master of the Capital without shedding a drop of Blood.

Our[1] people, with drawn sword and target, with a hideous yell and their particular manner of making ane attack (they not knowing what resistance they might meet with in the town), marched quickly up street, no one leaving their rank or order, and forced their way into the city guard-house, and took possession. The main body drew up in the Parliament closs, and guards were immediatly placed at every gate of the city; and the inhabitants cannot in justice but acknowledge that the behaviour of our Highlanders was civil and innocent beyond what even their best freinds could have expected.

I[2] entered the town by the Bristol port, which I saw to my indignation in the keeping of these caterpillers. A boy stood with a rusty drawen sword, and two fellows with things licke guns of the 16 centurie sat on each syde the entry to the poors howse, and these were catching the vermin from ther lurking places abowt ther plaids and throwing them away. I said to Mr Jerdin [John Jardine], minister of Liberton, 'Ar these the scownderalls [who] have surprised Edinburgh by treachery?' He answered, 'I

---

[1] *L. P.* ii, 488. From the Highland Officer's Journal already quoted.
[2] *W. M.* 25. See *supra*, p. xii.

had reither seen it in the hands of Frenchmen, but the divell and
the deep sea are both bad.'

When I came to the head of the stairs [that] leads to the
Parliament Closs I cowld scarce pass for throng, and the Parliament Closs was crowded with them, for they were to make
the parad at reading the manefesto and declaration from the
Cross. I saw from a window near the Cross, north syde of the
High Streeat, this commick fars or tragic commody. All these
mountain officers with there troupes in rank and fyle marched
from the Parliament Closs down to surrownd the Cross, and
with there bagpipes and loosie crew they maid a large circle from
the end of the Luickenboths to half way below the Cross to the
Cowrt of Gaird, and non but the officers and speciall favowrits
and one lady in dress¹ were admitted within the ranges. I observed
there armes: they were guns of diferent syses, and some of
innormowows lengh, some with butts turned up lick a heren,
some tyed with puck threed to the stock, some withowt locks
and some matchlocks, some had swords over ther showlder
instead of guns, one or two had pitchforks, and some bits
of sythes upon poles with a cleek, some old Lochaber axes.
The pipes plaid pibrowghs when they were making ther circle.
Thus they stood rownd 5 or six men deep. Perhaps there was
a stratagem in this appearance, to make us think they were a
rabbell unarmed in this publick parad show, for a greate many
old men and boys were mixed, and they certanly conceiled there
best men and armes thus; for they have 1400 of the most daring
and best melitia in Europe.

However, the parad went on. The Crosse to the east was
covered with a larg fine Persian carpet. The Lyon Heralds in
there formalities, coats on, and bleasons displayed, came attended
but with one trumpet to the theatur or to the Cross....All the
streat and the windows and forstairs were crowded, and sylence
being made, the manefesto was read. In the name of James 8 of
Scotland, England, France, and Ireland King, was a full indemnity and pardon granted for all crimes committed, I presume,
prior to this publication; the malt tax and all other grivences to

¹ Probably Mrs Murray of Broughton.

be removed; the churches secured, the Church of England as by
law established, and these of Scotland and Ireland according to
the lawse of the severall kingdoms...and all this given owt at
Rome, December 1743, and the 43 year of owr reigne. The
Prince Regent's declaration was a reswming all and confirming
it, and dated from Paris [May 16, 1745]. Thus the winds blew
from Rome and Paris were to work owr thraldome. The papers
were cairfully dispersed every where amongst the people, and in
the little armie the King had, and emissaries had been bussie
every where. [Roderick] Chalmers the herald pronunced all this
manefesto and declaration with ane awdable strong voice. I cowld
hear at my distance distinctly, and many much further, for there
was profownd silence. After all these, military [were] dismissed
with bagpipes playing and a fashion of streamers over ther
showlders, and the chime of bells from the High Church steaple
gave musicall tunes all the whill.

About[1] ten o'clock [that day, September 17] the main body
of the rebels, marching by Duddingston (to avoid being fired
upon by the Castle), entered the King's Park, and halted in the
hollow between the hills, under the peak called Arthur's Seat.
By and by Charles came down to the Duke's Walk, accompanied
by the Highland Chiefs, and other commanders of his army.

The Park was full of people (amongst whom was the Author
of this history), all of them impatient to see this extraordinary
person. The figure and presence of Charles Stuart were not ill
suited to his lofty pretensions. He was in the prime of youth, tall
and handsome, of a fair complexion; he had a light coloured
periwig with his own hair combed over the front; he wore the
Highland dress, that is, a tartan short coat without the plaid, a
blue bonnet on his head, and on his breast the star of the order of
St Andrew. Charles stood some time in the park to shew himself
to the people; and then, though he was very near the palace,
mounted his horse, either to render himself more conspicuous, or
because he rode well, and looked graceful on horseback....

When Charles came to the palace he dismounted, and walked
along the piazza, towards the apartment of the Duke of Hamilton.

[1] *H. H.* 99.

When he was near the door, which stood open to receive him, a
gentleman stepped out of the crowd, drew his sword, and raising
his arm aloft, walked up stairs before Charles. The person who
enlisted himself in this manner was James Hepburn of Keith....
He had been engaged when a very young man in the rebellion of
the year 1715, and...condemned the Union between England
and Scotland, as injurious, and humiliating to his Country; saying
(to use his own words), that the Union had made a Scotch gentleman of small fortune nobody, and that he would die a thousand
times rather than submit to it.

The[1] Croud Continued all that night in the outward Court of
the Abbey and huzza'd Every time the Prince Appeared at the
Window....There was a paper given about which had been wrote
in the Highlands Upon the Princes hearing that the Lords of
the regency had put a reward upon his head of 30,000p^d. This
paper offer'd the like sum to any body that would secure the
person of the Elector of Hanover (as his Majesty was at the time
of the Princes Landing Abroad, but Arrived at London soon
after). At night their came a Great many Ladies of Fashion to
Kiss his hand, but his behaviour to them was very Cool: he had
not been much used to Womens Company, and was always em-
barrassed while he was with them. The 18 in the morning the
Prince sent Lord Elcho to the Magistrates, who were Assembled
at provost Steuarts, to demand, under pain of Military execution
(if not Comply'd with) 1000 tents, 2000 targets, 6000 p^r of
Shoes, and 6000 Cantines[2]. The Magistrates Agread to it, and
the workmen were immediatly sett to work....The 18 Lord
Nairn arrived at Dediston [Duddingston] with a thousand Athole
men...which was the Usual Guard [of the town] ever after—
100 men at the Abby, 50 at the Cannon gate guard, 50 at the
City Guard, 100 at the Weigh house, and 25 at the foot of the
Bow. The rest were Lodged in the parliament house and As-
sembly room.

In[3] the meantime, Sir John Cope, whom we left on the road
to Inverness, continued his march thither. He soon became

[1] *E. J.* 259.
[2] *W. M.* 32, calls them 'pans for readying victwals.'
[3] *M. K.* 38.

sensible of the blunder he had committed in letting the Prince getting south of him, and resolved to do what he could to repair it. He marched with all expedition to Aberdeen, where [on September 15] he embarked his troops, and landed them at Dunbar [on September 17]. Tho' he came too late to defend Edinburgh, which the Prince was already in possession of, he resolved to prevent his penetrating into England, which he apprehended was his intention.

Whilst[1] the Heralds were proclaiming King James at Edinburgh [on September 17], Sir John Cope was landing his troops at Dunbar: the two regiments of dragoons had come there on the morning of the 17th in a condition not very respectable. The disembarkation of the troops, artillery, and stores was not completed till the 18th. That day a volunteer[2] from Edinburgh was introduced to Sir John Cope, who told the General that he... was persuaded that the whole number of Highlanders, whom he saw, within and without the town, did not amount to 2000 men[3]; but he was told that several bodies of men from the North were on their way, and expected very soon to join them at Edinburgh....

On the 19th of September, Sir John Cope with his army left Dunbar, and marched towards Edinburgh. This little army made a great show—the cavalry, the infantry, the cannon, with a long train of baggage carts, extended for several miles along the road....

That day the army encamped in a field to the west of the town of Haddington....Next day [September 20] the army moved again, directing their movement towards Edinburgh by the post road, till they came near Huntington; and turning off there, took the low road by Saint Germains and Seaton....

The Van of the army was entering the plain between Seaton and Preston, when Lord Loudon, who had been sent on to reconnoitre the ground, came back at a good pace, and informed the General that the rebels were in full march towards the King's army....

Sir John Cope...thought that the plain between Seaton and

---

[1] *H. H.* 102.   [2] Probably Home himself.

[3] The Atholl contingent had not yet arrived.

Preston, which he saw before him, was a very proper piece of ground to receive them, and continued his march along the high road to Preston, till he came to the place since well known by the name of the field of battle, and there he formed his army, fronting the west, from which the enemy was expected[1]. In a very short time after Sir John Cope had taken his ground, the Highland army came in sight....

As the Highlanders in marching from Duddingston had made a circuit, they did not come from that quarter whence they were expected; and Sir John Cope, as soon as he saw them appear on his left, put his troops in motion, and changing the front of his army from west to south, faced the enemy. On his right was the village of Preston; and still nearer his right, the East Wall of Mr Erskine of Grange's Park....On his left was the village of Seaton; in his rear, the village of Cockenzie and the sea; in his front, the rebels and the town of Tranent. Between the two armies was a morass; the ground on each side of it was soft, boggy, and full of springs that formed a run of water, which went down in a ditch to Seaton, where it ended in a mill-dam. In this boggy ground there were a great many cuts and drains which had made some parts of it more firm; and in these places there were several small inclosures with hedges, dry stone dykes, and willow trees. In the front, and but a few paces from the front of the King's army, there was a ditch, with a thick and strong hedge.

On[2] Thursday the 19th, in the evening, the Chevalier had certain intelligence that G[ll] Cope had marched that morning from Dunbar, and was to encamp that night att Haddingtown, upon which he immediately gave orders for the gaurds of the Citty to retire early next morning, and he went himself that night to Duddingston....

[1] Cope was marching due west in his advance from Dunbar upon Edinburgh; his right flank on the sea-coast, his left inland. The appearance of the Prince's army upon his left (*i.e.* south) flank compelled him to re-form facing south. Sweeping round, the Highlanders again threatened a flank attack upon the left (*i.e.* east) of his second position. A third time he formed, faced east, and fought the battle with Edinburgh in his rear.

[2] *M. B. M.* 198.

In obedience to the orders given, on the morning of the twentieth the gaurds retired from the Citty and joined the Army att Duddingston, and brought alongst with them some Surgeons, with whom the Army was then very ill provided, and some Coaches and Chaises were likewise ordered for the Conveniency of the wounded, so certain was the prospect of a battle, and even a succesfull one. Thus all things being prepared, about nine in the morning...the Chevalier putt himself att the head of his small army, drawing his sword, said with a very determined Countenance, 'Gentlemen, I have flung away the Scabbard, with Gods assistance I dont doubt of making you a free and happy people, Mr Cope shall not escape us as he did in the Highlands,' and then began his march, ordering the few horse he than had, not above fifty in number, to advance att some small distance in front, and to detach a few to discover the Enemys march. In this manner, with the Camerons in front, he marchd in good order, crossing Musselburogh bridge by Pinkey park wall.

I[1] had the van, and when we were upon the south side of Pinkey gardens, we had certain information Sir John Cope was at or near Preston, and that, in all appearance, he would endeavour to gain the high ground of Fawside. There was no time to deliberate, or wait for orders; I was very well acquainted with the grounds, and as I was confident that nothing could be done to purpose except the Highlanders got above the enemy, I struck off to the right hand through the fields, without holding any road....In less than half an hour, by marching quick, I got to the eminence....We then marched in order, advancing towards Tranent, and all the way in sight of the enemy. They were drawn up in the plain betwixt Preston Grange and Tranent; but there were meadows, and deep broad ditches, betwixt us and them. Mr O'Sullivan then came up, and, after taking a look of the enemy, he took fifty of Lochiel's people who had the van, and placed them in a churchyard at the foot of the town of Tranent, for what reason I could not understand. I sent Colonel Ker [of Graden] into the meadows to observe well the grounds. ...In the mean time, the enemy brought some of their cannon

---

[1] *J. M.* 36. From Lord George Murray's Journal.

to bear upon the men that were placed at the foot of Tranent. They...soon wounded a man or two. One of Lochiel's officers came to him and told him they were much exposed, and did not see what good they could possibly do in that place. Lochiel went himself and viewed it, and brought me word that nothing could dishearten men more than to be placed in an open exposed part, when they could not advance[1]. Mr O'Sullivan was then gone to the rear, so, as I was sure the only way to come at the enemy was upon the other side of Tranent, I desired Lochiel to march those men through the village, and I should march the line and join them. Of this I sent word to his Royal Highness; and, it being evening, and no time to be lost, I marched accordingly. When I was in the middle of the village, and joined by those fifty men, Mr O'Sullivan came up and asked what I was doing. I told him...that as there were exceeding good fields on the east side for the men to lie well and safe all that night, I should satisfy his Royal Highness how easy it would be to attack the enemy by the east side. I took the ground I designed; and when all were past the village except the Atholl brigade, who were to continue on the west side above Colonel Gardner's enclosures, his Royal Highness came up to the front of the line. The men lay all down in rank and file. The place was perfectly dry, with stubble, and a small rising in their front, just enough to cover them.

It was now night, and when all the principal officers were called together, I proposed the attacking the enemy at break of day....I told them I knew the ground myself....There was, indeed, a small defile at the east end of the ditches[2], but once that was past, there would be no stop, and though we should be long on our march, yet when the whole line was past the defile, they had nothing to do but face to the left, and in a moment the whole was formed, and then to attack. The Prince was highly pleased with the proposal, as indeed the whole officers were; so, after placing a few piquets, every body lay down at their posts,

[1] By a curious coincidence, Lochiel had to make a similar recommendation to Lord George at Culloden.

[2] This was pointed out to Murray by Robert Anderson of Whitburgh, East Lothian, who had been 'out' in the '15. Cf. *Waverley* (ed. 1830), vol. ii, chap. viii, Note 1.

and supped upon what they had with them. At midnight the principal officers were called again, and all was ordered as was at first proposed. Word was sent to the Atholl brigade to come off their post at two in the morning [September 21], and not to make the least noise. Before four the army began to march, and the Atholl men came up in good time, who were to be the second line, or corps de reserve; those of the first line who had the van and the right the day before were now, according to what was agreed formerly upon, to have the rear and the left; so the line marched from the left, and passed close in the front of what had been the right; this was done without the least noise or confusion. The Duke of Perth went in the front, and I gave him my guides. The Atholl men marched at the same time, in a different line, a little behind the first....When we were past about a hundred paces from the ditches, I immediately concluded, if we went farther, we should leave the enemy upon our left flank. I therefore called to face about, and the word went from the left to the right. We immediately marched on to the attack; and I desired Lochiel to call to his men, in going on, to incline to the left; and I believe, by the time we came up to the enemy, the Camerons had gained half the ground we had left betwixt us and the main ditch.

The[1] Army march'd of from the left in one Colum (this was done in order to Give the Macdonalds, who were on the left, the right). The Duke of Perth Commanded the right wing and Lord George Murray the left. The first line was Composed of the following regiments, Viz. Clanronald 250, Glengarry 350, Kepoch and Glenco 450, Perth 200, Appin 250, and Lochyell 500. The Prince himself Commanded the second line, which was Composed of three regiments, viz. Lord George Murray's 350, Lord Nairnes 350, Menzies of Shians 300, and Lord Strathallan with his troop of 36 horse was orderd to remain near Tranent in order to take prisoners in case of a Victory.

[Meanwhile][2] Sir John Cope, to secure his army during the night [of the 20th], [had] advanced piquets and out-guards of horse and foot along the side of the morass, very near as far east

[1] *E. J.* 269.　　　　　　　　[2] *H. H.* 113.

as the village of Seaton. He ordered fires to be kindled in the front of his army, and sent down the baggage and the military chest to Cockenzie, guarded by forty men from one of the regiments of the line, and all the Highlanders of his army, who were two companies of new raised men, belonging to Lord Loudon's regiments, and the two additional companies of Lord John Murray's [42nd] regiment, that had marched with Sir John Cope from Stirling to Inverness, and by desertion were reduced to 15 men a company.

The line of battle, formed along the side of the morass, consisted of five companies of Lee's [44th] regiment on the right, of Murray's [46th] regiment on the left, of eight companies of Lascelles's [47th] and two of Guise's [6th] regiment in the centre. On the right of the line of foot were two squadrons of Colonel Gardner's regiment of dragoons [13th Hussars]; and on the left, two squadrons of General Hamilton's [14th Hussars], having the third squadron of each regiment placed in the rear of the other two squadrons without any infantry. The cannon were placed on the left of the army (near the waggon road from Tranent to Cockenzie), guarded by a company of Lee's regiment, commanded by Captain Cochrane, under the orders of Lieutenant-Colonel Whiteford....

[But] Sir John Cope, informed by the dragoons, who had seen the Highlanders, that they were coming from the east, immediately...changed the front of his army from south to east. The disposition was the same, and each regiment in its former place in the line; but the out-guards of the foot, not having time to find out the regiments to which they belonged, placed themselves on the right of Lee's five companies, and did not leave sufficient room for the two squadrons of dragoons to form; so that the squadron which Colonel Gardner commanded was drawn up behind the other squadron commanded by Lieutenant-Colonel Whitney. The artillery with its guard, which had been on the left and very near the line, was now on the right, a little farther from the line, and in the front of Lieutenant-Colonel Whitney's squadron.

The ground between the two armies was an extensive corn field, plain and level, without a bush or tree. Harvest was just got in, and the ground was covered with a thick stubble, which rustled under the feet of the Highlanders as they ran on, speaking and muttering in a manner that expressed and heightened their fierceness and rage. When they set out the mist was very thick; but before they had got half-way, the sun rose, dispelled the mist, and showed the armies to each other. As the left wing of the rebel army had moved before the right, their line was somewhat oblique, and the Camerons...came up directly opposite to the cannon, firing at the guard as they advanced. The people employed to work the cannon, who were not gunners or artillery men[1], fled instantly. Colonel Whiteford fired five of the six field pieces with his own hand, which killed one private man, and wounded an officer in Locheil's regiment. The line seemed to shake, but the men kept going on at a great pace; Colonel Whitney was ordered to advance with his squadron and attack the rebels before they came up to the cannon: the dragoons moved on and were very near the cannon, when they received some fire which killed several men and wounded Lieutenant-Colonel Whitney. The squadron immediately wheeled about, rode over the artillery guard, and fled. The men of the artillery guard, who had given one fire, and that a very indifferent one, dispersed. The Highlanders going on without stopping to make prisoners, Colonel Gardner was ordered to advance with his squadron, and attack them disordered, as they seemed to be, with running over the cannon and the artillery guard. The Colonel advanced at the head of his men, encouraging them to charge; the dragoons followed him a little way; but as soon as the fire of the Highlanders reached them, they reeled, fell into confusion, and went off as the other squadron had done[2]. When the dragoons on the right of the King's army gave way, the Highlanders, most of whom had their pieces still loaded, advanced against the foot, firing as they went on. The soldiers, confounded and terrified to see the cannon taken, and the dragoons put to flight, gave their fire, it is said, without orders; the companies of the

[1] They were four old soldiers and some sailors from the man-of-war which had escorted Cope's transports from Aberdeen.

[2] Gardiner fell shortly after. Doddridge's account of his death is quoted in *Waverley* (ed. 1830), vol. ii, chap. viii, Note 11.

outguard, being nearest the enemy, were the first that fired, and the fire went down the line as far as Murray's regiment. The Highlanders threw down their musquets, drew their swords, and ran on; the line of foot broke as the fire had been given from right to left; Hamilton's dragoons seeing what had happened on the right, and receiving some fire at a good distance from the Highlanders advancing to attack them, they immediately wheeled about and fled, leaving the flank of the foot unguarded. The regiment which was next them (Murray's) gave their fire and followed the dragoons. In a very few minutes after the first cannon was fired, the whole army, both horse and foot, were put to flight; none of the soldiers attempted to load their pieces again, and not one bayonet was stained with blood.

We[1] on the left pursued to the walls and lane near Colonel Gardner's house. A lieutenant-colonel, with five other officers, and about fourteen common men of the enemy, got in over the ditch and fired at us. I got before a hundred of our men, who had their guns presented to fire upon them, and, at my desire, they kept up their fire, so that those officers and soldiers surrendered themselves prisoners....I was told that a number of the enemy were gathering in a body near to Tranent, and I perceived a good many people on the height. I immediately marched, with Lochiel and his regiment, back to the narrow causeway that led up to Tranent; but when I was half way up, we found those who were taken for enemies were mostly servants belonging to our army, and some country people. I got intelligence, at the same time, that a number of the enemy were at Cockenny [Cockenzie]. I immediately made the rear the front of Lochiel's men, and went with Lochiel straight to Cokenny, leaving our prisoners with a guard. This place was about a mile to the right of where we first engaged. There were about three hundred of the enemy there, above the half of them being their Highlanders. As they were within walls, they thought of defending themselves; but hearing that we were masters of their cannon, and as they could expect no assistance, they surrendered at discretion. The baggage of their army was all at that place. By the list I caused take that

[1] *J. M.* 40. From Lord George Murray's Journal.

afternoon, by their own sergeants and corporals, we had made betwixt sixteen and seventeen hundred prisoners, of which about seventy [were] officers.

This[1] Battle, which the Princes army call'd Gladsmuir and other people Preston...ended just as the sun gott up: it did not last full a quarter of an hour. The Prince from this Battle entertained a mighty notion of the highlanders, and ever after imagin'd they would beat four times their number of regular troops....The 22 [September] he March'd into Edinburgh with about 800 foot Carrying the trophies of the victory, he himself and all his principall officers on horseback. When he Came near the town he was mett by a multitude of people who huza'd him quite into the palace.

[1] *E. J.* 277.

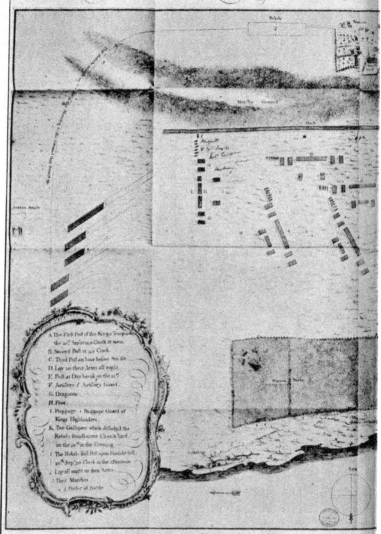

Plan of the Battle of Preston 21.st Septem.r 1745.

A The First Post of the Kings Troops on
   the 20.th Sep.at 4. a Clock at noon.
B. Second Post at 2.a Clock.
C. Third Post an hour before Sun set.
D. Lay on their Arms all night.
E. Post at Day break on the 21.st
F. Artillery & Artillery Guard.
G. Dragoons.
H. Foot.
I. Baggage & Baggage Guard of
   Kings Highlanders.
K. Two Gallopers which dislodg'd the
   Rebels from Tranent Church Yard
   on the 20.th in the Evening.
L The Rebels first Post upon Fauside hill,
   20.th Sep.30 a Clock in the afternoon.
   2 Lay all night on their Arms.
   3 Their Marches.
   4, 5 Order of Battle.

y an Officer of the Army Who was present —

CHAPTER IV

DERBY

While[1] the young Pretender endeavoured to improve the advantages he had gained, the Ministry of Great Britain took every possible measure to retard his progress. Immediately after the defeat of Cope, six thousand Dutch troops arrived in England, and three battalions of guards, with seven regiments of infantry, were recalled from Flanders for the defence of the kingdom. They forthwith began their march to the North, under the command of General Wade, who received orders to assemble an army, which proceeded to Newcastle [by October 29]. The parliament meeting on the [seventeenth] day of October, his Majesty gave them to understand, that an unnatural rebellion had broke out in Scotland, towards the suppression of which he craved their advice and assistance. He found both Houses cordial in their addresses, and zealous in their attachment to his person and government. The commons forthwith suspended the Habeas Corpus act; and several persons were apprehended on suspicion of treasonable practices. Immediately after the session was opened, the Duke of Cumberland arrived [October 19] from the Netherlands, and was followed by another detachment of dragoons and infantry[2]. The trained-bands of London were reviewed by his Majesty: the county regiments were completed: the volunteers in different parts of the kingdom employed themselves industriously in the exercise of arms; and the whole English nation seemed to rise up as one man against this formidable invader.

About[3] a fortnight[4] after the battle [of Prestonpans], there

---

[1] *S. H.* xi, 222.

[2] On October 25, Sir John Ligonier's horse [7th D.G.], Bland's dragoons [3rd H.], St Clair's [1st], Harrison's, Huske's, and Beauclerk's foot, and a troop of hussars, arrived in the Thames from Flanders. *S. M.* 1745, p. 489.

[3] *M. K.* 50.   [4] On October 7. *E. J.* 294.

arrived at Montrose a ship from France with arms and ammunition and a small sum of money. Aboard this ship came [Alexandre de] Boyer, Marquis D'Équilles [d'Éguilles], sent by the Court of France. I dont know what kind of credentials he had[1], but his arrival was represented as a thing of great consequence, and he passed for a public minister. This ship was soon followed by another, that, besides the same cargo, brought a few Irish officers, and then by a third, with much the same cargo as the two former. These succours, tho' trifling, were welcome, as they were looked upon as an earnest of more substantial ones, of which Monsieur D'Equilles gave the strongest assurances. An officer that came from France said, that every thing was getting ready at his departure for a great embarkation of troops. One of the French ships brought over some cannoniers and six field pieces, which, with the seven pieces taken from Cope, made a fine train of artillery.

All this time the Prince's army was increasing every day. My Lord Ogilvie, who had joined at Perth, and remained in the country to raise and bring up his men, was arrived with betwixt three and four hundred men. [John] Gordon of Glenbucket had brought up about three hundred. John Roy Stuart had a commission to raise a regiment of foot, and had got together two hundred. A hundred and fifty horse arrived in a body from the shires of Banff and Aberdeen, all gentlemen and servants, well armed and accoutred. Lord Pitsligo was at the head of his corps. The Macphersons were within a few days march. The Duke of Athol was likewise upon the road at the head of the rest of the Atholmen. The officers that had been sent to the West Highlands to bring back such of the men as had returned after the battle sent very good news of their success. Lord Lewis Gordon, brother to the Duke of that name, had joined the Prince, and was gone north to raise the followers of that family, who were generally well inclined, but wanted one of that family to head them; and there were certain accounts that the Frazers and Mackintoshes were in arms and ready to set out to join the Prince; the former had been raised by Lord Lovat's eldest son,

---

[1] His narrative of his embassy is in *Revue Rétrospective*, 1885–6.

and the latter by the Lady Mackintosh, whose husband, chief of
that name, was actually in the service of the Government, but
it was through the influence of this heroine, endowed with [the]
spirit and vigour of our sex, and all the charms and graces of her
own, that the Mackintoshes took arms, not only without the
countenance of their chief, a thing very rare among the Highlanders, but what is perhaps without example, against him.
Though this was not such an insurrection as was expected after
so complete a victory, there was, nevertheless, a prospect of
having soon a pretty good army.

When[1] Charles with his army returned to Edinburgh, after
the battle of Preston, the friends of Government were extremely
apprehensive that the rebels would march immediately to the
southward, and make a dangerous progress in England, before the
arrival of the British troops from Flanders. But Charles and his
Counsellors did not think it adviseable to march into England
with so small an army, whose appearance might discourage their
friends in that part of the country from declaring themselves.
They therefore resolved to remain some time in Scotland, and
wait for an accession of force which they expected [and received]
in consequence of their victory. Messengers were forthwith dispatched to France, and to the Highlands, with accounts of the
battle of Preston, calculated to obtain the assistance which they
required, to render, they said, their success certain and infallible.
From the time that the rebel army returned victorious to Edinburgh, Prince Charles, as Prince Regent, exercised every act
of sovereignty, ordering regiments to be levied for his service,
and troops of horse-guards to be raised for the defence of his
person. To carry on business with the appearance of royalty, he
appointed a Council to meet in Holyrood House, every day at
ten o'clock.

The[2] Council mett regularly every morning in his drawing
room. The Gentlemen that he Call'd to it Were The Duke of
Perth, Lord Lewis Gordon, Lord George Murray, Lord Elcho,
Lord Ogilvy, Lord Pitsligo, Lord Nairn, Lochyell, Keppoch,
Clanronald, Glenco, Lochgary, Ardshiel, Sir Thomas Sheridan,

    [1] H. H. 123.   [2] E. J. 288.

Coll O'Sulivan, Glenbuckett, and Secretary Murray. The Prince, in this Councill, used Always first to declare what he was for, and then he Ask'd Every bodys opinion in their turn. Their was one third of the Councill whose principals were, that Kings and Princes Can never either act or think wrong; so, in Consequence, they always Confirmed whatever the Prince Said. The other two thirds, who thought that Kings and Princes thought sometimes like other men, and were not altogether infallable, and that this Prince was no more so than others, beg'd leave to differ from him when they Could give Sufficient reasons for their difference of Opinion. Which very often was no hard matter to do; for as the Prince and his Old Governor, Sir Thomas Sheridan, were altogether ignorant of the Ways and Customs in Great Britain, and both much for the Doctrine of Absolute monarchy, they would very often, had they not been prevented, have fall'n into Blunders which might have hurt the Cause. The Prince Could not bear to hear any body differ in Sentiment from him, and took a dislike to Every body that did; for he had a Notion of Commanding this army As any General does a body of Mercenaries, and so lett them know only what he pleased, and [expected them to] obey without inquiring further about the matter. This might have done better had his favourites been people of the Country; but as they were Irish, And had nothing at Stake, the People of Fashion that had their all at Stake... thought they had a title to know and be Consulted in what was for the Good of the Cause in which they had so much Concern; and if it had not been for their insisting Strongly upon it, the Prince, when he found that his Sentiments were not always approved of, would have Abolish'd this Council long ere he did.

About[1] the end of October [the Prince] review'd his Army at Dediston and found them to be 5000 foot and 500 horse. A day or two after the review he proposed to his Council to March the Army into England, where, he Said, he was sure all the Country would join him. His reasons for Thinking so were, that in his Youth his Governors and Flatterers amongst his Fathers Courtiers had always talk'd of the Hanover Family as

[1] *E. J.* 301.

Cruel Tyrants hated by every body, and only kept possession of the crown because they had enslaved the people, and that if he or any of his Family were ever to appear in Britain, that they would flock to him & Look upon him as their deliverer and help him to chase away the Usurpers family (as they call'd him). The way he had been received upon his Entring Edn^r, and the success he had had against Gen: Cope, not only Confirm'd him in all the ideas he had when he came into the country, but he likewise now believed the regular troops would not fight against him, because of his being their natural Prince.

[General[1] Cope's defeat], however unimportant it at first seemed, made the Prince the entire master of Scotland, where the only English troops which remained were the garrisons of the castles of Edinburgh and Stirling. The whole of the towns of Scotland having been obliged to recognise the Prince as regent of the kingdom in the absence of his father, King James, then at Rome, all that he had to do now was to retain possession of it. His chief object ought to have been to endeavour, by every possible means, to secure himself in the government of his ancient kingdom, and to defend himself against the English armies, which would not fail to be sent against him, without attempting, for the present, to extend his views to England. This was the advice which every one gave the Prince; and, if he had followed it, he might still perhaps have been in possession of that kingdom.

[The[2] Prince] called a Councill of war the night of [October] the 30th, where were present his Grace the Duke of Athol, D. of Perth, L. George Murray, Lord Elcho, L. Pitsligoe, Cameron of Locheil, M^cdonald of Kepock, M^cdonald of Clanronald, M^cdonald of Lochgaray, etc., to consult of his march Southwards...whither to march the east road towards Newcastle, and there give General Wade Battle, or to march the west by Carlile. The Chevalier him self was clear for marching towards Newcastle, first, because Mr Wade could only arrive there a day or two before him, and Consequently his troops must have been very much fatigued with their long march after a Campaigne in Flanders. Secondly, having been unsuccessful there, together

[1] J. 34. [2] M. B. M. 231.

with Copes defeat then quite recent, made it reasonable to believe that they would not act with that vigour they might do if let to rest for any time; thirdly, their numbers were not so greatly superior to his own...4thly, to march towards Carlile would be a means to dishearten his own Army, as it would look like shunning Wade...5^{thly}, the advantages following a victory in these parts would be innumerable; the reduction of Newcastle, besides giving a Charracter to his arms, would enable him to strecken the Citty of London and very probably create the utmost Confussion amongst the inhabitants, which might have...made him absolute master of all Northumberland and the County of Durham, with Cumberland to the gates of Carlile, and...given the fairest opportunity to all his friends to join him from Lancashire, Yorkshire, etc., and Could then have left a garrison in the place and marched forward before any Considerable force could be got together to oppose him....

On the other hand, my Lord George Murray, with most of the Cheifs, argued that his marching into England being Cheifly to give his friends there an opportunity to join him, they thought he ought not to risque a battle unless upon good terms....That should he be defeated his affairs would be totally ruined, and a retreat very difficult should the Enemy follow the strock, having the river of Tweed to cross....That the road by Ouler [Wooler] and Whitingham...was extremely bad, and as some rains had lately faln, might be impassible with his Cannon and other Carriages...and therefore they was of opinion that by marching to Carlile and being there joined by his freinds from Lancashire, Northumberland, &c., as he expected, they might then Choose to march to NewCastle and give Mr Wade Battle or not as should be thought most advisible....

After a very long debate on both sides, the Council was adjourned till next morning at nine aClock....But when the Chevalier had retired to his own apartment he begun to reflect, that as the most if not all the Cheifs were for marching to Carlile, his forcing them the other road contrary to their inclinations might be of bad Consequences...as it might thereby enduce some of the Solgers to desert, thinking them selves warranted to do it as being against their Cheifs opinion....Accordingly next day [October 31], how soon the Council had mett, he told them …that he was ready to follow their advice.…This condescention on his part, made in so oblidging a manner, and as if proceeding from the Superior strength of their arguments, seemed to give great contentment..

He then told [the Council]…that what to him[1] appeared the most proper Step to be taken was to march at the head of the Clans to Kelsoe, which would cover his design, it being on the Road to Newcastle, and probably bring Wade to Morpeth to meet him, the ground being much stronger there than att Newcastle, by which means it would not be in his power, however willing, to gett to Carlile before him, and that the other Column with the Cannon and heavy baggage should march to Peebles, which…could not for the first day discover their intentions—so, halting one day with the Clans att Kelsoe, or even two if found necessary, would effectually disappoint Mr Wade, and give the 2^d Column time to march up the Tweed by Drumelzier to Moffat, and join him at Carlile. This proposal…was universally approven of by all present…and D. of A[tholl] Charged with the Command of the 2^d Column, D. of P[erth] under him; the Chevalier the first, L. G[eorge Murray] under him. The first was composed of the Camerons, M^{c}donalds of Glengary, M^{c}donalds of Kappoch, M^{c}donalds of Clanronald, M^{c}donalds of Glencoe, the Steuarts, M^{c}grigors—and M^{c}kinnons. The 2^d was composed of the Athol Brigade, D. of Perths Regiment, Glenbuckets, Roy Steuarts, Lord Ogilveys and the M^{c}pharsons. Lord Elchoes and Balmerinoes [Life-guards], [Lord Kilmarnock's] Perthshire horse. L[ord] Pitsligoes troop with the Hussars commanded by Major Bagg[o]t marched with the first Column. The Carriages having been all previously provided with a large quantity of biscuit, and nothing further requisite to be done, it was determined to evacuate the Citty of Edinburgh the 4th of November.

When[2] the rebels began their march to the southward, they were not 6000 men complete; they exceeded 5500, of whom 4 or 500 were cavalry; and of the whole number, not quite 4000

1 The plan, in fact, was Lord George Murray's. *J. M.* 47.
2 *H. H.* 137.

were real Highlanders, who formed the Clan regiments, and were indeed the strength of the rebel army[1]. All the regiments of foot wore the Highland garb: they were thirteen in number, many of them very small. Besides the two troops of horse-guards, there were Lord Pitsligo's and Strathallan's horse, Lord Kilmarnock's horse grenadiers, and a troop of light horse or hussars to scour the country and procure intelligence. The pay of a captain in this army was half a crown a day; the pay of a lieutenant, two shillings; the pay of an ensign, one shilling and sixpence; and every private man received sixpence a day, without deduction. In the Clan regiments, every company had two captains, two lieutenants, and two ensigns. The front rank of each regiment consisted of persons who called themselves gentlemen, and were paid one shilling a day; these gentlemen were better armed than the men in the ranks behind them, and had all of them targets, which many of the others had not....

The train of artillery which belonged to this army of invaders consisted of General Cope's field pieces, taken at the battle of Preston, and of some pieces of a larger caliber, brought over in the ships from France, amounting in all to 13 pieces of cannon.

Our[2] march was very judiciously planned, and equally well executed....There are three great roads from Edinburgh to London: one of them runs along the eastern coast of Scotland, enters England at Berwick-upon-Tweed, and passes through Newcastle-upon-Tyne. This is the road generally taken. Another goes along the western coast of Scotland, which enters England at Carlisle, a city formally the frontier defence of the English against the incursions of the Scotch on the west, as Berwick was on the east. The third road lies between the other two. Our army was formed into three columns, each of which took a separate road on setting out from [Edinburgh], with the view of keeping the enemy, by this stratagem, ignorant of the place where the Prince intended to enter England. This plan succeeded so well, that Marshal

[1] According to *E. J.* 310, as many as 1000 men deserted on the march, so that at Carlisle the army was reduced to 4500.
[2] *J.* 41.

The Prince a

Fitsligo
150

Lochyel
500

appin
150

Clunie
300

Claron
200

Hussars
70

Ogilvy
500

R: Stuart
200

Glenbucket
200

Perth
300

L⁰ J.
3

Total 4000 foot 500

+ + + + + + + + +
13 Cannon
Colonel Gro

Grant Colonel of Artillery

O'Sullivan Quarter master General

Sullivan Quarter master
General

little Commisary General

Colonel of fort
Lochyel
Stafford
Glenerronald
Ardshiel
Lochgarry
Keppoch Menzies
Lord Ogilvy
Rory Stuart
Clunie

rmy that marched to Derby

al｜ Clenroch. glangarry
150 500

guards Ld Elcho
150

Paion Skian Ld G: Murray
150 300   350

Kilmarnock
perthshire 59:
530

horse & j8 Cannon

L + +
n, 4, 2, 3, yu
int

129

Principal Officers
The Prince General
The Duke of Athole
Lord George Murray

Lt Generals {

Major General Gordon of Glenbucket

Brigadeer ... Lord ...
the attuls ...

Colonels of
horse
Lord Elcho
Lord Balmerino
Earl of Kilmarnock
Lord Pitsligo
M Murray

Wade, who was at Newcastle with eleven thousand men, whom he had lately brought from Flanders, including a corps of Swiss troops in [? Dutch] pay, continued to cover and protect that city, which is one of the most important in England. Secrecy, in this case, was so well observed, that hardly any person in our army had the least idea of the place where the junction of the three columns would take place; and we were very much surprised on finding ourselves all arrive, on the 9th of November, almost at the same instant, on a heath in England, about a quarter of a league from the town of Carlisle....

Carlisle, a considerable town, and capital of the county of Cumberland, is only about a league and a half distant from the borders of Scotland. The river Esk, which is fordable, and about half the breadth of the Seine at Paris, here separates the two kingdoms, as the river Tweed does on the side of Berwick. The fortifications are in the old style, and have been entirely neglected for several centuries, in consequence of the cessation of the long wars between the two countries, and the final union of the crowns, on the death of Queen Elizabeth. It is surrounded by walls flanked with towers, and a fosse, and contains a castle well furnished with artillery, and defended by a garrison of invalids. This castle was formerly a place of considerable strength; but at present its walls, like those of the town, are falling from age into decay. We opened our trenches before this place, under the orders of the Duke of Perth, on the night of the 10th of November.

On[1] Sunday the 10th, the main body of the Rebels were seen passing at a distance from [Carlisle], having crossed the river Eden below the town; we were told the Pretender himself had lodged the night before at Moor House. That day there being a thick fogg, we could not see them so distinctly from the batterys as we might otherwise have done; but when we saw them...they were fired upon from the Castle, Citadell, and every part where the guns could bear upon them....

About 3 o'clock that afternoon, one Robinson, a countryman, who said he was compelled to come, brought in a letter directed

    [1] *M. C.* 63. From the narrative of Dr Waugh, Chancellor of the Diocese of Carlisle.

to the Mayor, from the young Pretender...which was immediately shown to the Governor, the officers of the Militia, and Garrison, the Magistrates, etc.; who were all called together at the Bush, and without the least hesitation agreed, that no answer ought to be sent....Several parties that were seen about the town were fired upon the next day, Monday the 11th, particularly a party that came to Stanwix, said to be commanded by Glenbucket....On Tuesday [November 12] all was quiet, and several accounts, from spies we sent out and others, agreed that the main body of the Rebels had gone over Warwick Bridge towards Brampton....But on Wednesday the 13th, several accounts were brought us, that a party about Warwick were very busy making scaling ladders....About 4 or 5 o'clock this afternoon I was sent for to the King's Arms, where Col. Durand[1] was at dinner, with several of the Militia officers, when he received an answer from Marshal Wade to a letter he had sent him by an express, to acquaint him with what we had done for our defence, and with the whole force of the rebels being then before us....

Upon the reading of it, [wherein Wade held out no hope of speedy relief], several of the militia officers...desired the Col. would open the gates and let them go out in the night, in order to save themselves and their men; which he refusing absolutely to comply with...they were again prevailed with to stand to their arms that night; and did their duty more regularly, making fewer alarms than any night before....The Rebels, before morning, were returned, and a party of them were working at a trench for erecting a battery, behind a hedge opposite to the Cittadell. In the morning of Thursday, the 14th, Col. Durand...received a paper from the militia officers, [and] went immediately up to the room in the King's Arms where these officers were met; and (as it appeared from what passed after they came out of that room to all of us that were in the house) had been endeavouring to induce them not to think of giving up when there was so little appearance of danger....

[1] Carlisle was garrisoned by the Cumberland and Westmorland Militia. Colonel Durand was in command.

In this situation we had a meeting in the Town Hall, where many of the people seemed quite desperate, as thinking they were ruined and undone in case the Rebels entered. [The acting Mayor, Thomas] Pattinson came there, took the direction on himself, and...said the question was, *Whether we should open the gates to the Rebels, or not open the gates?* Mr Tullie, the Recorder, Mr Wilson, myself, and many others, told him that was not the question; the thing we came there to consider was, what could be done in the present situation, as the Militia would do no more?...that all that now appeared to us rational to be done for the service of the Government was to retire into the Castle, to defend that, which we were resolved to do....

We immediately removed what valuable effects we could into the Castle, which was pretty well supplied with stores of provisions....Some of the principal of the Militia officers having joined us...and having brought in about 400 men...with which we were so confident that we were able to make a good defence, all agreed to Col. Durand's sending...to Mr Wade with an account of our resolution, and of the steps that had been taken. ...Some time after we were in the Castle, towards evening, the Mayor came to demand the keys of the town, as Col. D[urand] had retired into the Castle; and John Davinson, merchant, John Graham, apothecary, and Doctor Douglass, a physician, were sent out [to Charles's camp]....About the time they went out, Col. Durand sent the engineer to spike the guns on the Town Walls and Cittadell....

About ten o'clock the messengers who had been sent out by the Militia and the Mayor being returned, said that the flags had been sent to the Pretender's son at Brampton, and that the answer was—*That he would grant no terms to the Town, nor treat about it at all unless the Castle was surrendered; likewise if that was done all should have honourable terms; the inhabitants should be protected in their persons and estates, and every one be at liberty to go where they pleased*....I received a message from Col. Durand to desire I would come to the Castle. I met, as I went into the guard room, most of the officers of the Militia, and several of the principal inhabitants coming out; and was told by Col. Durand that they had acquainted him what the answer was from the Rebels; and that they had begged he would take it into consideration...[and] that he had called a Council of War, at which I might be present; the result of which was, that the Castle was not to be held.

In[1] persuance to the Capitulation [November 15], the Mayer, with some other of the Magistrates, came to Brampton and delivered the Keys to the Chevalier, which he returned them, assuring them in a very obliging manner of his future favour and Protection, upon which they were dismissed, and returnd home. In the evening the D. of P[erth] took possession of the Town and Castle, [the] Capitulation being signd by both parties, and the Governour, Col. Durand, had his horses and baggage given him, with a passport to go where he pleased.... The day after that Surrendery of the Town the Chevalier made his entery [November 17], and Continued there till the 20th, having his Army Cantoned in the Villages adjacent.

Before[2] Charles set his foot on English ground, all the infantry of the British troops in Flanders had arrived in England, two battalions excepted; and these troops, with the Dutch auxiliaries and the new raised regiments, formed three armies, each of them superior in number to the rebel army. One army, commanded by General Wade, covered Newcastle. Another army, advancing towards Lancashire, was commanded at first by General Ligonier, and afterwards by his Royal Highness the Duke of Cumberland. Besides these two armies, a number of old regiments, both horse and foot, that had served abroad, were quartered at Finchley, Enfield, and other villages near London, ready in case of need to form a third army, which was to have been commanded by the King and the Earl of Stair.

Upon[3] the eighteenth [of November] a Council of war was Called [at Carlisle] to determine of what was next to be done, and after some deliberation it was agreed on to march into Lancashire. Tho the Chevalier in all appearance had little reason to expect any considerable assistance from his freinds there, if held in the same light with those in Northumberland, where only two gentlemen joind him, yet he was determined that they should not have it to say that it was oweing to the difficulty of passing the militia in the Country, and that their people were unwilling to rise without some troops to make a head for them, and therefore fixed his departure for the 20th. To have laid there [Carlisle] any longer would have been both idle and dangerous...Mr Wade [being] at Newcastle, and the 2 Regiments with the foot detached to Scotland on his left. So, to prevent a junction of the D[uke of Cumberland's] and Mr Wade's armies, his only proper methode was to march forward, that in case he came to action he might only have one army to deal with, whereas had they Continued [at Carlisle] till the D. [of Cumberland']s march north, who would have been joind by Mr Wade from Newcastle near to Carlile, he had only 3 things to choose upon—first, to fight with an army more than 3 times his number, give them the Slip if possible, and march South, where it was most certain nobody would join him, seeing such a powerfull army in his rear, which he must one day have engaged, or lastly, to have retired to Scottland where he must have encountered [Handasyde] with [Price's] and Ligonier's Regiment of foot, the Glasgow, Paisley and Lothian militia, & Hamiltons & the Late Gardners Dragoons, who were Sufficient to Stop his passage over the Firth till the D[uke] and Mr Wade had comed up; besides, he must have had the whole horse of these armies harassing his rear the whole way on his march from Carlile[1].

Our[2] cavalry left Carlisle on the 20th of November, and marched that day to Penrith....It consisted of two companies of life-guards, composed of young gentlemen. Lord Elcho, now Earl of Wemyss and a peer of Scotland, a nobleman equally distinguished for his illustrious birth and his singular merit, commanded the first company; and Lord Balmerino commanded the second. Besides the life-guards, there was a body of one hundred and fifty gentlemen on horseback, commanded by Lord Pitsligo. On the 21st, the Prince followed with the infantry, and passed the night at Penrith; Lord Elcho, with the cavalry which he

[1] *E. J.* 323, adds that want of money compelled an advance. Lord George Murray urged caution. He had already tendered and recalled his resignation as Lieutenant General, recognizing Charles' lack of confidence in him.　　　　　　　　　　　　　　[2] *J.* 46.

commanded, as first captain of the life-guards, passed the night at Shap, a village eight miles south from Penrith. The Prince, on quitting Carlisle, left a garrison of two or three hundred men in the castle.

On the 22d, the cavalry advanced to Kendal, and the infantry, with the Prince, remained at Penrith; and on the 23d the cavalry and infantry met at Kendal. On the 24th, the cavalry passed the night at Lancaster, whilst the infantry rested at Kendal; and on the 25th, the cavalry advanced to Preston, and the infantry passed the night at Lancaster.

The cavalry, having passed the bridge of Preston on the 26th, occupied a village near the suburbs, and our infantry arrived at Preston[1]. The Prince held here a council of the chiefs of clans; gave them fresh hopes of being joined by his English partisans on their arrival at Manchester; and persuaded them to continue their march. The whole army was allowed to rest itself during the 27th at Preston. On the 28th our army left Preston, and passed the night at Wigan; and on the 29th we arrived at Manchester, where we remained during the 30th....

One of my serjeants, named Dickson, whom I had enlisted from among the prisoners of war at Gladsmuir, a young Scotsman, as brave and intrepid as a lion, and very much attached to my interest, informed me, on the 27th, at Preston, that he had been beating up for recruits all day without getting one; and that he was the more chagrined at this, as the other serjeants had had better success. He therefore came to ask my permission to get a day's march a-head of the army, by setting out immediately for Manchester...in order to make sure of some recruits before the arrival of the army....

He had quitted Preston in the evening, with his mistress and my drummer; and having marched all night, he arrived next morning at Manchester...and immediately began to beat up for recruits for 'the yellow-haired laddie.' The populace, at first, did not interrupt him, conceiving our army to be near the town; but as soon as they knew that it would not arrive till the evening,

[1] Lord George Murray at once led his troops across the Ribble, 'to convince them that the Town Should not be their *ne plus ultra*,' as it had been in the invasions of 1648 and 1715. *M. B. M.* 246.

they surrounded him in a tumultuous manner, with the intention of taking him prisoner, alive or dead. Dickson presented his blunderbuss, which was charged with slugs, threatening to blow out the brains of those who first dared to lay hands on himself or the two who accompanied him; and by turning round continually, facing in all directions, and behaving like a lion, he soon enlarged the circle, which a crowd of people had formed round them. Having continued for some time to manœuvre in this way, those of the inhabitants of Manchester who were attached to the house of Stuart, took arms, and flew to the assistance of Dickson, to rescue him from the fury of the mob; so that he soon had five or six hundred men to aid him, who dispersed the crowd in a very short time. Dickson now triumphed in his turn; and putting himself at the head of his followers, he proudly paraded undisturbed the whole day with his drummer, enlisting for my company all who offered themselves....

I did not derive any advantage from these recuits, to the great regret of Dickson. Mr [Francis] Townley, formerly an officer in the service of France, who had joined us some days before, obtained the rank of colonel, with permission to raise a regiment entirely composed of English; and the Prince ordered me to deliver over to him all those whom Dickson had enlisted for me. It was called the Manchester regiment, and never exceeded three hundred men; of whom the recruits furnished by my serjeant formed more than the half. These were all the English who ever declared themselves openly in favour of the Prince; and the chiefs of the clans were not far wrong, therefore, in distrusting the pretended succours on which the Prince so implicitly relied.

The[1] 29 [November], when the Prince arrived with his army at Manchester, the Mob huzza'd him to his Lodgings, the town was mostly illuminated, and the Bells rung. Their were several substantial people came and kis'd his hand, and a vast number of people of all sorts came to see him supp....The Prince was so far deceved with these proceedings of bonfires and ringing of bells (which they used to own themselves they did out of fear of being ill Used) that he thought himself sure of Success, and his Con-

[1] *E. J.* 330.

versation that night at Table was, in what manner he should
enter London, on horseback or a foot, and in what dress....The
Principall officers of the army, who thought otherwise upon
these topics, mett at Manchester and were of Opinion that now
they had marched far enough into England, and as they had
received not the least Encouragement from any person of distinction, the French not landed, and only joined by 200 vaga-
bonds, they had done their part; and as they did not pretend to
put a King upon the throne of England without their consent,
that it was time to represent to the Prince to go back to Scotland.
But after talking a great deal about it, it was determin'd to
March to Derby, that so neither the French nor the English
might have it to Say, the army had not marched far Enough into
England to give the one Encouragement to Land and the other
to join.

When[1] we came to Macclesfield [December 1], we had certain intelligence that the Duke of Cumberland's army was on
its march, and were quartered at Litchfield, Coventry, Stafford,
and Newcastle under Line. We resolved to march for Derby;
and to cover our intentions, I offered to go with a column of the
army to Congleton, which was the straight road to Litchfield,
so that the enemy would have reason to think we intended to
come upon them, which would make them gather in a body, and
readily advance upon that road, so that we could get before them
to Derby. This was agreed to. A little before I came to Congleton, the Duke of Kingston and his horse retired towards Newcastle under Line, where Mr Weir with one or two others were
taken, and some escaped out of windows. This Weir was principal
spy. We heard afterwards that the body of the enemy, who were
at Newcastle under Line, retreated towards Litchfield, and other
bodies of them that were farthest back advanced, so as to gather
their army into a body about that place, which entirely answered
our design; for next morning early, I turned off to the left, and
passing through Leek, got that evening to Ashburn. His Royal
Highness, who had halted a day at Macclesfield, came the next
[December 3] to Leek, a little after I passed through it.

    [1] *J. M.* 53. From Lord George Murray's Journal.

I got to Derby about mid-day on the [4]th[1] December, and his Royal Highness, with the other column, came that evening.

On[2] Wednesday the 4th of December, about eleven o'clock, two of the rebels vanguard entered this town [Derby], inquired for the magistrates, and demanded billets for 9000 men or more. A short while after, the vanguard rode into town, consisting of about 30 men, clothed in blue faced with red, and scarlet waistcoats with gold lace; and being likely men, made a good appearance. They were drawn up in the market-place, and sat on horseback two or three hours. At the same time the bells were rung, and several bonfires made, to prevent any resentment from them that might ensue on our shewing a dislike of their coming among us. About three after noon, Lord Elcho, with the life-guards, and many of their chiefs, arrived on horseback, to the number of about 150, most of them clothed as above. These made a fine shew, being the flower of their army. Soon after, their main body marched into town, in tolerable order, six or eight abreast, with about eight standards, most of them white flags and a red cross; their bagpipers playing as they marched along. While they were in the market-place, they ordered their Prince to be publickly proclaimed before he arrived; which was accordingly done by the common cryer. They then insisted upon the magistrates appearing in their gowns; but being told they had sent them out of town, were content to have that ceremony excused. Their Prince did not arrive till the dusk of the evening. He walked on foot, attended by a great body of his men, who conducted him to his lodgings....At their coming in, they were generally treated with bread, cheese, beer, and ale, whilst all hands were aloft getting their suppers ready. After supper, being weary with their long march, they went to rest, most upon straw, and others in beds.

Next[3] day [December 5], when most of the officers were at the Prince's quarters [at Derby], it was considered what next was to be resolved on. We did not doubt but that the Duke of

[1] Cf. *B. I.* 30.

[2] *S. M.* 1745, p. 615. An unexpurgated version of this letter is in the *Gentleman's Magazine*, 1745, p. 708.

[3] *J. M.* 54. From Lord George Murray's Journal.

Cumberland would be that night at Stafford, which was as near
to London as Derby. Mr Wade was coming up by hard marches
the east road, and we knew that an army, at least equal to any of
these, would be formed near London...so that there would be
three armies, made up of regular troops, that would surround us,
being above thirty thousand men, whereas we were not above
five thousand fighting men, if so many....His Royal Highness
had no regard to his own danger, but pressed with all the force
of argument to go forward. He...was hopeful there might be a
defection in the enemy's army, and that severals would declare
for him. He was so very bent on putting all to the risk, that the
Duke of Perth was for it, since his Royal Highness was. At last
he proposed going to Wales, instead of returning to Carlisle, but
every other officer declared their opinions for a retreat, which
some thought would be scarce practicable. I said all that I thought
of to persuade the retreat, and indeed the arguments to me seemed
unanswerable.

The[1] Prince heard all these arguments with the greatest impatience, fell into a passion, and gave most of the Gentlemen
that had Spoke very Abusive Language, and said that they had
a mind to betray him. The Case was, he knew nothing about
the country nor had not the Smallest Idea of the force that was
against him, nor where they were Situated. His Irish favourites,
to pay court to him, had always represented the whole nation as
his friends, had diminished much all the force that was Against
him, & he himself believed firmly That the Soldiers of the
Regulars would never dare fight against him, as he was Their
true prince. For all the Success he had had as yett he attributed
more to the mens Consciences not Allowing them to fight
against him, than to The power of the Broad Sword, and he
always believed he Should enter St James's with as little difficulty
as he had done Holyrood house. He Continued all that day
positive he would march to London. The Irish in the army were
always for what he was for, and were heard to say that day that
they knew, if they escaped being killed, the worst that could
happen to them was some months imprisonment. The Scots were

[1] *E. J.* 340.

all against it. So at Night the Prince Sent for them and told them he consented to go to Scotland. And at the same time he told them that for the future he would have no more Councills, for he would neither ask nor take their Advice, that he was Accountable to nobody for his Actions but to his Father; and he was as good as his word, for he never after advised with any body but the Irish Officers, Mrs Murray & [John] Hay [of Restalrig][1], and never more summons'd a Councill[2].

The[3] retreat was begun on the 6th. To conceal it from the enemy as long as possible, a party of horse was ordered to advance some miles towards them, while the army took the road to Ashborn; and to keep the army in suspense, powder and ball were distributed as before an action, and it was insinuated that Wade was at hand, and they were going to fight him; but when the soldiers found themselves on the road to Ashborn, they began to suspect the truth, and seemed extremely dejected. All had expressed the greatest ardour upon hearing at Derby that they were within a day's march of the Duke of Cumberland; they were at a loss what to think of this retreat, of which they did not know the real motives; but even such as knew them, and thought the retreat the only reasonable scheme, could hardly be reconciled to it. When it was question of putting it in practice, another artifice was thought of to amuse them. It was given out that the reinforcements expected from Scotland were on the road, and had already entered England; that Wade was endeavouring to intercept them, and the Prince was marching to their relief; that as soon as they had joined him, he would resume his march to London. This pretext was plausible....The hopes of returning immediately made them somewhat easy under their present disappointment, but still all was sullen and silent that whole day.

The[4] Duke of Cumberland, when he heard of the Princes retreat, had put himself [on December] the 8 at the head of all his horse and Dragoons and 1000 foot, which he had mounted on horseback, to pursue the Prince, with orders for Sir John

[1] He had joined Charles at Edinburgh and acted on occasion as Broughton's deputy. *E. J.* 286.

[2] This is not correct. See *infra*, p. 110.

[3] *M. K.* 78.   [4] *E. J.* 344.

Ligonier to follow with the rest of the army. He marched by
Uttoxeter & Cheadle and came into Maclesfield the 10th.
Marechal Wades army was at Wakefield on the 10th, in order
to Gett into Lancashire before the Princes; he detached Major
General Oglethorpe with Wades [3rd Dragoon Guards] &
Montagus [2nd Dragoon Guards] horse, St George's dragoons
[8th Hussars], & the Yorkshire rangers to see & gett to Preston
before the Prince, but he only arrived at Wigan the 12th. The
11th the Prince Marched into Preston, and the rear guard to
Charly, & next day they arrived at Preston. The Dukes troops
were at Manchester on the 11th. The Prince halted the 12th at
Preston and the Guards were order'd to guard Ripple Bridge.
He would absolutely remain here, and sent of the Duke of Perth
with the Hussars with orders to bring up the army to Scotland.
It was represented here to him likewise that Wades Army might
gett to Lancaster [and] so putt him betwixt two fires. Upon
which he Agreed to Go to Lancaster, and the Army march'd
their the next day. An hour after the rear of the army left the
town, General Oglethorp took possession of it, and the Duke of
Cumberland came to Wigan. At Supper at Lancaster the Prince
talk'd much about retiring so fast, and said it was a Shame for to
go so fast before the son of an *Usurper*, and that he Would stay
at Lancaster. The principal Officers, who were not at all against
fighting when it was reasonable, mett and Agreed, since Wades
army could not now gett in betwixt them and Scotland, that they
would remain and fight the Duke at Lancaster, which at the
Same time would Show them whither it was great Stoutness or
Contradiction that made the Prince & his Irish favourites for
Stoping in Every town. And Accordingly Lord George Murray
went & ask'd the Princes leave to Go next morning and reconnoitre a field of Battle, which he consented to. Lord George
went next morning with a party of the Guards to Chuse
the Ground, and they made some of the Yorkshire rangers
prisoners, who informed them that General Oglethorp was at
Garstang. He sent them in with an escort to the Prince, who
after he had examin'd them, order'd the Baggage to march, and
the rest of the army to move early next morning towards Kendal,
which they accordingly did.

On[1] the 15th we reached Kendal, where we received certain information that we had left Marshal Wade behind us, and that we were no longer in any danger of having our retreat to Scotland cut off....

On the 16th, our army passed the night at Shap; but our artillery remained at the distance of a league and a half from Kendal, some ammunition waggons having broken down, so that we were obliged to pass the whole night on the high-road, exposed to a dreadful storm of wind and rain. On the 17th, the Prince, with the army, arrived at Penrith; but the artillery, with Lord George, and the regiment of the Macdonalds of Glengary, consisting of five hundred men, who remained with us to strengthen our ordinary escort, could only reach Shap, and that with great difficulty, at night-fall.

We [of the rear-guard] set out from Shap by break of day, on the 18th, to join the army, which waited for us at Penrith; but we had scarcely begun our march when we saw a great number of the enemy's light [militia] horse continually hovering about us; without venturing, however, to come within musket shot. The appearance of these light horse appeared the more extraordinary, as, hitherto, we had seen none in the whole course of our expedition in England. Having arrived, at mid-day, at the foot of an eminence [Thrimby Hill], which it was necessary to cross in our march to Penrith, about half-way between that town and Shap, the moment we began to ascend, we instantly discovered cavalry, marching two and two abreast on the top of the hill, who disappeared soon after, as if to form themselves in order of battle, behind the eminence which concealed their numbers from us, with the intention of disputing the passage. We heard at the same time a prodigious number of trumpets and kettle-drums. Mr Brown, colonel in the train of Lally's regiment, was at the head of the column, with two of the companies which the Duke of Perth had attached to the artillery, and of which mine was one. After them followed the guns and ammunition-waggons, and then the two other companies attached to the artillery. Lord George was in the rear of the column, with the regiment of Macdonalds.

[1] *J.* 63.

We stopt a moment at the foot of the hill, every body believing it was the English army, from the great number of trumpets and kettle-drums. In this seemingly desperate conjuncture, we immediately adopted the opinion of Mr Brown, and resolved to rush upon the enemy sword in hand, and open a passage to our army at Penrith, or perish in the attempt. Thus, without informing Lord George of our resolution, we darted forward with great swiftness, running up the hill as fast as our legs could carry us. Lord George, who was in the rear, seeing our manœuvre at the head of the column, and being unable to pass the waggons in the deep roads confined by hedges in which we then were, immediately ordered the Highlanders to proceed across the inclosure, and ascend the hill from another quarter. They ran so fast that they reached the summit of the hill almost as soon as those who were at the head of the column. We were agreeably surprised when we reached the top to find, instead of the English army, only three hundred light horse and chasseurs, who immediately fled in disorder....

We immediately resumed our march....When we had advanced about two miles...the Duke of Cumberland, having followed us by forced marches, with two thousand cavalry, and as many foot soldiers mounted behind them, fell suddenly on the Macdonalds, who were in the rear of the column, with all the fury and impetuosity imaginable. Fortunately, the road running between thorn hedges and ditches, the cavalry could not act in such a manner as to surround us, nor present a larger front to us than the breadth of the road. The Highlanders received their charge with the most undaunted firmness. They repelled the assailants with their swords, and did not quit their ground till the artillery and waggons were a hundred paces from them, and continuing their rout. Then the Highlanders wheeled to the right, and ran with full speed till they joined the waggons, when they stopt again for the cavalry, and stood their charge as firm as a wall. The cavalry were repulsed in the same manner as before by their swords. We marched [to Clifton] in this manner, about a mile, the cavalry continually renewing the charge, and the Highlanders always repulsing them, repeating the same manœuvre, and behaving like lions.

When[1] I came to Clifton, I sent off the cannon and other carriages to Penrith, being two miles farther; and as I believed these light horse that had met me would probably be near Lord Lonsdale's house at Lowther, as he was Lord Lieutenant of the county, I went a short way with the Glengary men to that place, through several enclosures, it being not above a mile. Lord Pitsligoe's horse had joined me....We got sight of severals hard by Lord Lonsdale's house [Lowther Hall], but could come up with few: at a turn of one of the parks, one like a militia officer, clothed in green, and a footman of the Duke of Cumberland's, were taken. We understood by them, that the Duke of Cumberland, with a body of four thousand horse, as they said, were about a mile behind. I sent Colonel Roy Stewart with the prisoners to Penrith, and to know his Royal Highness's orders, and [said] that I would stop at Clifton, which was a good post, till I heard from him. When I came back to Clifton, the Duke of Perth was there; and, besides Colonel Roy Stewart's men, being about two hundred, that I left there, Cluny, with his men, and Ardsheil, with the Appin men, were [come from Penrith] with them. The Duke of Perth...had been persuaded that it was only militia that had appeared, but he then saw, upon an open muir [Clifton Moor], not above cannon-shot from us, the enemy appear and draw up in two lines, in different divisions and squadrons. His Grace said he would immediately ride back [to Penrith], and see to get out the rest of our army....

After an hour they [the enemy] dismounted, as near as we could guess, about five hundred of their dragoons, which came forward to the foot of the muir they were upon, and to a ditch, which was the last of three small enclosures from the places where we were posted at the village. My men were so disposed, that the Glengary men were upon the enclosures on the right of the highway, and Appin's men, with Cluny's, in the enclosures upon the left; Colonel Roy Stewart's men I placed on the side of the lane, or highway, close to the village. I was about a thousand men in all. Pitsligoe's horse and hussars,...upon seeing the enemy, went off to Penrith....

[1] *J. M.* 65. From Lord George Murray's Journal.

Colonel Roy Stewart returned to me from Penrith. He told
me his Royal Highness resolved to march for Carlisle immediately...and desired me to retreat to Penrith. I shewed Colonel
Stewart my situation, with that of the enemy. They were, by
this time, shooting popping shots among us....I told him, I was
confident I could dislodge them from where they were by a brisk
attack, as they had not, by all that I could judge, dismounted
above five hundred. Their great body was on horseback, and at
some distance; and Cluny and he owned, that what I proposed
was the only prudent and sure way; so we agreed not to mention
his message from the Prince....I now went over again to where
the Glengary men were placed, and ordered them to advance, as
they should observe me do on the other side, and to keep up their
fire as much as they could, till they came to the bottom ditch;
and that, if we beat the enemy from their hedges and ditches,
they had a fair sight of them, and could give them a flank fire,
within pistol-shot; but I gave them particular injunctions not to
fire cross the lane, nor to follow the enemy up the muir. I left
Colonel Car [Ker] with them....After having spoke with all the
officers of the Glengary regiment, I went to the right of the
lane. The dismounted dragoons had not only lined the bottom
enclosures, but several of them had come up to two hedges that
lay south and north; the others, where we were, and the dragoons
at the bottom, lay east and west. The Appin battalion were next
the lane upon that side, and Cluny's farther to their left.

In[1] this posture we[2] continued for some minutes, prepared to
receave the enemy, and by this time it was quite night upon us;
and the Generall [Murray] finding it proper that we should
break our then situation by penetrating through our hedge, and
advancing therefrom to another that was situate in a hollow
halfway betwixt us and the enemy, we being both on eminences,
and this hollow interjected, through the hedge we made our
way with the help of our durks, the prictes being very uneasy, I
assure you, to our loose tail'd lads. But before we broke through,
his lordship, suspecting that we might be met with in our way to

[1] *L. M.* ii, 88.

[2] Captain John Macpherson of Strathmashie is the writer. His account
of the engagement was delivered to Bishop Forbes in 1748.

the other hedge, said to our colonel: 'Cluny, if such will happen, I'll attack on the right of your regiment, and doe you the same on the left of it, and we'll advance soe, if you approve of it.' To which Cluny readily answered, he was very well satisfied to attack when his lordship pleased. The disposition thus made, when with great rapidity we were makeing our way towards the other hedge, the advanced parties of the enemy, being dismounted dragoons, met us full in the teeth, who fired upon us; which they scarcely did, when they were answered with the little we had without ever as much as stoping to doe it, but goeing on in our rapid way; by which it soe happened they soon turned their backs to us. The General, how soon we had given our little fire, ordered us to draw our broad-swords, which was readily done, and then we indeed fell to pell-mell with them. But the poor swords suffered much, as there were noe lesse than 14 of them broke on the dragoons' skull caps (which they all had) before it seems the better way of doing their business was found out....There was also a detachment of them sent from their main body in order to have flanked us on the right; but it haveing been their luck to pass by the stone dyke which the Glengarrie regiment lined, they got such a smart fire from that brave corps, that such as outlived it were fain to make the best of their way back to their army; by which means we got none of their trouble, and to which our safety was in a very great measure oweing. After we had chaced the swiftest of those with whom we had to doe in amongst the heart of their friends, we retired to our own first hedge, where we charged our pieces, meaning to maintain that post till daylight, when we expected the whole army would have been up with us for disputing the main point. But soon we receaved orders by ane aid de camp from the army to return to Penrith to join them there, which was accordingly done.

Our[1] army did not withdraw from Clifton-hall till some hours after the night had set in; but our artillery was sent off in the beginning of the action, with orders to continue to advance to Carlisle, without stopping at Penrith....

As we very much dreaded the junction of Marshal Wade

[1] *J.* 70.

with these four thousand men, whom the Duke of Cumberland
had brought with him to Clifton-hall by forced marches, to
harass us in our retreat, as well as the arrival of the rest of his
army, which he had left behind him, we marched all night, and
arrived at Carlisle about seven o'clock in the morning of the
19th of December.

When[1] we came to Carlisle, where we halted [December 19],
I was clear for evacuating it, but it seems another resolution was
taken[2], and I was ordered to speak with some of the officers
that were appointed to stay. The Duke of Perth was very unwilling to leave any of his men; as, indeed, it was no wonder.
In the Prince's presence he asked me, why so many of the
Atholl people were not desired to stay. I told him, if his Royal
Highness would order me, I would stay with the Atholl brigade,
though I knew my fate; for so soon as they could bring cannon
from Whitehaven, I was sure it was not tenable....I do not
know who advised leaving a garrison at Carlisle; I had been
so much fatigued for some days before, that I was little at the
Prince's quarters that day, but I found he was determined in
the thing. It was very late next day [December 20] before we
marched...and when we came to the water Esk...no concert had
been taken what rout we were next to follow. His Royal Highness...desired to know my opinion, which...was, that I should
march with six battalions that night to Ecclefechan; next day for
Moffat, and then halt a day; and after making a feint towards
the Edinburgh road, turn off to Douglas, then to Hamilton and
Glasgow; that his Royal Highness would go with the clans and
most of the horse that night to Annan, next day to Dumfries,
where they would rest a day, then to Drumlanrig, Lead Hills,
Douglas, and Hamilton, so they would be at Glasgow the day
after us. This was immediately agreed to. I passed the water.
We were a hundred men abreast, and it was a very fine show;
the water was big, and took most of the men breast-high. When
I was near cross the river, I believe there were two thousand
men in the water at once; there was nothing seen but their heads
and shoulders; but there was no danger, for we had caused try

[1] *J. M.* 73. From Lord George Murray's Journal.
[2] Before Lord George's arrival.

the water, and the ford was good, and Highlanders will pass a
water where horses will not, which I have often seen....The
pipes began to play so soon as we passed, and the men all danced
reels, which in a moment dried them, for they held the tails of
their short coats in their hands in passing the river, so when
their thighs were dry, all was right. It was near night. Those
who went to Ecclefechan had a very bad march....We halted a
day at Moffat. It was Sunday, and having episcopal ministers
along with us, we had sermon in different parts of the town,
where our men all attended. Our people were very regular that
way, and I remember at Derby, the day we halted, many of our
officers and people took the sacrament. We marched next to
Douglas, then to Hamilton, and arrived at Glasgow, 25th
December. His Royal Highness came there next day[1], with the
other column of the army, by the route above mentioned.

Here[2] [at Glasgow] the Prince resolved to give some days
rest to his army, which really stood in need of it, after such a
long march performed in the severest season; though the fatigue
had been sometimes excessive, few complaints were ever heard.
The Prince's example contributed not a little to the alacrity and
cheerfulness the common men expressed on all occasions. After
a few days the Prince reviewed his army on Glasgow Green,
and had the satisfaction to find he had lost very few men during
this expedition. It was the first general review he had made since
he left the Highlands. Hitherto he had carefully concealed his
weakness; but now thinking himself sure of doubling his army
in a few days, he was not unwilling to let the world see with
what a handful of men he had penetrated so far into England,
and retired almost without any loss. It was indeed a very extraordinary expedition, whether we consider the boldness of the
undertaking, or the conduct in the execution.

Two days after the Prince left Carlisle, the Duke of Cumberland invested it, and having got from Whitehaven some eighteen
pounders, began to batter that part of the wall that is towards
the Irish gate. There was as yet no breach when the Governor
desired to capitulate; but the Duke of Cumberland would grant

[1] Cf. *B. I.* 34.   [2] *M. K.* 89.

no terms, they must submit to his father's clemency, to which he would recommend them. The Governor[1] called a council of all the officers to deliberate upon what was to be done. [Francis] Townley and several others were for defending themselves to the last extremity, rather than give themselves up prisoners at discretion; and they were in the right. They might have held out several days, perhaps obtained terms...But the Governor, and a few that adhered to him, presumed upon the clemency of the father, to which the son was to recommend them, and surrendered upon this condition only—that they should not be stripped by the soldiers. Thus the Prince lost Carlisle [December 30], with upwards of three hundred men, among whom were some good officers and a great many brave fellows.

The[2] garrison of Carlisle was confined in the prisons of London; and the Duke of Cumberland, on his arrival there, on the 5th of January, had so little regard for good faith as to maintain that they were not bound in honour to observe a capitulation with rebels[3]. Thus twelve of the unfortunate officers of the English regiment, with Messieurs Townley and [John] Hamilton at their head, were afterwards hanged and quartered in London; and the head of Townley still remains exposed on Temple-bar, one of the gates of the city.

[1] John Hamilton.   [2] *J.* 81.
[3] This is not accurate. The garrison surrendered on the condition that 'they shall not be put to the sword, but be reserved for the King's pleasure.'

CHAPTER V

FALKIRK AND AFTER

The[1] Prince gott intelligence before he left Carlisle That the Justice Clerk, Lords of the Session, & the Sheriffs of the Lothians had returned back to Edn[r] attended by a great number of other gentlemen, that they had reassumed the government of the town, & had order'd the 1000 men formerly agreed upon to be Levied and to be under the command of the Commander in cheif in Scotland. That L[t] General Handasyde had marched on the 14 [November] into Edn[r] with Price and Legoniers foot and Hamiltons and Ligoniers (Late Gardners) Dragoons, and that the town of Glasgow was raising their militia to be under the Command of the Earls of Home and Glencairn. The towns of Sterling, Paisley, & Dumfries were likewise raising their Militia, and General [John] Campbell [of Mamore] was arrived at Invereray in order to raise the Argyleshire militia. Lord Loudoun was at Inverness. So that Scotland was divided in the Following manner.

Lord Loudoun Commanded all to the north of Inverness, together with the Shires of Nairne & Moray. General Campbell had Argyleshire, and the Government possess'd all to the south of Forth. Lord Lewis Gordon commanded in Bamff & Aberdeenshire for the Prince, and as he was Lord Lieutenant of the county had raised three battalions by obliging every body to furnish so many men for so much valued rent. The three regiments were Abuchies [John Gordon of Avochy's] 300 men, [Francis] Farquharson of Monalt[rie's] 200, and [James] More [Moir] of Stonywood's 300. Sir James Kinloch had raised by L[d] Ogilvys orders, in the same way a regiment of 600 men and possess'd Angus: the remainder of the Princes Troops lay at Perth...[and] Consisted of the following men, viz. The Master

[1] *E. J.* 318.

of Lovat with 300 Frazers, [Alexander] Macgilvray of [Dun-maglass] with 200 Mackintoshes, [James] Farquharson of Bamurel [Balmoral] with 200 Farquharsons, [Coll] Macdonald of Bar[i]sdale with 200, a son [Angus] of Glengary with 100 Macdonalds, [Malcolm] Macleod of Raasa with 100, 150 Macdonalds of Clanronald, Glenco with a 100, [Alexander] Steuart of Inernoyel [Invernahyle] with 150 of Appins men, and [Ludovick] Cameron of Torcastle with 300 Camerons, all which putt together made 3400 men fully as good as the Prince had with him, and it was a most extrodinary thing not to wait for them. Whoever [However] at Carlisle the Prince dispatched Colonel Maclauchlan of that ilk with orders for them to march and join him....The reasons they gave afterwards for not joining the Prince were that they wanted money for such a march; then again, as the Prince had left Carlisle & was making forced marches every day, they Could have no thoughts of overtaking him....Had [he] had them with him in England he might very possibly have beat the Duke of Cumberlands army and gone on to London.

The[1] army would have been more affected with [the loss of Carlisle] but for the news of a victory gained by Lord Lewis Gordon over McLeod at Inverury, which came to Glasgow a few days before the other....To understand the situation of affairs in the north, and what gave the occasion to the action at Inverury, we must look back to the time the Prince marched out of the Highlands. About that time, Duncan Forbes, Esquire, Lord President of the Session, proposed to Sir John Cope to send some notable man to Inverness, who might, under the protection of that fort and garrison, assemble a body of forces for the service of the Government....Sir John Cope approved of the proposal, but being at a loss to find a proper person, the President offered his service, which being accepted of, he went to Inverness. Sir J. Cope left him there when he marched [to Aberdeen]. The President was soon joined by the Earl of Loudon, who had a commission to raise a regiment in that country....It's certain this body was of vast service to the established government. While it

[1] M. K. 91.

was at Inverness, it was impossible for those that lived beyond that town to rise; they must be crushed before they could assemble and be in a position of defence....

While Lord Loudon was busy at Inverness, Lord Lewis Gordon had been very active in Aberdeenshire, raising men and money for the Prince's service. He had got together about eight or nine hundred men, and had taken up his quarters at Aberdeen.

[Meanwhile,][1] upon the news of the march of the rebels into England, and some pretended successes gained by them, the Frasers, headed by Lord Lovat's son, [had] formed a sort of blockade of Fort Augustus....On the 3d of December, the Earl of Loudon, with 600 of the well-affected clans, marched, in a very severe frost, from Inverness, thro' Stratherrick, part of Lord Lovat's estate, on the South-side of Loch-ness, to the relief of Fort Augustus. He met with no opposition, supplied the place with what was wanting, and returned to Inverness on the 8th; after letting the inhabitants of Stratherrick know what they were to expect if they joined the rebels.

This detachment, after one day's rest, was ordered to march to relieve Banff and Aberdeenshire. For this end, two companies of Mackenzies, who had been posted near Brahan, were called into Inverness on Monday the 9th. On the 10th, the Lord Loudon, with 800 men, marched out to Lord Lovat's house of Castle-Dounie, to obtain the best security he could for the peaceable behaviour of the Frasers. At the same time, the Laird of Macleod was detached with 500 men (400 whereof were of his own kindred) towards Elgin, in their way to Banff and Aberdeenshire, to prevent the rebels recruiting there; and they were to be followed by Lord Loudon, and as many men as could be spared from Inverness. Lord Loudon prevailed with Lord Lovat, upon Wednesday the 11th, to come into Inverness along with him, and to live there under his eye until he should bring in all the arms which the clan was possessed of; which he promised to do against Saturday night following, and highly condemned the behaviour of his son. Whilst Lord Loudon waited for the delivery

[1] *S. M.* 1745, p. 588.

of these arms, 200 men, under Capt. Monro of Culcairn, were detached by his Lordship to follow Macleod to Elgin and Aberdeen. Lord Lovat, after delaying to fulfil his promise from time to time, at last found means to get out of the house where he was lodged, at a back passage, and made his escape.

In the mean time, Macleod marched forwards to Elgin; and from thence, hearing that 200 rebels had taken possession of the boats of Spey at Fochabris, and pretended to dispute the passage with him, he advanced on Sunday the 15th to the banks of that river; which the rebels on his approach quitted, leaving him a quiet passage. From thence he advanced on the 16th and 17th to Cullen and Banff, whilst Capt. Monro with his 200 men, on the 17th and 18th, advanced by Keith to Strathbogie; and the rebels, who were in possession of those places, retired towards Aberdeen. Mr Grant of Grant joined Capt. Monro with 500 of his clan, and marched with him to Strathbogie. Upon the 19th it was resolved by Macleod and Capt. Monro to march the next morning, the first from Banff to Old-Meldrum, twelve miles off Aberdeen, and the last from Strathbogie to Inverury, which is at the like distance.

Upon[1] Friday the 20th of December 1745, the Laird of MacLeod marched from Old Meldrum to Inverurie with 500 men, [and] was joined nixt day by [Captain Monro of] Culkern with 200 Minroos, who were quartered upon the farmers neerest to that village. They continowed there in great security untill Munday [December 23], about four in the afternoon, that there centrie in the south end of the town was surprized with the white [Jacobite] flag turning the firpark of Kethall in forward march upon the village, upon which he fir'd his pice to give the alarm, whereupon, as the townsmen say, they turn'd out in great conffusion. (This firpark was within half a mile of the village.) The reason of this security of theirs might proceed from their freinds at Aberdeen making them believe they had nothing to fear from Lord Lewis [Gordon], as he was preparing to march south. But therein were they deceived.

For upon Saturday [December 21] came two companies of

L. M. ii, 344. From a narrative sent to Bishop Forbes in 1749.

L[ord] J[ohn] D[rummond]'s men from Minrose¹, with [Sir
Alexander Bannerman of] Elsick's men from the Mearns, so
that he might have numbered about 900 men, part of which
were left to keep guard at Aberdeen; and upon Munday about
ten did he march by the bridge of Don, with Stonnywood's
regiment, Minaltrie's, Elsick's men, and a few Mr Crichton²
had raised, with the two companies of Drumonds. Abichie
marched his men the Kintore road, and by that means had Don
to cross in sight of the enimie, as Lord Lewis had Urie. About
60 of the Macleods kept firing upon them crossing Urie, wherby
two men were wounded. The Macleods were drawn up upon the
east side of the town, against whom was sent Colonel Culbert
and Stonnywood. Minaltrie and [Gordon of] Blelack entered the
town; Abichie went up the west side to scour the yards, from
which they fired and galled Lord Lewis men in their coming up
from Urie to form agenst the enemie.

The³ action began near an hour after sunset with a clear
moonshine, by some passing shots from some ten or twelve of
the McLeods who advanced so far, some to the one Foord and
some to the other, and fired on the enemy as they were passing
and killed two or three men in the water, and immediately
retired. The Body that crossed Ury moved up first to attack,
but were received with two or three fires from the McLeods,
which they returned indeed two for one, but both were at too
great a distance to do great execution. But as the party from Don
was by this time coming to attack them in flanks, and as the French
were advancing with a close regular fire and like to bear very
hard on them, the McLeods found themselves unable to stand
this shock, and accordingly gave way; yet not so but that a party
of them loaded their pieces retiring, and finding some of their

¹ Lord John Drummond had arrived from France on November 22.
He brought about eight hundred men, including his French Royal
Scots regiment, and piquets from the six Irish regiments in the French
service, commanded by Brigadier Stapleton.
² Of Auchengaul, 'a Popish gentleman of a very small estate, but
representative of the Viscount Frendraught.' B. O. 130.
³ B. O. 143. The narrative appears to be by a local minister and to
have been written about the end of 1746.

men, especially the wounded, like to fall in the enemy's hands, they wheeled about before they were half way up the town, and made another fire, but immediately ran off. On this the French advanced through the town with an incessant street fire, and the rest divided themselves and went firing up each side of it, being too by this time joined by most of their skulking companions. After this, as some of the McLeods were running off on the stubble ground on the North end of the town, some person gave a cry that McLeod was taken, on which they turned about again and made another fire, but immediately marched off. The Rebels meanwhile being at a considerable distance and not observing them so exactly going off, but seeing a ridge with a few furrows in it amidst a great deal of unploughed stubble ground, and taking it by the moonlight for a row of men, they fired once or twice into it very successfully. And thus in whole the firing continued for more than twenty minutes. The companies of McLeods and Monroes that were cantonn'd out of the town had unluckily no Officers with them; these happened to be with McLeod in Inverury and went out to engage along with the men that were there.... These therefore, having no body to draw them together, ran up different ways on hearing the firing till they met some of their friends flying, or were informed of the event, and then they ran off. But had their officers been with them to bring them together, and lead them up in a body to meet their friends at the north end of the town, and support them, they very possibly might have turned the scale in their favours....

Among the prisoners...McLeods own piper [Donald Ban] McGrimman [MacCrimmon] happened also to be taken, and the piper is always looked on as a person of importance in a Highland Chief's retinue. But McGrimman especially was a respectable person, being esteemed the best piper in the Highlands, having had most of the Clan pipers as his scholars, and being looked on by them as a kind of chief. And the veneration they had for him appeared when he was carried prisoner to their army at Stirling; for it is said not a Highland piper would play a tune of them till McGrimman was allowed to be on his parole, and he himself behaved with so much state that he would play to no one of them till their prince himself desired him[1].

Soon[2] after the skirmish…Lord Lewis Gordon marched his men to join the forces at Perth, which was the place of general rendezvous. The number of troops there was continually fluctuating, but at last amounted to 4000 men. They consisted of the Clans that had come to Perth after Charles had left Edinburgh, that is, of the Macintoshes, the Frazers, the Mackenzies, and the Farquharsons; of the recruits sent from the Highlands to the Clan regiments that had marched to England with Charles; of the regiments and companies raised by Lord Lewis Gordon, Sir James Kinloch and others in the low country of the north; of the picquets of the Irish regiments in the service of France, commanded by General [Walter] Stapleton; and of the [French] Royal Scots, whose Colonel, Lord John Drummond, called himself Commander in Chief of His Most Christian Majesty's forces in Scotland….The Commander in Chief [was] Lord Strathallan.

[Meanwhile[3], three days after the skirmish at Inverurie, Prince Charles and his army arrived at Glasgow], one of the prittiest (but most whiggish) towns in all Scotland…on the [26]th of December, 1745, much to their confusion, and halted six or seven days. That Town had given, when the Prince marched for England, five thousand pounds for its good behaviour, and paid as now as much over again for breaking the same, rebelling against us, and raising the Militia in our absence. So we taught them more wit, how to break their words another time. The Army having been here provided with cloathing and other necessaries, of which they were very much in want, the Prince resolved to make a general inspection and review of them. Accordingly, orders were issued one morning for that purpose, for us all to repair to a place at a little distance from the Town. So we marched out with drums beating, colours flying, bag-pipes playing, and all the marks of a triumphant army, to the appointed

[1] MacCrimmon was killed shortly after in the fiasco at Moy on February 16.

[2] *H.H.* 159.

[3] *B.O.* 191. From the narrative of Captain John Daniel, who had joined the Prince in Lancashire.

ground, attended by multitudes of people who had come from all parts to see us, and especially the ladies, who before were much against us, were now, charmed at the sight of the Prince, become most loyal[1]; and many afterwards, when they could not testify it to us by their good offices, did it in imitation in their hearts. I am somewhat at a loss to give a description of the Prince at this Review. No object could be more charming, no personage more taking, no deportment more agreeable, than his at that time was; for being well mounted and princely attired[2], having, too, great endowments both of body and mind, he appeared to bear a sway above any comparison with the heroes of the last ages, and the majesty and grandeur he seemed to display most noble and divine. The Army being now drawn up in all form, and every one putting himself out for the best, the Prince rode through the ranks, greatly encouraging and delighting all who saw him.

Their[3] was a great many people of the [Prince's] army were for marching from Glasgow to take possession a second time of Edinburgh, or else to go to East Lothian to oblidge General Hawley, who was marching the army Wade commanded down to Scotland.

The[4] Prince, upon his arrival at Glasgow, had despatched a gentleman to Perth to get a particular state of his affairs in that country. When he found that his forces were so widely scattered that it would be a considerable time before they could all join him, he altered his plan, and laying aside for some time the project of returning to England, he resolved upon the sieges of Stirling and Edinburgh Castles. He depended upon the artillery and engineers Lord John Drummond had brought along with him, and upon repeated assurances he gave him of French succours. Having determined to begin with Stirling, he sent orders to Lord Lewis Gordon, Lord John Drummond...Lord Strathallan, and other commanders in these parts, to assemble their men and join him.

The[5] [3rd] of January [1746], we quitted [Glasgow] in two

[1] Other accounts declare that the Glasgow women were hostile.
[2] In his 'French dress.' *E. J.* 355.
[3] *E. J.* 361.   [4] *M. K.* 93.   [5] *J.* 82.

columns; one of which [Lord George Murray's] took the road to Cumbernauld, where it passed the night, whilst the other went to Kilsyth. By this movement the Prince, according to every appearance, seemed to entertain the intention of proceeding to Edinburgh, especially as Lord Elcho, with the cavalry, had advanced as far as the town of Falkirk....But the [Prince's] column, which had passed the night at Kilsyth, quitted the Edinburgh road next morning; and falling back upon its left, the two columns met in the evening at the village of Bannockburn, about half a league from Stirling.

The object of the Prince in approaching Stirling was to accelerate his junction with Lord John Drummond, whom he had ordered to repair to Alloa with the...artillery and stores which he had brought from France. The town of Stirling, protected by the castle, in which there was a strong garrison, commanded by General Blakeney, the governor, having refused to surrender, the Prince, on the 4th of January, ordered a part of his army to occupy the villages of St Dennis and St Ninians, which are within cannonshot of the town, on the south. By this position it was blockaded and invested on every side; the stone bridge, to the north of the town, having been broken down when General Cope was there with his army.

On our reaching Bannockburn, Lord George Murray...repaired immediately to Alloa, where Lord John Drummond had already arrived, in order to take measures for the speedy advance to Stirling of the troops and artillery brought by Lord John from France; and after giving the necessary directions for the conveyance of the guns, he returned next day to Bannockburn. He then put himself at the head of eleven hundred men, and stationed himself with them as a fixed post at Falkirk....Lord Elcho, with the cavalry, occupied the town of Linlithgow....The rest of our army was quartered in the villages of St Dennis and St Ninians, and at Bannockburn, two miles from Stirling, where the Prince had his headquarters.

Lord John Drummond immediately repaired to Bannockburn with his regiment of Royal Scots, and five piquets of the Irish brigade; as also with Lord Lewis Gordon, and six hundred vassals of his brother, the Duke of Gordon; Mr Fraser, the eldest son of Lord Lovat, and six hundred of his father's vassals; the Earl of Cromarty, his eldest son Lord Macleod, and his vassals, the Mackenzies. The Prince was then joined by many other Highlanders of the clans of Mackintosh and Farquharson: so that by this reinforcement our army was suddenly increased to eight thousand men, the double of what it was when we were in England....

On the 6th of January, we opened the trenches before the town of Stirling, under the direction of Mr [James Alexander] Grant; but the mere threat of laying siege to the town induced the magistrates to repair to Bannockburn and propose a capitulation; and the Prince having granted them the conditions which they required, we took possession of Stirling next day. The castle was not included in the surrender. General Blakeney answered very politely to the summons of the Prince, 'That His Royal Highness must assuredly have a very bad opinion of him were he capable of surrendering the castle in such a cowardly manner.'...

M. Mirabelle de Gordon, a French engineer, and chevalier of the order of St Louis, was sent into Scotland with Lord John Drummond, and arrived at Stirling on the 6th....It was supposed that a French engineer, of a certain age, and decorated with an order, must necessarily be a person of experience, talents, and capacity; but it was unfortunately discovered, when too late, that his knowledge as an engineer was extremely limited, and that he was totally destitute of judgment, discernment, and common sense. His figure being as whimsical as his mind, the Highlanders, instead of M. Mirabelle, called him always Mr Admirable.

Mr Grant had already communicated to the Prince a plan of attack of the castle, which was to open the trenches and establish batteries in the burying-ground, on that side of the town which is opposite to the castle gate....The inhabitants of Stirling having remonstrated with the Prince against this plan, as...the fire from the castle would, they said, reduce their town to ashes, he consulted M. Mirabelle...and as it is always the distinctive mark of ignorance to find nothing difficult, not even the things that are impossible, M. Mirabelle, without hesitation, immediately undertook to open the trenches on a hill to the north of the castle, where there were not fifteen inches depth of earth above the solid rock, and it became necessary to supply the want of earth with bags of wool, and sacks filled with earth, brought from a distance. Thus the trenches were so bad, that we lost a great many men, sometimes twenty-five in one day. The six pieces of artillery sent from France, two of which were eighteen, two twelve, and two six pounders, arrived at Stirling on the 14th.

We[1] had scarce got well into the siege of the Castle before news came that General Hawley was advancing towards us with about eleven or twelve thousand men....So, seing we must inevitably fight, we endeavoured to prepare ourselves in the best manner for that purpose.

The[2] 15 of Jan[r] 1746 The Prince drew up all his army in battle upon a plain a mile to the East of Bannockburn, and sent of a large body of horse to reconnoitre Falkirk, who brought back intelligence that they had perceived a large body of horse near that town, but no foot, upon which the Prince order'd his army back to their quarters, and a body of horse to patrouille all that night as near Falkirk as they could with safety. Next day, [January] 16, that party sent word to the Prince that all the foot of Hawleys army were arrived at Falkirk, that they had been joined by 1000 Highlanders under the command of Colonel Campbell, and that they had pitch'd their Camp a little to the north of Falkirk & had the town on their left and their horse advanced in their front at the brige of Carron. The Prince drew his army up in battle in the same place as the day before and waited upon the field untill three o clock, but upon hearing that their was no appearance of their moving that day, he order'd his army to their quarters, which were so dispersed, that if Gen: Hawley had marched his army that night forward to Bannockburn, where the Prince lay, it would have been impossible to have Assembled 3000 men together in any one place all night. Lord Lewis Gordon this day joined the army with 800 men, as did Sir James Kinloch with 600, and Lord John Drummonds regiment 350 men. So that at this period the Prince had an army of 8000 men, and all in very good Spirits....On the 17 the Prince drew up his army upon the same field he had done the day before,

---

[1] *B. O.* 194. Captain Daniel's narrative.   [2] *E. J.* 370.

and sent of a body of horse to see if their was any motion in General Hawleys Camp at Falkirk, and upon report that their was none, he held a council of war upon the field.

The[1] officers being called into his Royal Highness's presence, I observed how difficult it was to bring our men together from so many different cantonments...whereas the enemy...could march by break of day, and so be in the heart of our quarters before we could make head against them, there being but four miles from a great part of our cantonments and their camp....I said, that by holding above the Torwood, we would gain the hill of Falkirk as soon as them, as it was a thing they did not expect. ...This was approved of by every body, and his Royal Highness was much pleased with the design. I then asked if I should march off at the head of the two lines in the manner they were then drawn up, which the Prince agreed to, and it was done accordingly, for there was not a moment to be lost, it being then [January 17] betwixt twelve and one [mid-day]. After I had marched about half a mile, Mr O'Sullivan came up to me, and told me he had been talking with the Prince, and that it was not thought advisable to pass a water [Carron] in sight of an enemy, and therefore it was best delaying it till night, and then we could do it unperceived....I did not halt, and he went back to his Royal Highness, who...came up soon after, with Brigadier Stapleton, Mr O'Sullivan, and some others....I told him, so far from disputing our passing, that we were now within half a mile of the water, which then was very small, and that the enemy were full two miles off, and could not see us till we were very near it... and that probably they were then all at dinner, so that we must get up to the high ground before them. His Royal Highness and the Brigadier were entirely satisfied. We had not stopped all the time, and Lord John Drummond had been sent to make a feint with the horse below the Torwood. After we came in sight of the water, which was just below us, we had a view of Falkirk and the enemy's camp; and some scouts that were on the other side of the water...rode off at full gallop, and carried the alarm to them, which was the first notice they had.

[1] *J. M.* 79. From Lord George Murray's Journal.

[Already]¹ about 10 o'Clock Mʳ Hawley went out to a little eminence on the left of the Camp [at Falkirk] to reconnoitre the Grounds between our Camp and the Torwood; where I heard some of the Officers say, they saw them [the Highlanders] moving on this Side of the Torwood Southwards. This proved true; though I saw nothing, neither did Mʳ Hawley. However, about eleven o'Clock we got the alarm, & in a very short space were all under Arms, & remain'd so a quarter of an hour. Then we found out it was a false Alarm, & we all turn'd in again, & went to look out for Dinner, which was not easy to be found; & after it was found we got no time to eat it; for a little before two the last Alarm came, when the Enemy was within a Mile & a half of us. I never was used to these things; but I was sur-priz'd to see in how little time the regular troops were form'd (I think in less than half an hour) on the left of the Camp, in two Lines, with the Dragoons on the flanks; all fronting the South, & just along the side of the high road leading to Stirling; the Road in their front, & Falkirk on their left. We all thought that there we were to wait for the Enemy, who was now plainly in view, coming along the hills from the South-west. Mʳ Hawley, it seems, had another notion; for no sooner was the Army form'd, than he marched them straight up a steep Hill which lyes to the South-west of Falkirk, in two Columns; in order, I suppose, to gain a large Moor which they say is on the top of that Hill, and which may be so for me, & I believe for His Excellency too; for neither of us saw it, at least before the action. All the Dragoons were sent on before, & form'd upon the top of the Hill; and there the Action began.

I² have explained elsewhere the method of marching and form-ing among the Highlanders. The first and second column, or line, went along the moor, on the west side of the Torwood, whence they could not be seen from Hawley's camp; the third marched along the high road and joined the other two at Dunipace, where they all passed the Carron, and immediately began to stretch along the moor, on the other side, in lines parallel to the summit

¹ *C. P.* 270. The writer, William Corse, was serving in the Glasgow regiment.
² *M. K.* 99.

of the hill that was betwixt them and the enemy's camp. When they had gone as far as was necessary, they faced about to the left, and marched up the hill in battle [formation].

The first line was composed of the Clans: the McDonalds had the right, and the Camerons the left[1]; in the second line the Athol brigade had the right, Lord Lewis Gordon's men the left, and Lord Ogilvy's the centre; in the third Lord Elcho's and Lord Balmerino's guards, with the huzzars, had the right, Lord Pitsligo's and Lord Kilmarnock's horse the left, and the Prince was in the centre, with Lord John Drummond's grenadiers[2], a piquet of his regiment, and the three Irish piquets. As the first line was much more than double of either the other two, there were very large intervals betwixt the centre and wings of the second and third line.

The[3] infantry of the King's army was also formed in two lines, with a body of reserve. The first line consisted of a battalion of the Royal [Scots], of the regiments of Wolfe [8th], Cholmondley [34th], Pulteney [13th], Price [14th], and Ligonier [48th]. The Royal had the right of the first line, and Wolfe's regiment the left. The second line consisted of Barrel's regiment [4th], Blakeney's [27th], Monroe's [37th], Battereau's, and Fleming's [36th]; Barrel's regiment had the right of this line, and Blakeney's the left. Howards regiment [3rd] formed a body of reserve. The dragoons that were advanced before the infantry, and a good way to their left, having large intervals between their squadrons, extended so far that they covered a great part of the first line of the rebel army, for the left of the dragoons was opposite to Keppoch's regiment, and their right to the centre of Lord Lovat's, which was the third regiment from the left of the rebels. Behind the greater part of this body of cavalry there was no infantry but the Glasgow regiment, which, being newly levied, was not allowed to have a place either in the first or second line, but stood by itself near some cottages behind the left of the

[1] In some accounts Appin holds the extreme left.

[2] In some accounts Lord John Drummond is wrongly placed on the left of the Camerons. See *J. M.* 84; *J.* 94 *n.*; and *H. H.* 169 *n.*

[3] *H. H.* 169. Home was present at the battle, and was made prisoner.

dragoons. Most of the regiments of foot in the King's army were standing on the declivity of the hill. More than one regiment both of the first and second line stood higher up, and on ground somewhat more plain and level. The Highlanders towards the left of their first line saw the foot of the King's army; the High-landers on the right of the first line saw no foot at all; for besides the great inequality of the ground, the storm of wind and rain continued, and the darkness increased so much, that nobody could see very far. To conclude this account of the field of battle, and the position of the regiments, there was a ravine or gully which separated the right of the King's army from the left of the rebels. This ravine began on the declivity of the hill, directly opposite to the centre of Lord Lovat's regiment, and went down due north, still deeper and wider to the plain....

The infantry of the King's army not being completely formed (for several companies of Fleming's regiment were only coming up to take their place in the centre of the second line) when General Hawley sent an order to Colonel Ligonier, who com-manded the cavalry, to attack the rebels: Colonel Ligonier with the three regiments of dragoons advanced against the High-landers, who at that very instant began to move towards the dragoons. Lord George Murray was marching at the head of the Macdonalds of Keppoch, with his drawn sword in his hand, and his target on his arm. He let the dragoons come within ten or twelve paces of him, and then gave orders to fire. The Mac-donalds of Keppoch began the fire, which ran down the line from them to Lord Lovat's regiment. This heavy fire repulsed the dragoons. Hamilton's and Ligonier's regiments wheeled about, and fled directly back: Cobham's regiment wheeled to the right, and went off between the two armies, receiving a good deal of fire as they passed the left of the rebels. When the dragoons were gone, Lord George Murray ordered the Macdonalds of Keppoch to keep their ranks, and stand firm. The same order was sent to the other two Macdonald regiments, but a great part of the men in these two regiments, with all the regiments to their left (whose fire had repulsed the dragoons), immediately pursued. When they came near the foot of the King's army, some regiments of the first line gave them a fire: the rebels returned the fire, and throwing down their musquets, drew their swords and attacked the regiments in the left of the King's army, both in front and flank: all the regiments in the first line of the King's army gave way, as did most of the regiments of the second line. It seemed a total rout...But Barrel's regiment stood, and joined by part of two regiments of the first line (Price's and Ligonier's) moved to their left, till they came directly opposite to the Camerons and Stuarts, and began to fire upon them across the ravine. The...rebels, after losing a good many men, fell back a little, still keeping the high ground on their side of the ravine. ...Most of the men in those regiments which stood behind the Clans of the first line that attacked the foot of the King's army, seeing the wonderful success of that attack...[had] followed the chase; but many of the men belonging to the regiments that were thinned in this manner, hearing the repeated fires given by the King's troops across the ravine, thought it was most likely that the Highland army would be defeated; and that the best thing they could do was to save themselves by leaving the field when they might: accordingly they did so, and went off to the westward. At this moment the field of battle presented a spectacle seldom seen in war, whose great events Fortune is said to rule. Part of the King's army, much the greater part, was flying to the eastward, and part of the rebel army was flying to the westward. Not one regiment of the second line of the rebels remained in its place; for the Athol brigade, being left almost alone on the right, marched up to the first line, and joined Lord George Murray where he stood with the Macdonalds of Keppoch. Between this body of men on the right of the first line, and the Camerons and Stuarts on the left (who had retreated a little from the fire of the troops across the ravine)[1], there was a considerable space altogether void and empty, those men excepted who had returned from the chase, and were straggling about in great disorder and confusion, with nothing in their hands but their swords. By and by Lord George Murray with his men joined them, and

---

[1] These regiments on the left were outflanked by Hawley's line and suffered in consequence. Cf. *J. M.* 85.

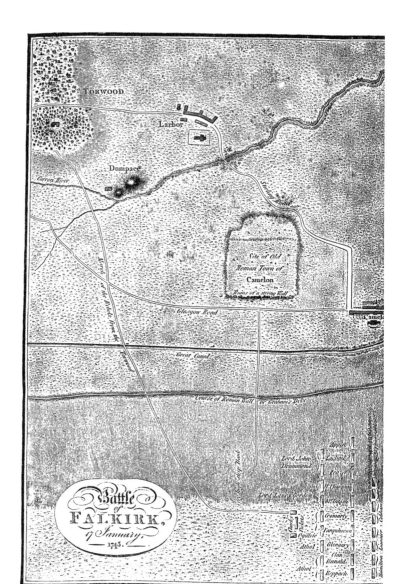

TORWOOD

Larbor

Dumpace

Carron River

March of the Rebels from the Torwood

Site of Old
Roman Town or
Camelon

Ruins of a strong Wall

Stirling Road

Camel

Glasgow Road

Great Canal

Course of Roman Wall or Graham's Dyke

March of the Royal Troops

Arpsie
Loeboul

Lord John
Drummond

M'Clarson

Lord Lewis Gordon

M'Intosh

Cromarty

Farquharson

Ogilvie

Glengary

Athol

Clan
Ranald

Athol

Keppach

Battle
of
FALKIRK,
17 January,
1745.

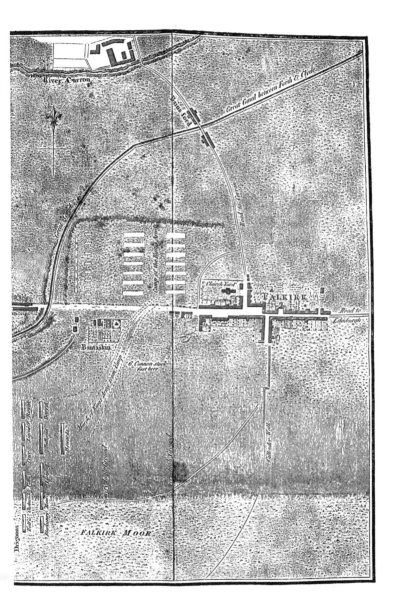

River Carron

Great Canal between Forth & Clyde

Dunn Pace

Road to Forth

Camp the Highlanders

Church Yard

FALKIRK

Road to Edinburgh

Bantaskin

6 Cannon stuck fast here

March of King James's Army from Camp

Callender Woods

Dragoons

FALKIRK MOOR

Charles with the Irish piquets, and some other troops of the reserve, came up from the rear. The presence of Charles encouraged the Highlanders: he commended their valour; made them take up the musquets which lay thick upon the ground; and ordering them to follow him, led them to the brow of the hill. At the approach of so considerable a body of men, Cobham's regiment of dragoons [10th Hussars], which, having always kept together, was coming up the hill again, turned back, and went down to the place where the regiments of foot were standing who had behaved so well, and retreating with them in good order, joined the rest of the army who had rallied on the ground in the front of their camp, where the Argyleshire Highlanders had been left by General Hawley, when he marched with his troops to meet the enemy. The storm of wind and rain continued as violent as ever: night was coming on, for the battle began a little before four o'clock. Before it grew dark, General Hawley gave orders to set fire to the tents, and marching his army through the town of Falkirk, retreated to Linlithgow, leaving behind him seven pieces of cannon, with a great quantity of provision, ammunition, and baggage.

The[1] enemy, finding they could neither possess nor save their camp...were just got to the east end of the toun of Falkirk when Lord John Drummond entered it on that side, Lord George Murray in the middle, and Lochiel in the west end of the toun. We took most of their cannon, ammunition, and baggage, which they had not themselves destroyed. We reckond about seven hundred of the enemy taken prisoners, and about six hundred men and between thirty or forty officers killed. We had not above forty men killed on our side, among whom were two or three captains and some subaltern officers.

His R. H.'s first care early next morning was to cause bury the dead, as well those of the enemy as our own people. Had not night come on and been very stormy, and our men engadged in pillaging the enemys camp, our army might have got betwixt them and Lithgow and would have entirely distroyed them; but they being in want of every thing, they thought fitt to retire

[1] *L. P.* ii, 502. By 'A Highland Officer.'

next day to Edinburgh, near twenty miles from the field of battle....

An unlucky accident happend amongst us [at Falkirk] next day; Colonell Enæas McDonald, second son to Glengarie, and who commanded the Glengarie men, a brave and good naturd youth, was unhappily shot by the accident of a Highlandmans cleaning his peice. This poor gentleman, satisfyed of the unhappy fellows innocence, beggd with his dying breath that he might not suffer; but nothing could restrain the grief and fury of his people, and good luck it was that he was a McDonald (tho not of his own tribe, but of Keppochs[1]), and after all they began to desert daily upon this accident, which had a bad effect upon others also, and lessend our numbers considerably.

However[2], the victory was complete....Several were for following the blow, and driving Mr Hawley out of Scotland. Some were for marching directly to London, without giving the enemy time to recover from their consternation....Those that were against this measure said that Stirling was the object at present; that it was never heard of that an army employed in a siege, having beaten those that came to raise it, had made any other use of their victory than to take the fortress in the first place; that any other conduct would argue a great deal of levity; that it was of the utmost importance to have the Castle, as it opened an easy and safe communication betwixt the Prince, wherever he might happen to be, and his friends in the north. In fine, this opinion prevailed so much the more readily, that Monsieur Mirabel, the chief engineer, had given the strongest assurance that the Castle would be forced to surrender in a few days, and if the Prince went immediately upon another expedition, his heavy artillery, which he could not carry about with him, would be lost.

The[3] Prince, who was determined to make the Siege of Sterling Castle, [accordingly] went back on [January] the 19 to Bannockburn, and order'd all the troops into their former quarters, the Clans to remain at Falkirk with Ld George Murray,

---

[1] Of Clanranald's, according to *E.J.* 380.
[2] *M. K.* 106.   [3] *E.J.* 381.

and a party of horse at Ld Napiers house on the road to Linlithgow. The Prince, upon his arrival at Bannockburn, order'd the Castle of Sterling to be Summon'd to surrender, but General Blakeney who Commanded it made answere that he would defend it to the last, Upon which the Trenches which were open'd on the 16 were Carried on with all diligence. Their was about 400 men mounted the trenches once in the four & twenty hours. General Blakeney firr'd upon them almost every day, but not much, and their was a great many shells thrown from Coehorns on both sides, but as they were very bad they did little mischief. The Prince came and visitted the trenches once[1]; provisions were very scarce during the Siege at Sterling, for General Blakeney had order'd an Arche of the Bridge to be Broke down, which prevented the Country people on that side of the river from coming to town.

On the 28 of Jan^r. Monsr de Mirabel had so far finished a battery (on the Gowan hill very near the Castle) as to begin to play upon it with three Battering Cannon, on the 29 in the morning; and the Shot he firr'd did the walls much damage. But Generall Blakeney firr'd against it with a Battery of nine nine pounders, and in a few hours time dismounted the three Guns and demolish'd the Battery. Monsr de Mirabell was much blamed for the unsufficiency of his Battery and for Beginning to play upon the castle with only three Cannon, when, if he had waited a day longer, he might have had seven mounted, and people did not hesitate to Say he had been bribed. The Princes army at this siege had 30 men kill'd and 50 wounded, which loss fell upon the Lowland foot and French piquetts, for the highlanders are not fitt for Sieges. The news of The Duke of Cumberland's arrival at Edn^r on [January] the 29 and of his intention to march to Sterling with Hawleys army, reinforced by the Scots fusileers & Sempills foot [25th] and Lord Mark Ker's dragoons [11th Hussars], putt a Stop to all further preparations about the Siege.

[It[2] was on January] the 28th the news came to Bannockburn

[1] He was residing near Stirling with Sir Hugh Paterson, whose niece, Maria Clementina Walkinshaw, a girl of twenty, later became his mistress. [2] *M. K.* 111.

that the Duke of Cumberland was to be at Edinburgh in a day or two at farthest, and that the army was ready, and only waited his arrival to march again to the relief of Stirling Castle, the reduction of which was not likely to be so sudden as Monsieur Mirabel had promised. The Prince sent his Secretary Murray that day to Falkirk, to acquaint Lord George with his intentions, which were to go and attack the Duke of Cumberland when he advanced as far as Falkirk, where Lord George was to remain till the Duke of Cumberland came to Linlithgow. Lord George seemed to approve of every thing, drew up a new plan of battle with some improvements upon the former, and sent it next day to the Prince for his approbation. The Prince was extremely pleased with the plan, and in the highest spirits to think he was to have to do with the Duke of Cumberland in person. But this joy was very short; for that very night he received a representation signed at Falkirk, by Lord George Murray and all the commanders of Clans, begging his Royal Highness would consent to retreat :

Falkirk, 29th January 1746.

We[1] think it our duty, in this critical juncture, to lay our opinions in the most respectful manner before your Royal Highness.

We are certain that a vast number of the soldiers of your Royal Highness's army are gone home since the battle of Falkirk; and notwithstanding all the endeavours of the commanders of the different corps, they find that this evil is encreasing hourly, and not in their power to prevent: and as we are afraid Stirling Castle cannot be taken so soon as was expected, if the enemy should march before it fall into your Royal Highness's hands, we can foresee nothing but utter destruction to the few that will remain, considering the inequality of our numbers to that of the enemy. For these reasons, we are humbly of opinion, that there is no way to extricate your Royal Highness, and those who remain with you, out of the most imminent danger, but by retiring immediately to the Highlands, where we can be usefully employed the remainder of the winter, by taking and mastering the forts of the North...and in spring, we doubt not but an army of 10,000 effective Highlanders can be brought together, and follow your Royal Highness wherever you think proper....

The hard marches which your army has undergone, the winter

[1] *H. H.* 352.

season, and now the inclemency of the weather, cannot fail of making this measure approved of by your Royal Highness's allies abroad, as well as your faithful adherents at home. The greatest difficulty that occurs to us is the saving of the artillery, particularly the heavy cannon; but better some of these were thrown into the River Forth as that your Royal Highness, besides the danger of your own person, should risk the flower of your army, which we apprehend must inevitably be the case if this retreat be not agreed to, and gone about without the loss of one moment....Nobody is privy to this address to your Royal Highness except your subscribers; and we beg leave to assure your Royal Highness, that it is with great concern and reluctance we find ourselves obliged to declare our sentiments in so dangerous a situation, which nothing could have prevailed with us to have done, but the unhappy going off of so many men.

These[1] reasons were plausible, but there were very strong arguments on the other side, such as the loss of reputation the Prince would sustain by retiring at the approach of the Duke of Cumberland, the various impressions this retreat would make upon the minds of his friends and enemies, and above all, the real dangers that attended such a retreat. It was to be apprehended that an irregular army would not keep together in a retreat so nigh their own country, and that it would be impossible to assemble it again in the Highlands, where the Prince had no magazine, and the country affords no kind of provisions in the winter and spring seasons, and the army could be assembled no where else but in the Highlands, if the Duke of Cumberland followed closely and occupied the low country along the coast.

Charles[2] was a-bed [when the letter from the Chiefs arrived] and Mr [John] Hay [of Restalrig] would not allow him to be called for some time. When he got up, Hay went into the room with the dispatch. Charles opened it, and found a paper signed by Lord George Murray and many of the Chiefs, advising a retreat to the North as absolutely necessary....When Charles read this paper he struck his head against the wall till he staggered, and exclaimed most violently against Lord George Murray. His words were, 'Good God! have I lived to see this?' He sent

[1] *M. K.* 112.
[2] *H. H.* 355. From John Hay of Restalrig's narrative.

Sir Thomas Sheridan to Falkirk to signify his opinion to the Chiefs:

Bannockburn, Jan. ye 30th.

GENTLEMEN[1],—I have received y^rs of last night and am extremely surprised at the contents of it, wch I little expected from you at this time. Is it possible that a Victory and a Defeat shou'd produce the same effects, and that the Conquerors should flie from an engagement, whilst the conquer'd are seeking it? Shou'd we make the retreat you propose, how much more will that raise the spirits of our Ennemys and sink those of our own People? Can we imagin that where we go the Ennemy will not follow, and at last oblige us to a Battel which we now decline? Can we hope to defend ourselves at Perth, or keep our Men together there better than we do here? We must therefore continue our flight to the Mountains, and soon find our selves in a worse condition than we were in at Glenfinnen. What Opinion will the French and Spaniards then have of us, or what encouragement will it be to the former to make the descent for which they have been so long preparing, or the latter send us any more succours?...Will they send us any more Artillery to be lost or nail'd up? But what will become of our Lowland friends? Shall we persuade them to retire with us to the Mountains? Or shall we abandon them to the fury of our Merciless Ennemies? What an Encouragement will this be to them or others to rise in our favour, shou'd we, as you seem to hope, ever think our selves in a condition to pay them a second visit....For my own Part, I must say that it is with the greatest reluctance that I can bring my self to consent to such a step, but having told you my thoughts upon it, I am too sensible of what you have already ventured and done for me, not to yield to y^r unanimous resolution if you persist in it.

[A[2] retreat having been agreed to] the Prince...and Lord George Murray concerted that on the first of Febrewary all the army should be order'd very early in the morning to cross the Forth at the Frews, that all the heavy Cannon Should be nail'd, and all the ammunition which could not be carried along should be destroy'd, and that Ld George Should have 1200 Chosen foot and Ld Elcho's troop, with which he undertook to wait a great while after the army and to make the arriere guard and prevent the Dukes horse from following. All this Schême was so far from being putt in Execution, that on the first of

[1] *B. I.* 76.   [2] *E. J.* 385.

Febrewary, when the troops at Sterling, who knew nothing of the Concert, gott orders to march by the Frews to Dumblain, every body was Struck with amazement, for Every body that did not know of the Clans representation [to Charles] Expected a battle, and it appeared very Strange to run away from the very army that had been beat only a fortnight before.

Never was their a retreat resembled so much a flight, for their was no where 1000 men together, and the whole army pass'd the river in Small bodies and in great Confusion, leaving Carts & Cannon upon the road behind them. Their was no Arriere Guard, & Lord Elcho's troop, who was order'd to wait at the Bridge of Carron untill further orders, was forgott, so that at two o clock, when they left it, they had near been intercepted by a Sally from the town and Castle of Sterling. All the battering Cannon at Sterling were naild, and the Amunition at St Ninians was destroy'd. In Blowing up the Gun powder, as it was near the Church, they blew up the Church.

Lord George blamed the Prince for this retreat, and he was so far blamable, that very often orders that had been Agree'd upon betwixt him & Ld George were changed afterwards by him & his favourites, Sir Thomas [Sheridan], Mrs Murray & Hay [of Restalrig], for Since the resolution he took at Derby to call no Councills, he never advised with or consulted any body but these Gentlemen, which the people of fashion of his army took very much Amiss, and undoubtedly in their Situation, fighting for their all without gain, they ought not to have been treated like mercenaries, as the Prince affected to do, so that this flight over the Frews, when without danger they might have gone Slowly and in order, or any other wrong Step that was taken, could never be laid to the Charge of the principal officers of the Princes army, as the orders always came from his quarters and he never Consulted any of them.

The[1] army was quartered that night [February 1] at Down, Dumblane, and adjacent villages, and continued to retire next day in a very disorderly manner. The horse and some of the Lowland regiments went to Perth [under Lord George Murray],

[1] M. K. 115.

but most of the foot [i.e. the Clans] assembled at Crieff. Here
the Prince reviewed them, and found the desertion was nothing
like what it had been represented—there did not appear to be a
thousand men wanting of the whole army. The Prince, who
had with reluctancy consented to the retreat, upon the supposition
he had lost one third of his army, was affected, as one may
imagine, on this occasion. Lord George Murray's enemies did
not let slip this opportunity of loading him, and indeed this
seemed to bear very hard upon him, and all those chiefs that had
signed the representation above mentioned. Nevertheless, their
mistake is far from being unaccountable, if people will divest
themselves of prejudice, and examine impartially the circumstances from the battle of Falkirk to the Duke of Cumberland's
march from Edinburgh. The country being absolutely secure,
the Highlanders indulged their restless disposition, and sauntered
about all the villages in the neighbourhood of their quarters, and
abundance of them had been several days absent from their
colours. Their principal officers, knowing for certain that some
were gone home, apprehended that was the case with all that
were not to be found in their respective quarters; but all the
stragglers had got to Crieff and appeared at the review there.

The Prince called a council at Crieff to deliberate upon what
was to be done; there never had been such heats and animosities
as at this meeting; however, after a great deal of wrangling and
altercation, it was determined that the horse and low country
regiments should march towards Inverness along the coast,
while the Prince, with the clans, took the Highland road thither.
The Prince's division was more than sufficient to drive Lord
Loudon from Inverness; but it was to be feared, that when
the Highlanders drew nigh their homes, it would be impossible
to prevent their making a visit to their families, whom many
of them had not seen for six months, so that the Prince might
have occasion for the other division to make himself master of
Inverness.

Accordingly[1] the Prince went the Highland way, with the
Highlanders and prisoners, for Inverness; and the Horse and

[1] *B. O.* 201. From Captain John Daniel's narrative.

Lowland Regiments [under Lord George Murray went] the Low-Country Road by the Sea-Coast, which was much longer, so that it was three or four weeks before we again formed a junction.

[Lord George Murray] marched from...Perth to Cowpar-in-Angus; from Cowpar to Glams; from Glams to Forfar; and so on to Montrose...a fine loyal seaport town and looked upon, as I was told there, to produce men of the greatest wisdom in Scotland. Having staid three days there...we arrived at Aberdeen [February 8], where we staid two or three days; and notwithstanding our being in the town, the Presbyterian Ministers ceased not to preach and pray publicly against us....When we marched out of Aberdeen it blew, snowed, hailed, and froze to such a degree, that few Pictures ever represented Winter, with all its icicles about it, better than many of us did that day; for here men were covered with icicles hanging at their eyebrows and beards; and an entire coldness seizing all their limbs, it may be wondered at how so many could bear up against the storm; a severe contrary wind driving snow and little cutting hail bitterly down upon our faces, in such a manner that it was impossible to see ten yards before us....

From Old Meldrum we marched the next day for Banff, a little pretty agreeable town [and]...after a short stay marched for Cullen; and by this time we heard that the Prince had made himself master of the Lord President's House [at Culloden on February 19], and, after some little resistance, forced the soldiers in the town of Inverness to retire into the Castle, which, after a regular siege, likewise soon surrendered at discretion [on February 20]....This rapid success of the Prince gave us great courage. So, marching from Cullen, through Fochabers, over the river Spey, Elgin, Forres, and Nairn, towns only ten miles distant from each other, we came to be greedy spectators of our dear Prince again.

[Meanwhile][1] the Prince march'd from Creif to Castle Menzies & then to Blair [February 4]...to Dalnacardock and to Dalwhiny and so to Ruthven of Badenoch, where he took &

[1] *E. J.* 387.

demolish'd the Barracks [February 10]....From Ruthven the Prince march'd to Moy Castle [February 16], the house of the Laird of Mackintosh. The Laird was a Captain in Lord Loudouns Regiment, but his Lady was at home, and so much attached to the Princes Cause that she raised all her husbands clan for his service. The Prince Loged in the Castle and about [thirty] men with him: the rest of his men were Scatterer'd about the Country at one or two miles distance in order to gett quarters. The Earl of Loudoun, who Commanded about 2000 Highlanders for the Government, was at Inverness, which place he had fortified with a ditch and pallisadoes at all the avenues. Hearing that The Prince was at Moy Castle (which is only eight miles from Inverness) with so few men with him, he form'd a Scheme to take him prisoner, and on the 16 at night, he march'd at the head of his men out of town for Moy Castle.

Old[1] Lady Macintosh, living in Inverness, and getting notice of Lord Loudon's design, dispatched a boy (Lachlan Macintosh) about fifteen years of age, to try if he could get past Lord Loudon's men, and to make all the haste he could to Moy to warn the Prince of what was intended against him. The boy attempted to pass by Lord Loudon and his command, but found he could not do it without running the risque of a discovery; and therefore, as he said, he lay down at a dyke's side till all Lord Loudon's men past him, and, taking a different road, came to Moy about five o'clock in the morning [of February 17].

[He][2] gave the cry as soon as he came to the Closs where the guards was standing and call'd out the enamie was withine a mille of us. And then he came into the kitchen, wher I [Alexander Stewart] was lying on the table head asleep, and awakned me by pulling and halling at my greatcoat, and desired me for Gods sake to go and waken the Prince, which accordingly I went upstairs and meet on of the guard comming down from the Princes roome dore, and I asked him if the Prince had made answer, and he said he hade, for which his highness heard us

[1] *L. M.* ii, 134. From the statement of James Gibb, Master of the Prince's Household.

[2] *L. M.* ii, 246. Alexander Stewart's narrative, communicated to Bishop Forbes in 1749.

speaking and call'd out who was their. Upon which I made answer, and he desired me to call the piperach, for which I did, and his highness went down stairs and his feet in his shooes by the way of slippers, and buckled them in the Closs. Upon which my Lady McIntosh and her sister and me went to the roome where he sleept and took all the most valuable things that were in the roome where he lay, and went upe to the garrats and hide them in fether stands that was almost full of feathers, and my Lady was always calling at me to follow with the curtains, for I would stay till they would take me by the neck, for by this time the Prince was more than a mile of, toward the southwast end of the loch thorrou a wood.

[Meanwhile][1] when the Prince was about going to rest, or rather when it became dark, Lady MacIntosh, [had] ordered one Frazer, a blacksmith (who happened to be there by chance, having a desire to see the Prince), and four servants, to get loaded muskets, and to go away privately beyond all the guards and sentries without allowing them to know anything about them or their design, and to walk on the fields all night, and to keep a good look-out....The blacksmith and his faithful four accordingly went pretty far beyond all the sentries, and walked up and down upon a muir, at the distance, Captain MacLeod said he believed, of two miles from MacIntosh's house. At last they spied betwixt them and the sky a great body of men moving towards them, and not at a great distance. The black-smith fired his musket and killed one of Loudon's men, some say, the piper[2]....The four servants followed the blacksmith's example, and it is thought they too did some execution. Upon this the blacksmith huzzaed and cried aloud, 'Advance, Advance, my lads, Advance! (naming some particular regiments), I think we have the dogs now.' This so struck Lord Loudon's men with horrour, that instantly they wheel'd about, after firing some shots, and in great confusion ran back with speed to Inverness.

Next[3] morning the Prince assembled all his column, who had

[1] *L. M.* i, 149. From the narrative of Captain Malcolm Macleod, communicated to Bishop Forbes in 1747.

[2] Macleod's piper, Donald Ban MacCrimmon. See *supra* p. 92.

[3] *J.* 113.

passed the night in the villages and hamlets some miles from Moy, and advanced to Inverness, with the intention of attacking Lord Loudon, and taking revenge for the attempt of the preceding night; but, as he approached the town, his Lordship retreated [February 18] across the arm of the sea, to the north of Inverness, after collecting and taking along with him to the other side all the boats, great and small, and other vessels that could aid us in pursuing him.

The castle of Inverness was fortified in the modern manner, being a regular square with four bastions, and it was advantageously situated on the top of an eminence, which commanded the town....The governor of the castle [Grant of Rothiemurchus], who was in a situation to stand a siege, at first refused to comply with the summons of the Prince; but two hours after the trenches were opened, he surrendered himself [February 20] with his garrison, which consisted of two companies of Lord Loudon's regiment. The Prince immediately gave orders to raze the fortifications, and blow up the bastions. M. L'Epine, a serjeant in the French artillery, who was charged with the operation, lost his life on the occasion. This unfortunate individual, believing the match extinguished, approached to examine it, when the mine sprung, which blew him into the air, with the stones of the bastion, to an immense height.

The[1] Prince established his quarters at Inverness, and laid the plan of his future operations. He had three things principally in view; to reduce Fort Augustus and Fort William on one side; on the other, to disperse Lord Loudon's army; and to keep possession, as much as possible, of the coast towards Aberdeen. He had no other resource for the subsistence of his army but that coast; and if any little succours came from France, they were directed thither by a gentleman he had sent to that Court upon his retreat from Stirling. The greatest part of that division of the army that had marched by Aberdeen was cantoned betwixt that town and Inverness, and occupied all the little towns along the coast; 'twas a great extent to be guarded by so few troops; but the country was generally well inclined, and such as

[1] M. K. 118.

were not, durst give no disturbance. There was nothing to be apprehended till the Duke of Cumberland's army came up, when these parties were to fall back from post to post as they were overpowered.

Things being thus settled on this side, the Prince, without loss of time, set about the execution of the rest of his plan, and, in a few days after the Castle of Inverness had surrendered, sent Lord Cromarty against Lord Loudon.

As[1] the former was obliged to go round the head of the first frith, the latter had abundance of time to retire across the frith that divides Ross-shire from Sutherland; he took up his quarters at Dornoch, where he seemed to be perfectly secure, as Lord Cromarty had no boats. It was not so easy to go round the head of this [Dornoch] frith, which reaches a great way into a mountainous country; and when Lord Cromarty attempted it, Lord Loudon sent some of his own men back by water to Ross-shire, which determined Lord Cromarty to return to Tain [about March 2], but Lord Loudon had already brought back his men to Dornoch. It was plain Lord Loudon would persist in this method of eluding his adversary, and it seemed impossible to force him either to come to an action, or to retire out of the country, without two detachments, one of which might guard the passage of the frith, while the other went about by the head of it. But the Prince could spare no troops at that time; he had hardly as many men at Inverness as were necessary to guard his person. Nevertheless, it was of the utmost importance to disperse Lord Loudon's little army; it cut off all communication with Caithness, whence the Prince expected both men and provisions, and Lord Loudon seemed disposed to return to Inverness upon the Prince's leaving it....

An expedient had been thought of, and preparations had been privately made for it some time ago, but the execution was extremely hazardous. All the fishing-boats that could be got on the coast of Moray had been brought to Findhorn: the difficulty was to cross the frith of Moray unperceived by the English ships that were continually cruizing there; if the design was

[1] *M. K.* 128.

suspected it could not succeed. Two or three North country gentlemen, that were employed in this affair, had conducted it with great secrecy and expedition; all was ready at Findhorn when the orders came from Inverness to make the attempt, and the enemy had no suspicion. Moir of Stonywood set out with this little fleet in the beginning of the night, got safe across the frith of Moray, and arrived in the morning at Tain, where the Duke of Perth, whom the Prince had sent to command this expedition, was ready.

During[1] the night between the 19th and 20th of March, we embarked as many men in [the boats] as they could contain, under the orders of the Duke of Perth....The Duke took with him about eighteen hundred men, and a very thick fog, which came on in the morning, having greatly favoured the enterprise, he landed his detachment very near the enemy, who did not perceive our troops till they were within fifty paces of them, advancing rapidly sword in hand. The enemy were so much confounded on seeing the Highlanders ready to fall on them, that the greater part threw down their arms, and surrendered themselves prisoners of war. A few escaped by flight, and Lord Loudon [with Lord President Duncan Forbes] was of the number. The Duke of Perth returned the same day to Inverness, with some hundred prisoners, without having fired a single shot, or shed one drop of blood.

[Five[2] days later] the *Hazard*, sloop of war, of about eighteen guns, which had been taken by the Highlanders [at Montrose] in a very singular manner [and renamed *Prince Charles*], and sent into France with news of our victory at Falkirk, was retaken by the English, on the 25th of March. Having been chased the whole of the 24th, by the English ship of war the *Sheerness*, it threw itself on the coast of Lord Ray's country, in the northern extremity of Scotland.

The[3] people on board of her, which consisted of some Spanish and French officers, fifty soldiers, and the rest Sailors, in all about 120, with 13,000 Lewis d'ors, landed, and intended to Endeavour to gett to Inverness, but they were attacked by Lord

¹ *J*. 121.   ² *Ibid.* 114.   ³ *E. J.* 410.

Rea's men, and after an engagement, where they had six or seven men kill'd and as many wounded, they surrender'd themselves prisoners, and were carried first to Tongue, Lord Reas house, and then putt aboard of the *Sheerness* and carried to Berwick. This was a great loss to the Prince, as he was in Great distress for want of money.

[Meanwhile,][1] a few days after the Castle of Inverness had surrendered, [the Prince] sent Brigadier Stapleton, who commanded the Irish piquets, with them and a detachment of Lord John Drummond's regiment, to Fort Augustus. He attacked the old barrack at his arrival without waiting for the artillery, and carried it immediately—the garrison retiring to the fort; the soldiers behaved with surprising intrepidity on this occasion. The 3d of March, a trench was opened before Fort Augustus, which held out but two days. What hastened the reduction of this place was, that some shells that had been thrown into it had set fire to the powder magazine and blown it up. Mr Grant was now chief engineer in room of Mirabel, who had been laid aside since the unfortunate siege of Stirling.

Brigadier Stapleton, having left Lord Lewis Drummond to command at Fort Augustus, marched to Fort William, and laid siege [March 5] to that important fortress. Besides the Irish piquets, and some piquets of the Royal Scots, the Camerons and McDonalds of Keppoch were ordered upon this enterprise. These people were particularly interested in the success of it, as Fort William commands their country; and during the Prince's expedition to England, the garrison made frequent sallies, burnt their houses, and carried off their cattle.

Fort William is the strongest fortress in the north of Scotland; it's situated on the western coast, at the mouth of the river Nevis; it's partly defended by that river and by the sea, and that side which is accessible from the land has a good wall, ditch, counterscarp, and bastions at proper distances, and a kind of ravelin before the gate. It seemed at first impossible to take such a place with six pounders, which were the heaviest pieces the besiegers had, and which could never make a breach; but the fort is

[1] *M. K.* 119.

domineered on the south-east side by a hill, whence one can discover every thing that passes in the fort.

On[1] the 20th of March Brigadeer Stapleton open'd the Siege by discharging 18 small mortars, but as the battery was 800 yards off they fell Short of the fort....On the 22 the Battery of small mortars was advanced 100 yards nearer the fort, and the same day Colonel Grant Erected a battery on Sugar loaf hill for three pieces of Cannon betwixt four and Six pounders....The 28 Colonel Grant, finding his Cannon could make no breach in the walls, Erected a new battery of three four pounders on a very high ground Call'd the Craigs at 100 yards distance from the fort. As this Battery swept the whole parade, Brigadeer Stapletons Schême was, by firing partridge shott, to destroy their men and make them Surrender that way. All the 29 and 30th this firing continued very briskly on both sides. On the 31 Captain Caroline Scott, at the head of 150 men, Sallied out from the fort and attacked the works at the Craigs, beat the men of from it with the loss of two or three men on both sides, and took the three Cannon and Carried them with him after demolishing the Battery....All the 1 & 2 of April the firing Continued as usuall, but the 3d, Brigadeer Stapleton, finding he Could not take it with the Cannon he had, and likewise that all provisions and amunition was most done, he Spiked up 5 Cannon and 9 Coehorns, raised the Siege, and marched to Inverness. The Besieged had about thirty men killed and wounded, and the Besiegers about as many.

As[2] all the male vassals of the Duke of Athol were in our army, with his brother, Lord George, the Duke of Cumberland [had meanwhile] sent a detachment of his troops into their country.

There[3] was about three hundred of the Argyleshire Highlanders at several posts in that country, and it was apprehended their numbers would increase; and it was given out that General Campbell [of Mamore] was coming from Argyleshire with one thousand more; and then the Hessians[4] were to march from

[1] *E. J.* 411.   [2] *J.* 116.
[3] *J. M.* 106. From Lord George Murray's narrative.
[4] On February 8, 4000 or 5000 Hessian troops under Prince Frederick of Hesse and the Earl of Crawford arrived at Leith.

Perth and join them, as also the garrisons of Blair [under Sir Andrew Agnew] and Castle Menzies, and to march together towards Badenoch; and by choosing a strong camp, they might harass us [in the north] much on that side, especially their Highlanders....

I was, therefore, [ordered] to see to surprise those Highlanders, and, if possible, to be master of Blair Castle, where there was three hundred regular troops. His Royal Highness had gone to Elgin [March 11], where he was very bad of a fever of cold. I made a very quick march; and, in one day and night, made above thirty miles. I had not above seven hundred men [of the Athol Brigade, Macphersons, and Mackintoshes[1]]; yet we laid our scheme so well, that, betwixt the hours of three and five in the morning [of March 17] we took their whole posts, though at many miles' distance one from another, having sent different parties to each, and I believe there were not under thirty, reckoning all the different houses they were quartered at.

About[2] break of day, before any of the parties had joined Lord George at the place of rendezvous, or any account had been received of their success, a common fellow from the town of Blair came to the Bridge of Bruer and informed Lord George Murray, that Sir Andrew Agnew had got his men under arms, and was coming to see who they were that had attacked his posts.

When Lord George and Cluny received this notice, they had with them only 25 private men, and some elderly gentlemen. They consulted together what should be done. Some advised, that without loss of time they should make the best of their way back to Drumochter. Others were of opinion, that it would be better to mount the hills that were nearest, and make their retreat by roads where they could not easily be followed. Lord George differed from every body who had given his opinion. 'If I quit my post (said he), all the parties I have sent out, as they come in, will fall into the hands of the enemy.'

It was day-light, but the sun was not up. Lord George, looking earnestly about him, observed a fold dyke (that is, a wall of sod

[1] E. J. 403. [2] H. H. 204.

or turf) which had been begun as a fence for cattle and left unfinished; it was of considerable length, and cut in two a field that was near the bridge. He ordered his men to follow him, and drew them up behind the dyke, at such a distance one from another thay they might make a great shew, having the colours of both regiments flying in their front. He then gave orders to the pipers (for he had with him all the pipers, both of the Athol-men and the Macphersons) to keep their eyes fixed upon the road from Blair, and the moment they saw the soldiers appear, to strike up with all their bagpipes at once. It happened that the regiment came in sight just as the sun rose, and that instant the pipers began to play one of their most noisy Pibrochs. Lord George Murray and his Highlanders, both officers and men, drew their swords, and brandished them about their heads. Sir Andrew, after gazing a while at this spectacle, ordered his men to the right about, and marched them back to the Castle of Blair. Lord George Murray kept his post at the bridge till several of his parties came in, and as soon as he had collected three or four hundred men, conscious of victory, and certain that his numbers would be greater very soon, he marched to Blair and invested the Castle.

Pretty[1] early in the forenoon of the 17th March, Lord George Murray, as Lieutenant General for the Prince-Regent, with Major-Generals Lord Nairne and Mr Macpherson of Clunie, and the principal part of the rebel forces, having established their headquarters in and about the village of Blair, nearly a quarter of a mile to the north of the castle, sent down a summons, written on a very shabby piece of paper, requiring Sir Andrew Agnew, Baronet, commanding the troops of the Elector of Hanover, to surrender forthwith....It appeared afterwards, that no Highlanders, from the impressions they had received of the outrageous temper of Sir Andrew Agnew, could be prevailed on to carry that summons; but a maid-servant from the inn at Blair (then kept by one McGlashan), being rather handsome, and very

[1] *S. M.* 1808, p. 332. From a narrative of the siege by 'a Subaltern Officer of his Majesty's Garrison, who served in the Defence, and has long since been a General in the first rank.' The writer was Ensign Robert, afterwards General, Melville.

obliging, conceived herself to be on so good a footing with some
of the young officers, that she need not be afraid of being shot,
and undertook the mission: taking care, however, when she
came near the castle, to wave the paper containing the summons
over her head, as a token of her embassy; and when she arrived
at one of the low windows in the passage, whither the furnisher
of these notes, with three or four more of the officers, had come,
the window was opened and her speech heard; which strongly
advised a surrender, promising very good treatment by Lord
George Murray and the other highland gentlemen: but denounced, if resistance were made, that as the highlanders were
a thousand strong, and had cannon, they would batter down or
burn the castle, and destroy the whole garrison.

That speech was received from Molly with juvenile mirth by
the officers, who told her, that those gentlemen would be soon
driven away, and the garrison again become visitors at McGla-
shan's, as before. She then pressed them much, that the summons
should be received from her and carried to Sir Andrew: but that
was positively refused by all, excepting a Lieutenant, who being
of a timid temper, with a constitution impaired by drinking, did
receive the summons, and after its being read, carried it up to
deliver it to Sir Andrew, with some hopes, doubtless, of its
having success. But no sooner did the peerless knight hear something of it read, than he furiously drove the Lieutenant out of
his presence, to return the paper, vociferating after him, so loud
on the stairs, strong epithets against Lord George Murray, with
threatnings to shoot through the head any other messenger whom
he should send, that the girl herself perfectly overheard him, and
was glad to take back the summons, and to return with her life
to Lord George; who, with Lord Nairne, Clunie, and some
other principal officers, were seen standing together in the
church-yard of Blair to receive her, and could be observed, by
their motions and gestures, to be much diverted by her report.

On[1] [March] the 18 Lord George begun to fire against the
Castell with two four pounders, and as he had a furnace along
with him, finding his Bulletts were too small to damage the

[1] *E. J.* 404.

walls, he endeavour'd, by firing red hott balls...to sett the roof on fire, but by the care of the Besieged it was always Extinguished. Their was a Constant fire of small arms kept against the windows, and the besieged kept a Close fire from the Castell with their Small arms. As the Castell is Situated upon a rocky ground, their was no blowing it up, so the only chance Ld George had to gett possession of it was to Starve it, which he had some hopes of. But on the 24 of March, the Hessians from Perth and Creif moved to its relief. They encamped the first night at Nairn house, and next day at Dunkeld, and their was some firing betwixt them and a party of Ld Georges at Dunkeld across the river. Those that marched from Creif encamp'd at Tay Bridge on the 27.

Upon this motion of the Hessians, Ld George sent an express to the Prince to tell him that if he would send him 1200 men he would pitch upon an advantageous ground and fight them; the Prince sent him word he Could not send him them in the way his army was then situated. On the 31, The Earl of Crawford marched with St George's Dragoons [8th Hussars], 500 Hessians and 60 Hussars, and encamped at Dowallie, four miles north of Dunkeld, and next day they advanced to Pitlochrie. Both these days Lord George had several schirmishes with the Hussars, but Suppose he laid several snares for them, he never could catch but one of them, who was an officer and a Swede, who had had his horse Shott under him. Ld George used him very civilly, and sent him back with a letter of Compliment he wrote to The Prince of Hesse.

On the 1 of April Lord George Murray drew his men up in Battle opposite to Lord Crawford at Pitlochrie, and then retreated before him, in order to draw him into the Pass of Killicrankie. But Ld Crawford never moved, but sent for reinforcements to The Prince of Hesse. Lord George, upon hearing of the march of that reinforcement to sustain Lord Crawford, and that The body of Hessians from Tay Bridge were marching to Blair by Kinachin, he quite[d] the Country and marched [April 2] his men into Strathspey and from thence to Spey side.

CHAPTER VI

CULLODEN

In[1] the meantime, the Duke of Cumberland had advanced with his army along the coast, and came to Aberdeen [on February 27], a few days after FitzJames' horse landed there[2], which obliged them, and a handful of men commanded by Moir of Stonywood, to retire towards the river Spey. It was every one's opinion that the Duke of Cumberland would come straight on to Inverness; it seems he did not think himself strong enough at that time, or was in hopes that want of money and provisions would soon disperse the Prince's army. Whatever was his motive, he stopped short at Aberdeen, and remained quiet with the main body of his army about five or six weeks.

On[3] the 15th of March I arrived [at Aberdeen]; at which Time his Royal Highness had ordered the Army to be divided into three Cantonments, and the Battalions were daily marching off; the whole first Line, consisting of six Battalions, the Duke of Kingston's Horse, and Lord Cobham's Dragoons [10th Hussars], were ordered to Strathbogie, within twelve miles of the Spey, under the Command of Lord Albemarle and Major-General Bland; the Reserve, consisting of three Battalions, with four Pieces of Cannon, under the Command of Brigadier Mordaunt, at Old Meldrum, half Way betwixt Strathbogie and [Aberdeen]; and the whole second Line, consisting of six Battalions, and Lord Mark Kerr's Dragoons [11th Hussars] were here.

There[4] are two roads that lead from Aberdeen to...the river

---

[1] *M. K.* 122.

[2] Part of the regiment of the Duke of FitzJames (1712–87; son of Marshal Berwick) landed on February 22. *M. K.* 121.

[3] *R.* 301.   [4] *M. K.* 122.

Spey: one goes by Old Meldrum and Cullen, and the other by Kintore, Inverury, and Huntly, otherwise called Strathbogie.... Lord John Drummond, whom the Prince had appointed to command on that side, finding the Duke of Cumberland did not advance, as was expected, stationed Lord Strathallan's horse, which were now divided from Lord Kilmarnock's, and the hussars, at Cullen, and sent Lord Elcho's troop of guards, with Avochie's and Roy Stuart's battalions, to Strathbogie. He took up his own quarters at Gordon Castle, hard by Fochabers, and cantoned the rest of the troops he had under his command at Fochabers, and in the villages along the river. The Prince's cavalry, which had never exceeded four hundred, was now re-duced to half that number. Lord Pitsligo's horse was dwindled away to nothing; several north country gentlemen had left that corps and joined some of the foot regiments. Lord Kilmarnock's were reformed; the men made in the beginning of a regiment of foot-guards, which that Lord was to command, and such of their horses as were fit for service were given to Fitzjames' troopers; but it was long before they could get all mounted and their horses trained for service. However, Lord John Drummond made the most of what horse he had to keep advanced post, and get intelligence.

All had been quiet in these parts, [and] the different parties had kept their posts without attempting any thing against one another, till the 16th of March, when the Duke of Cumberland sent orders to Major-General Bland, who commanded the troops at Old Meldrum and Inverury, to march to Strathbogie, with all the troops under his command...to surprise or attack the little party [under Roy Stewart] that was posted there; and sent Brigadier Mordaunt, from Aberdeen, with four battalions and four pieces of cannon, to sustain Major-General Bland. It was much more than was needful, for there were not above 500 foot and 50 horse at Strathbogie, which is open and defenceless on all sides.

Colonel[1] [John Roy] Stewart had news of their march, drew up his men, and waited their arrival, and when they were close

[1] *E. J.* 401.

by the town, he begun his retreat, the foot in the front and the few horse in the rear. Major General Bland dispatch'd the horse and Dragoons after him, but the retreat was made in such good order, that The Dragoons durst not attack him, and only fired their Carabines at a distance; he arrived that night at Keith and next day pass'd the Spey without the loss of a man. The 19 [of March] Lord John Drummond order'd all the troops to pass the Spey, and they were quarter'd mostly in hutts built on purpose, from Rothes quite to the mouth of the river, on the north side, and guards placed all along it.

On[1] the [20th] an advanced Party, consisting of a Captain, with 50 [Campbell] Highlanders, and 30 of Kingston's Light Horse, had been detached by General Bland to Keith, where a Party of Rebels were just preparing to sit down to Dinner. But on the Approach of the King's Men the Rebels fled, and left their Dinner to be eaten by those it was not intended for; but they, being informed of the Number of our Men, resolved to return and fall upon them in the Night; our loyal Highland men, who, to do them Justice, were always willing and ready to do the hardest Duty, had desired Kingston's Men to go to Bed, expecting all was safe, and that they would do the Duty for that Night; accordingly they fixed their Guard in the Church-Yard.

Lord[2] John [Drummond], having notice of it, order'd Major [Nicolas] Glascow [Glascoe], with 150 of Ld Ogilvy's men, 20 of Ld Elcho's troop, & 30 hussars, to march and attack them. The Detachment arrived at Keith at one o clock of the morning, and after taking possession of all the avenues leading to the town, they attacked the Churchyard, and the Campbells defended it for about half an hour, in which time their was six or seven men kill'd on both Sides. After making everybody prisoners in the Church, all those that were in town were taken except one or two who Escaped to Strathbogie, where ever after this Surprise they were very alert and very often kept the troops under arms all night....After the Surprise at Keith their never was any troops of either side pass'd the night there, but every day their

[1] R. 302.　　　　　[2] E. J. 401.

was parties of horse from Strathbogie & Speyside sent to Keith, and they Generaly mett on different sides of the river at Keith, & fired Guns and pistols across the river at one another, but neither party ever Cross'd the river.

Let[1] us take a general view of what we have seen in detail. Brigadier Stapleton was carrying on the siege of Fort-William, Lord George Murray that of Blair Castle, Lord John Drummond was making head against Major-General Bland, the Duke of Perth was in pursuit of Lord Loudon, and the Prince, as it were, in the centre, whence he directed all these operations. But this is the last favourable prospect we shall have of the Prince's affairs, which began visibly to decline about this time. Several things contributed to this change, but nothing so much as the want of money, the principal sinew of war. Since the Prince retired from before Stirling, he had constantly a great number of men in pay, and, except about one thousand five hundred pounds of Spanish money, which was found in the neighbourhood of Montrose, he had got no foreign supplies, and could get very little in the narrow country he was now confined to....The scarcity of money was concealed as long as possible; but when the common men were reduced to a weekly allowance of oatmeal, instead of their pay, which had formerly been very punctual, this sudden change was at first attended with discontent, murmurings, neglect of duty, and dismal apprehensions; nevertheless, the diligence of the officers, and the loyalty of the men themselves, got the better, and all was set to rights again. It was to be hoped that the army would be kept together and in good humour till the Duke of Perth, Lord George Murray, and Brigadier Stapleton returned after finishing their several expeditions, and [that] then the Prince would march to Aberdeen with all the forces he could muster up. But fortune, which had again begun to smile upon him, abandoned him at this critical juncture.

The[2] Prince...remain'd close at Inverness....He very often went a Shooting, and sometimes gave bals at night, where he danced himself, and Endeavour'd to keep up the peoples Spirits that aproach'd him by despising his Enemy, and Assuring that

[1] *M. K.* 130.   [2] *E. J.* 414.

the Duke of Cumberlands soldiers would be so conscious of the highness of the crime of fighting against their true & Lawfull Prince, that whenever he appear'd they would certainly run away. Suppose he himself believed this firmly, he had difficulty in persuading other people of these notions who were any ways acquainted with the English Soldiers.

Their was great discontent in his Army at this time, both amongst the Officers and Soldiers. As money was very Scarce with him, he paid his troops mostly in meal, which they did not like and very often mutiny'd, refused to obey orders, and Sometimes threw down their arms and went home; and it would have been impossible for him ever to have march'd the face of an Army over Spey without money, for people that would willingly have given a days fighting near Inverness would never have march'd out of the Country with him without pay.

What displeased the people of fashion was that he did not Seem to have the least Sense of what they had done for him, but on the contrary would often Say that they had done nothing but their duty as his fathers Subjects were bound to do. Then, as he had his head full of the notions of Commanding his army as if they had been mercinaries and had their fortunes depending upon his will and pleasure, he never Consulted with any of them or lett them know in the least any of his Schêmes, but managed all his Affairs in a hidden way with his favourites Sir Thomas Sheridan, M^{rs} OSullivan, Murray, and Hay, but particularly Mr Hay, who governed him entirely; and it was so far a great loss to him, that Suppose every body looked upon Mr Hay as a very honest man, yett he was Generally Esteem'd a man of neither parts nor Capacity, and as men of that kind are apt to Change their Behaviour with their fortune, he was reckoned to Carry it too high to his Superiors, which created him a great many Enemies....

Another thing the Officers took much amiss was the preference the Prince gave the Irish to the Scots, which he did upon all occasions; his reasons for that were, they were of his own religion, and paid always more Court to him in their discourse. As they had nothing at Stake and were only there to Gain his favour and protection, whatever he proposed they were for;

whereas, as many of his Schêmes were very ill formed, & as the Scots had their lives & fortunes depending, they Sometimes took the liberty of representing against them, which the Prince took highneously amiss. And then their was people about him that profited of his displeasure to represent The Scots to him as a mutinous people, and that it was not so much for him they were fighting as for themselves, and repeated to him all their bad Behaviour to King Charles the first, and Second, and putt it into the worst lights to him, which wrought upon him So far, that at the Battle of Culloden he thought all the Scots in generall were a parcell of Traitors, and he would always have Continued in the Same way of thinking if he had immediately gott out of the Country. But the care they took of his person while he was hiding made him Change his mind and fix treason only to particulars....

Prejudices in favours of Passive obedience, Absolute monarchy, the Roman Catholick Religion, and Consequently the Irish who professed it, had been Strongly inculkated into the Princes head by Sir Thomas Sheridan, who was infinitely fitter to bring up Jesuitts than Princes who Pretend to the British Crown; for Sir Thomas in Company always used to Argue that the Nation had Usurped every priviledge they possess from their Kings, for that all the Subjects of Great Britain are the Kings property, and in Consequence a parcel of Slaves. As most all the Gentlemen of the best fashion who had join'd the Prince had very different principles, it is Easy to Imagine what Uneasiness it gave them to be Governed by people who's heads were fill'd with these Idea's. But as the French Says, Le Vin etoit Versé il falloit le Boire, and as the Prince in his Conversation used always to Swear he would never lay down his arms, as long as too men would Stick by him, nobody ever thought of asking terms from the Government, but on the Contrary to Stand by the Cause, whither good or bad, as long as it would last. Private Gentlemen who had no Command in this Affair were very much to be pitied, and some such their were of very good Estates who never either Spoke to the Prince or Eat with him; and as he knew nothing of the familys of the Country, he used to look upon them in the light of Common Dragoons.

On[1] Tuesday the 8th of April, his Royal Highness [the Duke of Cumberland] marched from Aberdeen with six Battalions of Foot, and Lord Mark Kerr's Dragoons, in order to seek the Rebels. For some Days before we march'd, there were scandalous written Libels dropp'd about the Town by the Rebel Party: I happen'd to find one of them in the Lane going out of Broadstreet to the Duke's Quarters, where I carried it, the Substance of which was, to admonish our Soldiers of the Danger that attended us in the Pursuit of the Rebels; and that there were several Mines about the Spey ready for blowing us up on our Approach. In order to find the Authors of which several of the Inhabitants were oblig'd to shew their Hand-writing to People appointed for that Purpose, which, by comparing with the Libels, was hoped would be found out, but it proved ineffectual[2].

It being fine Weather, our Transports at the same Time moved along Shore, with a gentle Breeze and fair Wind. We marched throgh Old Aberdeen...to Old Meldrum, a poor old dirty Town, where the Army quarter'd the first Night after 12 Miles March. Our next March was to Bamff...where his Royal Highness gave the Army a Day's Rest....That Morning the Army marched from Bamff...we saw a great Fire burning vehemently, at about a Mile and a half Distance on our Left; the Officers not knowing what it was, I propos'd to go and see; when I came there, I found it to be a Nonjuring [Episcopal] Meeting-House, set on Fire by a Party of Kingston's Horse, that were reconnoitring the Hills. After about six Miles marching, in our Way to Cullen, we came to Portsoy, a pretty small Village, with the Sea coming full up to the Town. Here we were joined by the whole Army, which were too numerous to get Quarters, so that the Foot encamped that Night on some ploughed Grounds to the Right of the Town, and the Horse lay in the Towns [April 11]....

From Cullen, our next Day's March was to Fochabers, eight Miles. In the way thither we pass'd by large barren Mountains on our Left, and then came to some better Land, where we had

[1] R. 316.

[2] The passage 'For some Days...ineffectual' is interpolated from R. 313.

a pleasant Prospect of our Transports and Men of War standing in close to the Shore, who discharged some Shot at a Party of Rebel Hussars on the other Side of the Spey, which when we came in Sight of, we observed the Rebel Army were assembled with their white Flags displayed, making a formidable Appearance. Our Army continued their March to within half a Mile of the River, when the Duke of Kingston's Horse, which was the Advanced Guard, stopp'd for Orders at the Head of a plowed Field, above the Town of Fochabers....By this Time the Foot with the Cannon came up, when the Rebels set Fire to their Barracks, likewise to their Guard-House, which looked as if they did not intend to stand an Engagement. At this Time his Royal Highness gave Orders for the Duke of Kingston's Horse to advance. Accordingly we marched through the Town of Fochabers, which consists mostly of one long Street, where I observed several good Houses, and People of Fashion standing looking at us; but not one Person to wish us good Success....

We entered the River [Spey, on April 12] with a Guide, wading on Foot, to shew where the Ford lay; which was bad enough, having loose Stones at the Bottom, which made it very difficult for Man or Horse to step without falling; the Water Belly-deep, and very rapid; the Ford not lying right across, we were obliged to go Midway into the River, then turn to the Right and go down it for about sixty yards, and then turn to the Left, inclining upwards to the landing Place. In this Situation, had the Rebels stood us here, it might have been of bad Consequence to our Army, they having a great Advantage over us, and might have defended this important Pass a long Time, to our great Loss. But they wanted to draw our Army over, and further into their Country, from whence (in their Imagination) we were never to return. When we got up the Banks on the other Side of the River, the Rebels were all fled, and appeared on a Hill about half a Mile's Distance, from which they retreated out of Sight...After the Rebels were fled out of Sight, our Foot encamped on the North Side of the Spey....The Horse were ordered to repass the River and quarter in the Town of Fochabers. ...After that his Royal Highness had formed the necessary Dispositions, he took up his Quarters at the Minister's House on the North-Side of the Spey, which had been Lord John Drummond's Quarters.

On[1] Saturday morning, the 12th of April, intelligence was brought [to the Prince at Inverness] that the Duke of Cumberland was marching with his whole army. They had been, for a fortnight before that, lying all the way from Aberdeen to Strathbogie, at which last place near half of their army was. Expresses were sent every where, to bring up our men. Those who had been at the siege of Fort William were on their march; but Lord Cromarty was at a great distance, with a good body of MacKenzies; and also [Gregor Macgregor of] Glengyle and M'Kinnon, with their men. It seems they were left there, after the Duke of Perth had dispersed Lord Loudon's corps, and was returned himself to Inverness. The other men that had been with him were cantoned north from Inverness. His Grace was then gone to Speyside, where Lord John Drummond also was. They had the Duke of Perth's regiment, those of the Gordons, the Farquharsons, Lord Ogilvie, John Roy Stewart, the Atholmen besides, and some others, and all our horse. Had the rest of our army been come up, we were all to have marched there. Clanranald's and the MacIntoshes were sent to strengthen them; and they had orders to retire as the Duke of Cumberland advanced. On Sunday morning, the 13th, it was confirmed that the enemy were coming on, and passed the Spey. Many of our people, as it was seed time, had slipt home; and as they had no pay for a month past, it was not an easy matter to keep them together. On Monday, the 14th, Lochiel came up; and that day, his Royal Highness went to Culloden, and all the other men as they came up marched there; and that night, the Duke of Perth came back with all the body he had at Speyside. The Duke of Cumberland...encamped this night at Nairn. Many were for retiring to stronger ground till all our army was gathered; but most of the baggage being at Inverness, this was not agreed to. Early on Tuesday morning [April 15], we all drew up in a line of battle, in an open muir near Culloden. I did not like the ground: it was certainly not proper for Highlanders.

[1] *J. M.* 118. From Lord George Murray's Journal.

I proposed that Brigadier Stapleton and Colonel Ker should view the ground on the other side of the water of Nairn, which they did. It was found to be hilly and boggy; so that the enemy's cannon and horse could be of no great use to them there. Mr O'Sullivan had gone to Inverness, so he was not with them when they reconnoitred the ground. They were returned by two o'clock afternoon; but the same objection was made to taking up the ground as to retiring farther; the enemy might have marched to Inverness. When it was so far in the day, it was concluded the Duke of Cumberland would not move from Nairn till next day.

It was then proposed a night attack might be attempted. His Royal Highness and most others were for venturing it, amongst whom I was; for I thought we had a better chance by doing it than by fighting in so plain a field; besides, those who had the charge of providing for the army were so unaccountably negligent, that there was nothing to give the men next day, and they had got very little that day, even though meal should be brought, the men could not make it ready without dispersing, for several miles, to all the houses about, which could not be done when the enemy was so near. Keppoch came up that evening; but before the time the army was to march, a vast number of the men went off on all hands to get and make ready provisions; and it was not possible to stop them. Then, indeed, almost every body gave [a night march] up as a thing not to be ventured.

But[1] the Prince continued keen for the attack, and positive to attempt it, and said there was not a moment to be lost; for as soon as the men should see the march begun, not one of them would flinch. It was near eight at night when they moved, which could not be sooner, otherwise they might have been perceived at a considerable distance, and the enemy have got account of their march. Lord George Murray was in the van, Lord John Drummond in the centre, and the Duke of Perth towards the rear, where also the Prince was, having Fitz-James's horse and others with him.... There were about two officers and thirty men of the MacIntoshes in the front as guides, and some of the

[1] *L. M.* i, 258. Also in *L. P.* ii. 527. By 'A Highland officer.'

same were in the centre and rear, and in other parts, for hindering any of the men from straggling. Before the van had gone a mile, which was as slow as could be to give time to the line to follow, there was express after express sent to stop them, for that the rear was far behind...and of these messages I[1] am assured there came near an hundred before the front got near Culraick, which retarded them to such a degree that the night was far spent: for from the place the army began to march to Culraick was but six miles, and they had still four long miles to Nairn. It was now about one o'clock in the morning, when Lord John Drummond came up to the van and told...if they did not stop or go slower, he was afraid the rear would not get up. In a little time the Duke of Perth came also to the front, and assured that if there was not a halt the rear could not join. There was a stop accordingly. Lochiel had been mostly in the van all night, and his men were next the Athol men, who were in the front. These two bodies made about twelve hundred men. There were also several other officers that came up, there being a defile a little way behind occasioned by a wall of the wood of Culraick, which also retarded the march of those that were behind. The officers, talking of the different places of making the attack, said it was better to make the attempt with four thousand men before daybreak, as with double the number after it was light. Mr O'Sullivan [had] come up to the front, and it being now evident by the time the army had taken to march little more than six miles it would be impossible to make the other part of the road—which was about four miles—before it was clear day-light, besides the time that must be spent in making the disposition for the attack, as it could not be done by the army in the line by their long march. Mr O'Sullivan said he had just then come from the Prince, who was very desirous the attack should be made; but as Lord George Murray had the van, and could judge the time, he left it to him whether to do it or not....

Lord George Murray desired the rest of the gentlemen to give their opinions, for they were all deeply concerned in the consequence. It was agreed upon all hands that it must be sun-

---

[1] Possibly Lord George Murray, or one of his friends.

rise before the army could reach Nairn and form, so as to make
an attempt upon the enemy's camp; for one part was to have
passed the water a mile above the town, to have fallen upon them
towards the sea-side. The volunteers were all very keen to
march. Some of them said that the red-coats would be all drunk,
as they surely had solemnised the Duke of Cumberland's birthday....

But the officers were of different sentiments, as severals of
them expressed. Lochiel and his brother said they had been as
much for the night attack as anybody could be, and it was not
their fault that it had not been done; but blamed those in the
rear that had marched so slow, and retarded the rest of the army.
Lord George Murray was of the same way of thinking, and said
if they could have made the attack it was the best chance they
had, especially if they could have surprized the enemy. But to
attack a camp that was near double their number in day-light,
when they would be prepared to receive them, would be perfect
madness.

By this time Mr John Hay [of Restalrig] came up and told
the line was joined. He was told the resolution was taken to
return. He began to argue upon the point, but nobody minded
him....It was about two o'clock in the morning (the halt being
not above a quarter of an hour) when they went back in two
columns, the rear facing about, and the van taking another way.
At a little distance they had a view of the fires of the Duke of
Cumberland's camp....Day-light began to appear about an hour
after. They got to Culloden pretty early, so that the men had
three or four hours' rest.

Every[1] body seemed to think of nothing but Sleep. The men
were prodigiously tired with hunger and fatigue, and vast numbers of them went into Inverness, and the Villages about, both
to Sleep and to pick up what little nourishment they Could gett.
The principal officers went all to the house of Culloden and
were so much tired that they never thought of Calling a Councill
what was to be done, but Every one lay'd himself down where
he Could, some on beds, others on tables, Chairs, & on the floors,

[1] *E. J.* 428.

The Battle of

Wednesday 16

Culloden

Royal Scots 300 Pulteny Bligh 500 Cobham horse 1250

Monro Barrel Scots
Fusilier, Wolfe Sempill Ligonier
2000 300 500 500 500 300

500 Cholmondely 500 Regal 500 Pulteny 150 150 Kingston

500 ming 500 Howard 500 Blakeney 500 Battereau

Culloden fought on
of April 1746

for the fatigue and the hunger had been felt as much amongst the officers as Soldiers.

About two hours after the Princes Arrival at Culloden, a party of horse that had been left to Observe the Duke of Cumberland's motions, brought word that their was a party of his horse within two miles, and that his whole army was not above four miles off. Upon which the Prince and the Duke of Perth, Lord George Murray, and Lord John Drummond mounted their horses, ordered the drums to beat & the pipes to play, which Alarm Caused great hurry & Confusion amongst people half dead with fatigue. They Endeavoured to gett the men together as fast as possible, but as they were dispersed all over the Country as far as Inverness, their was near two thousand of them that was not at the Battle. So all The Prince Assembled was about five [or six] thousand men, which he march'd up the hill from Culloden, & drew them up in the same place they were drawn up in the day before, with their right to Some park walls[1]. It was a dark, misty, rainy day, & the wind blew in the face of the Princes army. Their was no manner of Councill held upon the Field, and indeed their was but one party to take, which was to have cross'd the water of Nairn, which was upon the right, and march'd up a hill where the Dukes army could not have follow'd, and have waited there untill night, and then attack'd him. But this Scheme was never Spoke of; [as] for retreating into the highlands, it was not possible, as the army for want of provisions must have dispersed. Besides, what putt a Stop to all Councills was that the Prince always believed firmly that the Dukes army would be Struck with a panick; so, with these notions, it was Equal to him to have nine or only five thousand men....But as was said before, their was two thousand absent on the 16, some asleep & others gone too far of in Search of provisions.

Besides[2] this deficiency in our severall regiments, which amounted to above a third, we likewise wanted Clunies brave clann of McPharsons, also Cromartys, which was surprized [on

[1] *i.e.* a field- or boundary-wall.
[2] *L. P.* ii, 509. By 'A Highland officer.' See *supra*, p. 133 n.

April 15, at Dunrobin] in Sutherland, Barisdales McDonalds, and Glengyle with his McGregors, &c., out upon command in the shire of Ross. All these unhappy circumstances for us considered, it is no wonder the event of this day proved so fatal to us as it did. Add to this, what we of the Clan McDonalds thought ominous, we had not this day the right hand in battle as formerly, and as we enjoyed in this enterprize when the event proved successfull, as at Gladsmuir and Falkirk, and which our clan maintains we had enjoyed in all our battles and struggles in behalf of our Royall family since the battle of Bannockburn, in which glorious day, Robert the Bruce bestowed this honour upon Angus McDonald, Lord of the Isles, as a reward for...protecting him for above nine months in his country of Rachlin, Isla, and Vist, as the same name has done since to his royall successor.

Betwixt[1] ten and eleven o'clock, we drew up in the muir, a little back from where we had been the day before. I told Mr O'Sullivan, who was placing the men in the order of battle, that I was convinced it was wrong ground; but he said that the muir was so interspersed with moss and deep ground, that the enemy's horse and cannon could be of little advantage to them. We had still time to cross the water [of Nairn] and take up the ground which Brigadier Stapleton and Colonel Ker had viewed the day before; for our right was within three hundred paces of the water, and the banks were very steep, which was nothing to hinder Highlanders, and our horse and cannon could have crossed at a small ford a mile farther back; but I reckon the belief that the enemy would have marched straight to Inverness was the occasion that we did not quit that plain muir....Cluny was within three or four miles, with above four hundred men, and was marching as quickly as possible, and many others were hourly expected....So I am persuaded that night, or next morning, we would have been near two thousand stronger; and had we passed that water, in all probability we would not have fought that day; so that if the Duke of Cumberland had encamped that night upon the muir, which very possibly he might, we would have had a fair chance next day.

[1] *J. M.* 123. From Lord George Murray's Journal.

About[1] half an hour after Eleven, the Duke of Cumberlands army appeared two miles off, Straight in front of the Princes, form'd in two lines with most all their horse upon their left [i.e. landward] wing. They march'd down the two miles form'd in the Same way. When they Came within a mile they detach'd a Small party of horse to reconnoitre the left of the Prince's army; when they Came within Cannon Shot their was a great many huzzas pass'd on both Sides. The Princes Cannon began to fire first, and presently after they fir'd theirs, which when they Came pretty near they charged with grape shott, and as they were well pointed they did great execution. The highlanders had orders not to move untill the word of Command to advance was given them, and then they were to give their fire very near, draw their Swords and rush in; they suffer'd the Cannonade very impatiently, a great many of them threw themselves down flatt upon the Ground, and some of them, but few, gave way and run off. When the Dukes army came within muskett Shott, they detach'd 600 Campbells and a Squadron of Dragoons to See and flank the Princes right wing.

This[2] made Lochiel send to Lord George Murray, then on the left with the Duke of Perth, to tell him of the danger. Lord George Murray (whom I heard formerly say that the park would be of great service to prevent our being flanked) on this took a narrower view of it, and sent three gentlemen, viz., Colonel Sullivan, John Roy Stewart, and Ker of Grydan [Graden] to view it down to the Water of Nairn. At their return they said it was impossible for any horse to come by that way. The men still believed they might be flanked, and some proposed lining the park wall. The Duke of Perth, who came from the left, was of their opinion. But Lord George Murray, thinking otherwise, ordered Lord Ogilvie's regiment to cover the flank, told there was no danger, and to Lord Ogilvie said, he hoped and doubted not but he would acquit himself as usual.

[The[3] Prince's] front was Straight East. His first line Con-

[1] *E. J.* 431.
[2] *L. M.* i, 86. From the Journal of John Cameron, chaplain at Fort William.
[3] *E. J.* 423.

sisted of the following regiments, viz. the Athole Brigade 600, which was Lord George Murrays, Lord Nairns & Shian Menzies's, Lochyells 700, Ardshiels 150, Roy Stuarts 200, Lovats 800, Mackintoshes 500, Farqursons 150, Macleans 150, Macklachlins 100, Glenbucketts 200, Perths 300, Chisholms 100, Keppochs 200, Clanronalds 200, & Glengarys 300, which made in all 4650 foot. The Second line was divided into three Bodies, one on the right, another on the left, and one in the Center. The right division was Composed of Elcho's and Fitz-james's horse 110, Lord Strathallans 70, Abuchies foot 300, Lord Ogilvys 500; the Centre division was formed of the Irish piquets 300, Lord John Drummonds regiment 300, and the Earl of Kilmarnocks 300; in the left division was the Hussars 60, Sir Alexander Bannermans[1] foot 150, Stoneywoods 200, which made the second line in all 2050 foot and 240 horse, So that the whole army made 6940[2]. The right Wing was Com-manded by Lord George Murray, and the left by the Duke of Perth, the Centre of the first line by Lord John Drummond, and the Centre of the Second by Brigadeer Stapleton. Their was five Cannon on the right and four on the left of the Army.

The[3] first line of the duke's army consisted of six regiments of foot. The Royal had the right. On their left stood Chol-mondely's [34th], Price's [14th], the Scots Fusileers [21st], Monro's [37th], and Barrel's [4th]. The second line consisted of the same number of regiments. Howard's regiment [3rd] had the right; on their left stood Fleming's [36th], Ligonier's [48th], Blyth's [20th], Sempill's [25th], and Wolfe's [8th]. The reserve consisted of Blakeney's [27th], Battereau's, and Pul-teney's [13th]. The Duke of Kingston's regiment of light horse, and one squardon of Lord Cobham's dragoons [10th H.], were placed on the right of the first line; Lord Mark Ker's regiment of dragoons [11th H.], and two squadrons of Lord Cobham's, on the left. When the King's army came within five or six hundred paces of the rebel army, part of the ground in their front

[1] He had joined the Prince after the retreat from Stirling. Cf. *E. J.* 393.

[2] The figure does not allow for desertions.

[3] *H. H.* 229.

was so soft and boggy, that the horses which drew the cannon sunk, and were obliged to be taken off: the soldiers, slinging their firelocks, dragged the cannon across the bog. As soon as the cannon were brought to firmer ground, two field pieces, short six pounders, were placed in the intervals between the battalions; and Colonel Belford of the artillery, who directed the cannon of the Duke's army, began to fire upon the rebels, who, for some time, had been firing upon the King's troops from several batteries; but the cannon of the rebels were very ill served, and did little harm. The Duke's artillery did great execution, making lanes through the Highland regiments. The Duke of Cumberland, observing the wall on the right flank of the Highland army, ordered Colonel Belford to continue the cannonade, with a view to make the Highlanders leave the ground where they stood, and come down to attack his army. During the cannonade, which began a little after one o'clock, and lasted till near two, the Duke made several changes in the disposition of his army. Wolfe's regiment, which stood on the left of the second line, and extended somewhat beyond the left of the first line, was moved from its place (where the men were standing in water up to their ankles) and brought to the left of the first line, where they wheeled to the right (and formed *en potence*, as it is called), making a front to the north, so as to fire upon the flank of the rebels, if they should come down to attack the King's army. The Duke, at the same time, ordered two regiments to move up from the reserve, so that Pulteney's regiment stood on the right of the Royal, which had the right of the first line before, and Battereau's regiment stood on the right of Howard's regiment in the second line. His Royal Highness, after making these changes in the disposition of his army, placed himself between the first and second line, in the front of Howard's regiment.

While these changes were making, Colonel Belford, observing the body of horse with Charles, ordered two pieces of cannon to be pointed at them; several discharges were made; and some balls broke ground among the horses' legs. Charles had his face bespattered with dirt; and one of his servants, who stood behind the squadron with a led horse in his hand, was killed. Meanwhile the cannonade continued, and the Highlanders in the first line, impatient of suffering without doing any harm to their enemies, grew clamorous to be led on to the attack. A message was sent to Locheil, whose regiment stood next the Athol brigade, desiring that he would represent to Lord George Murray the necessity of attacking immediately[1]. While Locheil was speaking with Lord George, the Macintosh regiment brake out from the centre of the first line; and advanced against the regiment opposite to them, which was the 21st. But the fire of the field-pieces, and the small arms of the 21st, made the Macintoshes incline to the right, from whence all the regiments to their right, with one regiment to their left, were coming down to the charge. These regiments, joining together, advanced under a heavy fire of cannon (loaded with grape shot) and musketry in their front, and a flank fire when they came near Wolfe's regiment. Notwithstanding which they still advanced, and attacking sword in hand, broke through Barrel's and Monro's in the first line, and pushed on to the second. In the second line, immediately behind Barrel's, stood Sempill's regiment, which during the attack had advanced fifty or sixty paces; and their front rank kneeling and presenting, waited till Barrel's men got out of their way. For the soldiers of Barrel's and Monro's did not run directly back, but went off behind the battalions on their right. The Highlanders, who had broke through the first line, were got close together, without any interval between one Clan and another; and the greater part of them came on directly against Sempill's regiment, which allowed them to come very near, and then gave them a terrible fire that brought a great many of them to the ground, and made most of those who did not fall turn back. A few, and but a few, still pressed on, desperate and furious, to break into Sempill's regiment, which not a man of them ever did, the foremost falling at the end of the soldiers' bayonets.

Blyth's regiment, which was on the right of Sempill's, gave their fire at the same time, and repulsed those that were advancing against them. When the Highland regiments on the right of their first line made this attack, the regiments on the left, the Farquharsons, and the three Macdonald regiments, did not ad-

---

[1] Perhaps this is the incident already referred to on p. 137.

vance at the same time, nor attack in the same manner. They came so near the King's army, as to draw upon themselves some fire from the regiments that were opposite to them, which they returned by a general discharge, and the Macdonalds had drawn their swords to attack in the usual manner; but seeing those regiments, that had attacked sword in hand, repulsed and put to flight, they also went off. When the Highlanders in the first line gave way, the King's army did not pursue immediately. The regiments of foot, from right to left, were ordered to stand upon the ground where they had fought, and dress their ranks. The horse on the right of the King's army were the first that pursued, and they were very near the Macdonalds, when the Irish piquets came down from their place in the second line, and fired upon the dragoons, who halted, and the Macdonalds fell back to the second line. The two lines joined formed a considerable body of men; but their hearts were broken, and their condition was altogether hopeless and irretrievable: in their front they saw the infantry which had defeated them, and reduced their two lines to one, preparing to advance against them. On their right flank, and somewhat behind them, they saw a body of the Duke's cavalry ready to fall upon them as soon as the infantry should advance.

Such was the condition of the rebels, when the Duke of Cumberland, with his infantry, advanced towards them. At his approach they began to separate, and go off in small parties, four or five together. The rest made two large bodies; one of these, in which were most of the Western Highlanders, directed their course towards Badenoch, and the hills of their own country. The other, and much the smaller body, in which were the Frasers, Lord John Drummond's regiment, and the Irish piquets, marched straight to Inverness.

The[1] Highlanders who attacked sword in hand were the Maclachlans and Macleans (making one regiment), the Macintoshes, the Frasers, the Stuarts, and the Camerons.

Most of the Chiefs who commanded these five regiments were killed, and almost every man in the front rank of each

[1] *H. H.* 238.

regiment. Maclachan, Colonel of the united regiment, was killed
by a cannon ball, and the Lieutenant-Colonel, Maclean of
Drimnin, who succeeded to the command, bringing off his
shattered regiment, and missing two of his sons, for he had three
in the field, turned back to look for them, and was killed by a
random shot. Macgillivray of Drumnaglass, Colonel of the Macintosh regiment, was killed in the attack, with the Lieutenant-
Colonel, the Major, and all the officers of his regiment, three
excepted. Charles Fraser, younger of Inverallachie, who was
Lieutenant-Colonel, and commanded the Fraser regiment, was
killed. The Stuart regiment had a number, both officers and men,
killed in the attack; but Stuart of Appin, their Chief, never
having joined the standard of Charles, the regiment was commanded by Stuart of Ardshiel, who escaped from the field.
Cameron of Lacheil, advancing at the head of his regiment, was
so near Barrel's, that he had fired his pistol, and was drawing his
sword when he fell, wounded with grape-shot in both ankles.
The two brothers, between whom he was advancing, raised him
up, and carried him off in their arms. When the Macdonalds'
regiment retreated, without having attempted to attack sword
in hand, Macdonald of Keppoch advanced with his drawn sword
in one hand, and his pistol in the other; he had got but a little
way from his regiment, when he was wounded by a musket shot,
and fell. A friend who had followed, conjuring him not to throw
his life away, said that the wound was not mortal, that he might
easily join his regiment, and retreat with them. Keppoch desired
him to take care of himself, and going on, received another shot,
and fell to rise no more.

The[1] Prince, who at the beginning of the Action was behind
the Irish piquetts guarded by Sixteen of Fitzjames's horse, turn'd
about his horse and went off as soon as the left wing gave way,
and never offer'd to rally any of the broken Corps; but indeed it
would have been to no purpose, for none of the highlanders who
Escaped ever Stop'd untill they gott home to their own houses.
As the Dukes army after the deroute Continued to pursue in
order of Battle, always firing their Cannon and platoons in

[1] *E. J.* 434.

Advancing, their was not so many people kill'd or taken as their would have been had they detach'd Corps to pursue, but Every body that fell into their hands gott no quarters, except a few who they reserved for publick punishment; the Earl of Kilmarnock and Colonel [Francis] Farquharson [of Monaltrie] were taken on the field. The Princes army had about a Thousand men kill'd. …The Dukes army lost Lord Robert Ker and about 250 men, some officers included.

In the Flight of the Princes army most of the left wing took the road to Inverness; the right wing Cross'd the Water of Nairn and went to Ruthven of Badenoch; the rest, to the number of 500, mostly Officers, follow'd the Prince into Stratharick, where he had Stop'd about four miles from the field of Battle. As he had taken it into his head he had been betray'd, and particularly by Lord George Murray, he Seemed very diffident of Every body Except the Irish officers, and he appeared very anxious to know whither he had given them all higher Comissions then they had at their Arrival, on purpose that they might gett them Confirm'd to them Upon their return to France. He nether Spoke to any of the Scots officers present, or inquired after any of the Absent, (nor at any of the preceding battles he never had inquired after any of the Wounded Officers). He appeared very Uneasy as long as the Scots were about him, and in a Short time order'd them all to go to Ruthven of Badenoch, where he would Send them orders; but before they had rode a mile, he Sent Mr Sheridan after them, to tell them that they might disperse and every body Shift for himself the best way he could….

The Prince kept with him some of Fitzjames's horse, and went that night to a house [Gortleg] in the head of Strathyrick, where he mett Lord Lovatt, and a great many other Scots Gentlemen, who advised him not to quit the Country, but Stay and gather together again his Scatter'd forces. But he was so prepossess'd against the Scots, that he was Affraid they would give him up to make their peace with the Government.…Untill the fidelity of the Highlanders, Show'd him during the long time he was hid in their Country, Convinced him and every body else of the Contrary. The 17 [of April] early in the morning he Sent away all Fitzjames people from him (who went and Surrendered themselves to the Duke at Inverness), and he himself, disguised like a Servant, and mounted before a portmanteau, and only attended by Mr OSullivan and [Edward Burke] a guide, [rode off towards Arisaig].

Much[1] the smaller body, in which were the Frasers, Lord John Drummond's regiment, and the Irish piquets, marched straight to Inverness. The dragoons, both from the right and left of the Duke's army, pursued, and did great execution upon the straggling parties. Kingston's light horse followed the chace, till they came within a mile of Inverness. At a mill, which is about that distance from the town, lay the last of the slain. The Duke of Cumberland, marching on towards Inverness, was met by a drummer with a message from General Stapleton, offering to surrender and asking quarter. The Duke made Sir Joseph Yorke alight from his horse, and with his pencil write a note to General Stapleton, assuring him of fair quarter, and honourable treatment. The drummer went off with his answer. The Duke then sent forward Captain [James] Campbell of Sempill's regiment, with his company of grenadiers, who took possession of Inverness. The French and Irish laid down their arms.

Four[2] of their principal Ladies also fell into our Hands, viz. Lady Ogilvie[3], Lady Gordon[4], Lady Kinloch[5], and Lady Mackintosh, who was at the Head of the Clan of that Name. The Ladies, after Tea, were preparing to dress for a Ball in the Evening, expecting the Rebels had gain'd the Victory; but the King's Red-Coats were so rude as to interrupt them, and lead them up a Dance they did not expect. The Rebels had ordered the Inhabitants of Inverness to provide all the Oatmeal they could spare, and with it bake Bannocks for their Suppers, against their Return from the Victory; but their Disappointment was very pleasing to us, who came to eat it in their Stead.

[1] *H. H.* 235. [2] *R.* 343.
[3] Margaret Johnstone, daughter of the Laird of Westerhall, wife of David Lord Ogilvy, titular Earl of Airlie.
[4] Janet Duff, daughter of William Lord Braco (1st Earl of Fife), wife of Sir William Gordon of Park.
[5] Janet Duff, half-sister of William Lord Braco (1st Earl of Fife), wife of Sir James Kinloch of Kinloch.

I[1] arrived, on the 18th, at Ruthven, which happened by chance to become the rallying point of our army, without having been previously fixed on. There I found the Duke of Athol, Lord George Murray, the Duke of Perth, Lord John Drummond, Lord Ogilvie, and many other chiefs of clans, with about four or five thousand Highlanders, all in the best possible dispositions for renewing hostilities and taking their revenge....

We passed the 19th at Ruthven without any news from the Prince. All the Highlanders were cheerful and full of spirits, to a degree perhaps never before witnessed in an army so recently beaten, expecting, with impatience, every moment the arrival of the Prince; but, on the 20th, Mr Macleod, Lord George's aide-de-camp, who had been sent to him, returned with the following laconic answer: 'Let every man seek his safety in the best way he can'—an inconsiderate answer, heart-breaking to the brave men who had sacrificed themselves for him[2]....

We were masters of the passes between Ruthven and Inverness, which gave us sufficient time to assemble our adherents. The clan of Macpherson of Clunie, consisting of five hundred very brave men, besides many other Highlanders, who had not been able to reach Inverness before the battle, joined us at Ruthven; so that our numbers increased every moment, and I am thoroughly convinced that, in the course of eight days, we should have had a more powerful army than ever....But the Prince was inexorable and immoveable in his resolution of abandoning his enterprise, and terminating in this inglorious manner an expedition, the rapid progress of which had fixed the attention of all Europe....

Our separation at Ruthven was truly affecting. We bade one another an eternal adieu. No one could tell whether the scaffold would not be his fate. The Highlanders gave vent to their grief in wild howlings and lamentations; the tears flowed down their cheeks when they thought that their country was now at the discretion of the Duke of Cumberland, and on the point of being plundered; whilst they and their children would be reduced to slavery, and plunged, without resource, into a state of remediless distress.

[1] *J.* 148.   [2] Cf. *B. I.* 45, note 1.

CHAPTER VII

IN THE HIGHLANDS

Our[1] small, hungry, and fatigued army being put into confusion and overpowered by numbers, was forced to retreat. Then it was that Edward Bourk fell in with the Prince, having no right guide and very few along with him.... Edward Bourk, being well acquainted with all them bounds, undertook to be the Prince's guide and brought him off with Lord Elcho, Sir Thomas Sheridan [and others]. Afterwards they met with O'Sullivan, when they were but in very bad circumstances. The Prince was pleased to say to Ned, 'If you be a true friend, pray endeavour to lead us safe off.' Which honour Ned was not a little fond of, and promised to do his best. Then the Prince rode off from the way of the enemy to the Water of Nairn, where, after advising, he dismist all the men that were with him, being about sixty of Fitz-James's horse that had followed him. After which Edward Bourk said, 'Sir, if you please, follow me. I'll do my endeavour to make you safe.' The Prince accordingly followed him, and with Lord Elcho, Sir Thomas Sheridan, O'Sullivan, and Mr Alexander MacLeod, aid-de-camp, marched to Tordarroch, where they got no access, and from Tordarroch through Aberarder, where likewise they got no access; from Aberarder to Faroline, and from Faroline to Gortuleg, where they met with Lord Lovat, and drank three glasses of wine with him.

About 2 o'clock next morning [April 17] with great hardships we arrived at the Castle of Glengary, called Invergary, where the guide (Ned Burk) spying a fishing-net set, pulled it to him, and found two salmonds, which the guide made ready in the best manner he could, and the meat was reckoned very savoury and acceptable. After taking some refreshment the Prince wanted to be quit of the cloathing he had on, and Ned gave him his own coat. At 3 o'clock afternoon, the Prince,

[1] *L. M.* i, 190. From Edward Burke's Journal.

O'Sullivan, another private gentleman[1], and the guide set out and came to the house of one [Donald[2]] Cameron of Glenpean.

He[3] arrived [at Glenpean] on the 18th at two in the morning, and went to sleep, which he had not done for five days and nights. ...He remained there till 5 o'clock in the afternoon in hopes of obtaining some intelligence, but gaining none, he set out from thence on foot, and travell'd to the Glens of Morar, over almost inaccessible mountains.

Upon[4] Saturday's morning, being the 19th, he came to Oban in Kinlochmors, a corner of Clanranald's estate, and for their further security contented themselves that night for their lodgment with a small sheal house near a wood.

Early upon the 20th his royal highness got up and went straight to Arisaig, to a town called Glenbiastill [Glenbeasdale[5]], where the Prince got a sute of new Highland cloaths from Angus MacDonald of Borodale's spouse, the better to disguise him and to make him pass for one of the country. At Glenbiastill the few gentlemen (that happened to come home from that unlucky battle of Culloden) of Clanranald's men assembled about the Prince, in order to consult and lay their schemes for his present and future safety, being convinced that the enemy would probably soon be about them if not resisted. His royal highness stayed at Glenbiastill for four nights, and upon the 24th then instant his royal highness concurred in their opinions that he should leave the mainland and go to the Isles.

Upon the said 24th day, as young Clanranald was absent at the beginning of their consultation, he finds great fault with his royal highness's resolution of leaving the continent so abruptly, but that he should tarry for some time to see what might cast up; and that he would immediately cause four small bothies to be built at competent distances in different woods where he might with all imaginable security skulk for some time, and that he himself (young Clanranald) and some other chosen men

[1] Captain Allan Macdonald, of Clanranald's family and a priest. *L. M.* i, 163, 321.
[2] *B. O.* 229.   [3] *L. M.* i, 68.
[4] *L. M.* i, 322. From Captain Alexander Macdonald's Journal.
[5] Cf. *L. M.* iii, 375.

would take a trip to the Isles to look out for a ship for his transportation, if seen requisite. But then his royal highness was so far overswayed by Colonel O'Sullivan, &c., that he would by no means stay. Upon this, young Clanranald immediately prepares a boat and shippage, Donald MacLeod of Gualtergill in Sky being appointed pilot and steersman.

About[1] the beginning of April, 1746, Æneas MacDonald (one of Kinlochmoidart's brothers, and a banker at Paris) [had] sent for Donald MacLeod and told him that he heard that he (Donald) knew the coast well, and likewise the course to the different Isles, and that as he was upon going to the island of Barra for a small sum of money that was lying there, only about £380 Sterling, he was desirous to have him for his pilot and guide. Donald MacLeod very frankly agreed to do that, or anything else in his power to promote the Prince's interest. On board they go, and...had the good luck to get safe to Barra, where they got the money....From thence they sailed to the island of Egg...and from Egg they steered their course to the mainland, where they arrived at Kinlochmoidart's house....

About four or five days after they came to Kinlochmoidart... several messages (for the greater security, lest any one of them should happen to miscarry or come by any misfortune) came to Donald MacLeod desiring him forthwith to go to the Prince at Boradale, which order he obeyed directly.

When Donald came to Boradale, the first man he met with was the Prince in a wood, all alone.

The Prince, making towards Donald, asked, 'Are you Donald MacLeod of Guatergill in Sky?' 'Yes,' said Donald, 'I am the same man, may it please your Majesty, at your service. What is your pleasure wi' me?'...'Why,' said the Prince, 'the service I am to put you upon I know you can perform very well. It is that you may go with letters from me to Sir Alexander MacDonald and the Laird of MacLeod....' 'What,' said Donald, 'does not your excellency know that these men have played the rogue to you altogether, and will you trust them for a' that? Na, you mauna do't.'...

[1] *L. M.* i, 159. From Donald Macleod's Journal.

When Donald MacLeod had absolutely refused to go any message whatsomever to Sir Alexander MacDonald and the Laird of MacLeod, the Prince said to him, 'I hear, Donald, you are a good pilot; that you know all this coast well, and therefore I hope you can carry me safely through the islands, where I may look for more safety than I can do here.' Donald answered...that he most willingly undertook to do his best in the service he now proposed. For this purpose Donald procured a stout eight-oar'd boat, the property of John MacDonald, son of Æneas or Angus MacDonald of Borodale....Donald took care to buy a pot for boyling pottage or the like when they should happen to come to land, and a poor firlot of meal was all the provision he could make out to take with them.

April 26th. They go on board in the twilight of the evening in Lochnannua[gh], at Boradale, being the very spot of ground where the Prince landed at first upon the continent....There were in the boat the Prince, Captain O'Sullivan, Captain [Felix] O'Neil[1], Allan MacDonald, commonly called Captain Mac-Donald (of the family of Clanranald, and a clergyman of the Church of Rome); and Donald MacLeod, for pilot, managing the helm, and betwixt whose feet the Prince took his seat. The names of the boatmen are: Rhoderick MacDonald, Lauchlan MacMurrich, Rhoderick MacCaskgill, John MacDonald, Murdoch MacLeod (son of the pilot), Duncan Roy, Alexander MacDonald, and Edward Bourk or Burk, a common chairman in Edinburgh....

They had not rowed far from the shore till a most violent tempest arose....When the Prince saw the storm increasing still more and more, he wanted much to be at land again, and desired Donald to steer directly for the rock which runs for no less than three miles along one side of the loch. 'For,' said the Prince, 'I had rather face canons and muskets than be in such a storm as this.' But Donald would not hear of that proposal at all....

After this all was hush and silence; not one word more

---

[1] O'Neil joined the Prince 'at Knoidart,' having been left by him at Invergarry 'to direct such as pass'd that way the road he took.' *L.M.* i, 367. Cf. *A. P.* i, 71.

amongst them, expecting every moment to be overwhelmed with the violence of the waves, and to sink down to the bottom. To make the case still worse, they had neither pump nor compass nor lantern with them....'But,' to use Donald's words, 'as God would have it, by peep of day we discovered ourselves to be on the coast of the Long Isle, and we made directly to the nearest land, which was Rushness [Rossinish] in the Island Benbecula. With great difficulty we got on shore, and saved the boat, hawling her up to dry land, in the morning of April 27th.'...

When they landed at Rushness in Benbecula, they came to an uninhabited hut where they made a fire to dry their cloaths, for all of them were wet through and through in to the skin, and an old sail was spread upon the bare ground, which served for a bed to the Prince, who was very well pleased with it, and slept soundly. Here they kill'd a cow, and the pot which Donald had brought served them in good stead for boyling bits of the beef. In this poor hut they remained two days and two nights[1].

April 29th. In the evening they set sail from Benbecula on board the same eight-oar'd boat for the island Scalpay, commonly called the Island Glass, where they landed safely about two hours before daylight next day, the Prince and O'Sullivan going under the name of Sinclair, the latter passing for the father, and the former for the son....In this island Donald MacLeod had an acquaintance, Donald Campbell, to whose house he brought the Prince and his small retinue before break of day, April 30th. Being all cold and hungry, Donald MacLeod desired immediately to have a good fire, which was instantly got for them. Donald MacLeod was here only one night, but the Prince remained four nights, and was most kindly entertained by his hospitable landlord....

May 1st. Donald MacLeod was dispatched by the Prince to Storn[o]way in the island of Lewis, in order to hire a vessel under a pretence of sailing to the Orkneys to take in meal for the Isle of Sky, as Donald used to deal in that way formerly....Donald left the eight-oar'd boat at Scalpay, and got another boat from his friend, Mr Campbell, in which he sailed for Stornway, where

---

[1] Here they were visited by Old Clanranald. *L. M.* i, 323.

he remained some time without making out the design on which he was sent. But at last he succeeded, and then dispatched an express to the Prince in Scalpay...to inform him that he had got a vessel to his mind.

May 4th. The Prince (leaving Allan MacDonald, the Popish clergyman, in Scalpay, who afterwards returned to South Uist) set out on foot for Stornoway, attended by O'Sullivan and O'Neil, taking a guide along to direct them the right road. This guide, in going to the Harris...took them eight miles out of the way. In coming from Harris to the Lewis they fell under night, and a very stormy and rainy night it was, which fatigued them very much; their journey, by the mistake of their guide, being no less than thirty-eight long Highland miles.

May 5th. When in sight of Stornway the Prince sent the guide to Donald MacLeod to inform him that he and the two captains were at such a place, desiring withal that he would forthwith send them a bottle of brandy and some bread and cheese, for that they stood much in need of a little refreshment. Donald immediately obeyed the summons and came to the Prince, bringing along with him the demanded provisions. He found the Prince and his two attendants upon a muir all wet to the skin, and wearied enough with such a long journey through the worst of roads in the world. Donald told the Prince that he knew of a faithful and true friend to take care of him till things should be got ready for the intended voyage. This was the Lady Killdun at Arynish [Mrs Mackenzie of Kildun House in Arnish], to whose house Donald conducted the Prince and his two attendants. Here the Prince was obliged to throw off his shirt, which one of the company did wring upon the hearth-stone, and did spread it upon a chair before the fire to have it dried.

The same day, May 5th, Donald was sent back to Stornway to get things in readiness. But when he came there, to his great surprize he found no less than two or three hundred men in arms...for that they were well assured the Prince was already upon the Lewis, and not far from Stornway, with five hundred men. This they said exposed them to the hazard of losing both their cattle and their lives, as they heard the Prince was come with a full resolution to force a vessel from Stornway. Donald very gravely asked, How sorrow such a notion could ever enter into their heads?...They replied that Mr John MacAulay[1], Presbyterian preacher in South Uist, had writ these accounts to his father in the Harris, and that the said father had transmitted the same to Mr Colin MacKenzie, Presbyterian teacher in the Lewis. Donald saned these blades, the informers, very heartily, and spared not to give them their proper epithets in strong terms. 'Well then,' said Donald, 'since you know already that the Prince is upon your island, I acknowledge the truth of it; but then...he has only but two companions with him, and when I am there I make the third. And yet let me tell you farther, gentlemen, if Seaforth himself were here, by G—— he durst not put a hand to the Prince's breast.'...

Donald desired they would give him a pilot, but they absolutely refused to give him one...such was the terror and dread the people were struck with. Donald then returned to the Prince, and gave him an honest account how matters stood, which made them all at a loss to know what course to take, all choices having but a bad aspect....

In this great difficulty the Prince declared, let the consequence be what it would, he could not think of stirring anywhere that night till he should sleep a little, so much was he fatigued with the late tedious journey. And the two captains were no less wearied, being quite undone[2]. To make their case still worse, two of the boatmen had run away from Stornway, being frighted out of their wits at the rising of the men in arms.

May 6th. About eight o'clock in the morning the Prince, O'Sullivan, O'Neil, Donald MacLeod, and the six boatmen (two whereof were Donald's own son and honest Ned Bourk), went on board Donald Campbell's boat, which they had got at Scalpa, and sailed for the Island Euirn [Iubhard], twelve miles from Stornway, and landed safely. This Euirn is a desert island round which the people of the Lewis use to go a fishing....

Upon the desart island they found plenty of good dry fish.... As they had plenty of brandy and sugar along with them, and

---

[1] Lord Macaulay's grandfather.
[2] Cf. *L. M.* i, 191, 369.

found very good springs upon the island, they wanted much to have a little warm punch to chear their hearts in this cold remote place. They luckily found a earthen pitcher which...served their purpose very well for heating the punch. But the second night the pitcher by some accident or another was broke to pieces, so that they could have no more warm punch....

Upon this uninhabited island they remained four days and four nights in a low, pityful hut, which the fishers had made up for themselves; but it was so ill-roofed that they were obliged to spread the sail of the boat over the top of it. They found heath and turf enough to make a fire of; but had nothing but the bare ground to lie along upon when disposed to take a nap, without any covering upon them at all....

May 10th. They set sail from the uninhabited island, when the Prince told his retinue he was determined to return to Scalpay or the Island Glass, in order to pay his respects to honest Donald Campbell....When they arrived at Scalpay, Donald Campbell was not at home, having gone a skulking for fear of being laid up, an account or rumour having passed from hand to hand that the Prince had been in his house, and that the landlord had entertained him kindly. The Prince was sorry at missing his hospitable friend, and set sail directly from Scalpa the same day, May 10th....In coursing along they happened to spy a ship at Finisbery, in the Harris, within two musket-shot, before they observed her. They were on the windward of the ship at the mouth of the said bay, and made all the haste they could along the coast to Benbicula. In this course they spied another ship in Lochmaddy, in North Uist, which occasioned them to make all the sail and rowing they could to get free of the mouth of the loch and out of sight of the ship.

May 11th. Being still upon the sea they fell short of bread; but having some meal on board, and the men turning very hungry and thirsty, they began to make Dramach (in Erse *Stappack*) with salt water, and to lick it up. The Prince said that was a kind of meat he had never seen before, and therefore he behoved to try it how it would go down. Donald said the Prince ate of it very heartily, and much more than he could do for his life. Never any meat or drink came wrong to him, for he could

take a share of every thing, be it good, bad, or indifferent, and
was always chearful and contented in every condition.

May 11th. They arrived at Lochwiskaway [Loch Uskavagh],
in Benbicula, and had scarce got ashore [on an island in the
Loch], when the wind proved quite contrary to what it had been,
blowing a hard gale, which served to make the ships they had
spied steer an opposite course.

[On¹ this island] we came to a poor grasskeeper's bothy or
hut, which had so laigh a door, that we digged below the door
and put heather below the Prince's knees, he being tall, to let
him go the easier into the poor hut. We stayed there about three
nights, and provided ourselves very well in victuals by fowling
and fishing, and drest them in the best shapes we could, and
thought them very savoury meat.

Thence we went [May 14] to the mountain of Coradale, in
South Uist.

[The² Prince] dispatched Donal MacLeod [from Coradale]
in Campbell's boat to the continent with letters to Lochiel and
John Murray of Broughton, in order to know how affairs stood,
and that Donald might bring along with him some cash and
brandy. Donald met with Lochiel and Murray at the head of
Locharkaig; but got no money at all from Murray, who said he
had none to give, having only about sixty louis d'ores to himself,
which was not worth the while to send. Donald received letters
from Lochiel and Murray to the Prince, and found means without much ado to purchase two anchors of brandy at a guinea
per anchor. Here Donald observed that the Prince had a very
good opinion of Murray, looking upon him as one of the
honestest, firmest men in the whole world.

Donald was absent from the Prince eighteen days or thereabouts, and upon his return he found the Prince where he left
him upon Coradale. During his abode on this mountain he lived
in a tenant's house [Ronald MacGachan]³, only a hut better
than ordinary, diverting and maintaining himself with hunting
and fishing.

¹ L. M. i, 193. From Edward Burke's Journal.
² Ibid. 174. From Donald Macleod's Journal.
³ A. P. i, 69, 74.

In[1] the Forrest house [at Coradale] the Prince (when resting himself) used to sit on a fail-sunk, *i.e.* an earthen seat, having some fog and plaids under him, and would step into a by-chamber, which served as a pantry, and (when he stood in need of it) put the bottle of brandy or whiskie to his head and take his dram without any ceremony. Upon the [3rd?][2] day of June, Mac-Donald of Boystil [Boisdale], Hugh MacDonald of Bailshair in North Uist, of the family of Slate [Sleat], James and Lauchlan MacDonalds, brothers of the often mentioned Captain Alexander MacDonald, and Ranald MacDonald of Torulum, of Clanranald's family, visited the Prince in his Forrest palace to pay him the compliments of the day. Their drink was only cold brandy out of a clean shell without any mixture at all, and the Prince stood it out better than any one of them in drinking the health of the day.

From[3] the foot of the mountain of Coradale they set sail [June 6] in Campbell's boat still, and landed in the Island Ouia [Wiay], at Benbicula, where they stayed four nights.

From thence [June 10] the Prince and O'Neil, with a guide, went to Rushness [Rossinish], where Lady Clanranald was. Donald [Macleod] and O'Sullivan were left at Ouia, where they abode two nights after the Prince had gone off to Rushness by land. The third night after the Prince had been at Rushness, he got information that it was advisable he should go back again to the place from whence he had come; but he knew not well what to do, as the boats of the militia had been all the time in the course between Ouia and Rushness. Donald and O'Sullivan, hearing of the Prince's situation, set sail [June 12] under favour of the night, and brought the Prince off from Rushness, steering their course from thence south again back towards Coradale hill. But meeting with a violent storm, and a very heavy rain, they were forced to put into Uishness Point, two miles and an half north of Coradale. The place they put up at in that night [June 13] is called Achkirsideallich [Acarseid Fhalaich], a rock

1 *L. M.* i, 326. From Captain Alexander Macdonald's Journal.

2 Macleod names the 10th, the Old Pretender's birthday, an impossible date. Cf. *B. I.* 51.

3 *L. M.* i, 268. From Donald Macleod's Journal.

upon the shore, in a clift of which they took up their quarters, the storm continuing for a whole day. At night, the enemy being within less than two miles of them, they set sail again, and arrived [June 14] safely at Ciliestiella [Kyle Stuley], from whence they steered their course towards Loch Boisdale. But one on board swore that there was a long-boat in their way, no doubt full of marines...and therefore they steered back to Ciliestiella and stayed there that night. Next day [June 15] they set out for Loch Boisdale.

All[1] that day we were obliged to keep in a narrow creek till night that we got into Loch Boisdale. Afterwards coming ashore very much fatigued, we came to an old tower in the mouth of the island, where we kindled fire, put on our pot in order to make ready some provisions; and Ned Burk went out to pull some heath for the Prince's bed. Meanwhile Donald MacLeod of Gualtergill said there were two French ships of war appearing; but to our great surprize they proved to be Englishmen. The Prince with three others took to the mountains, and the rowers went to the barge lying in the creek and steered up the loch.

The men-of-war steered to the main. At night [June 15] we all met again at our barge, wherein we had still some small provisions. We stayed in the open fields two nights, having only the sails of the boat for covers. On the third night [June 18] we went farther into the loch, and rested thereabouts for other two nights [June 19 and 20].

Besides[2] [the two ships of war] there was a command of above five hundred redcoats and militia within a mile and a half of them[3]. All choices were bad, but (under God) they behoved to remove from the place where they then were, and to do their best.

The Prince [June 21] called for the boatmen, and ordered O'Sullivan to pay every one of them a shilling sterling a day, besides their maintenance. He gave a draught of sixty pistols to Donald MacLeod to be paid by Mr John Hay of Restalrig, if he should happen to be so lucky as to meet with him upon the

[1] *L. M.* i, 195. From Edward Burke's Journal.
[2] *Ibid.* 177. From Donald Macleod's Journal.
[3] Under Captain Carolina Scott. Cf. *A. P.* i, 11.

continent. But as Donald never met with Mr Hay, the draught remains yet unpaid....

They parted [at Loch Boisdale] with a resolution to meet again at a certain place by different roads; Donald MacLeod, O'Sullivan, and the boatmen walking away and leaving O'Neil only with the Prince. Donald MacLeod went south about, but all the men left him, one only excepted; upon which he was obliged to sink the boat, and to do the best he could to shift for himself[1].

At[2] nightfall [June 21] we [the Prince and O'Neil] marched towards Benbecula, being informed [Captain Carolina] Scott had ordered the militia to come and join him. At midnight we came to a hut [near Milton], where by good fortune we met with Miss Flora MacDonald, whom I formerly knew. I quitted the Prince at some distance from the hut, and went with a design to inform myself if the Independent Companies were to pass that way next day, as we had been informed. The young lady answered me—Not—and said that they would not pass till the day after. Then I told her I brought a friend to see her, and she, with some emotion, asked me if it was the Prince. I answered her it was, and instantly brought him in. We then consulted on the imminent danger the Prince was in, and could think of a no more proper and safe expedient than to propose to Miss Flora to convey him to the Isle of Sky, where her mother lived. This seemed the more feasible, as the young lady's father, being captain of an Independent Company[3], would accord her a pass

[1] On July 5, 1746, Donald was taken prisoner in Benbecula. *L. M.* i, 178.

[2] *L. M.* i, 370. From Captain Felix O'Neil's Journal.

[3] Duncan Forbes of Culloden, remaining in the North after Cope's embarkation at Aberdeen in September, 1745, had summoned Sir Alexander Macdonald, Macleod of Macleod and others of the government's supporters to furnish companies of 100 men each. They assembled at Inverness in the course of October and November, and Lord Loudoun, arrived there early in October, took over the command of them. After Culloden these Independent Companies were employed in the islands and on the mainland in the search for Prince Charles and punishment of his partisans. Cf. *C. P.* 245 and *E. J.* 300.

for herself and a servant to go visit her mother. The Prince assented, and immediately propos'd it to the young lady, to which she answered with the greatest respect and loyalty; but declined it, saying Sir Alexander MacDonald was too much her friend to be the instrument of his ruin. I endeavoured to obviate this by assuring her Sir Alexander was not in the country, and that she could with the greatest facility convey the Prince to her mother's, as she lived close by the waterside. I then remonstrated to her the honour and immortality that would redound to her by such a glorious action, and she at length acquiesc'd, after the Prince had told her the sense he would always retain of so conspicuous a service. She promised to acquaint us next day when things were ripe for execution, and we parted for the mountains of Coradale.

Miss[1] MacDonald had gone from Sky to Milton in South Uist in order to visit her brother-german, who had about that time taken up house. She had not been long there till Captain O'Neil (by some happy accident or other) had become acquainted with her. When...Miss MacDonald had (with some difficulty) agreed to undertake the dangerous enterprize, she set out for Clanranald's house [Nunton], Saturday, June 21st, and at one of the fords was taken prisoner by a party of militia, she not having a passport. She demanded to whom they belonged? And finding by the answer that her step-father was then commander, she refused to give any answers till she should see their captain. So she and her servant[2], Neil MacKechan, were prisoners all that night.

Her step-father, coming next day, being Sunday, she told him what she was about, upon which he granted a passport for herself, a man-servant (Neil MacKechan), and another woman, Bettie Burk, a good spinster, and whom he recommended as such in a letter to his wife at Armadale in Sky, as she had much lint to spin....[He] set his step-daughter at liberty, who immediately made the best of her way to Clanranald's house, and acquainted

[1] *L. M.* i, 297. From Flora Macdonald's narrative.

[2] Neil Maceachain or Mackechan was schoolmaster in South Uist and tutor to Clanranald's family. His narrative is in *B. O.* 225 ff. Cf. *B. I.* 99.

the Lady Clanranald with the scheme, who supplied the Prince with apparel sufficient for his disguise, viz. a flower'd linen gown, a white apron, &c., and sent some provisions along with him.

During Miss MacDonald's stay at Clanranald's house, which was till the Friday, June 27th, O'Neil went several times betwixt the Prince and Miss, in which interval another scheme was proposed, that the Prince should go under the care of a gentleman[1] to the northward, but that failing them, they behoved to have recourse to that agreed upon before; and accordingly Lady Clanranald, one Mrs [John] MacDonald [of Kirkibost], O'Neil, Miss Flora MacDonald, and her servant, Neil MacKechan, went to the place where the Prince was, being about eight Scotch miles. He was then in a very little house or hut, assisting in the roasting of his dinner, which consisted of the heart, liver, kidneys, &c., of a bullock or sheep, upon a wooden spit. O'Neil introduced his young preserver and the company, and she sat on the Prince's right hand and Lady Clanranald on his left. Here they all dined very heartily.

Next morning, June 28, they heard of General Campbell's arrival at Benbecula, and soon after, a man came in a great hurry to Lady Clanranald, and acquainted her that Captain [John] Ferguson with an advanced party of Campbell's men was at her house, and that Ferguson had lain in her bed the night before. This obliged her to go home immediately, which accordingly she did, after taking leave of the Prince....

O'Neil would gladly have staid with the Prince and shared in his distresses and dangers, but Miss could by no means be prevailed upon to agree to that proposal.

When all were gone[2] who were not to accompany the Prince in his voyage to the Isle of Sky, Miss MacDonald desired him to dress himself in his new attire, which was soon done, and at a proper time they removed their quarters and went near the water with their boat afloat, nigh at hand for readiness to embark in case of an alarm from the shore. Here they arrived very wet and wearied, and made a fire upon a rock to keep them somewhat

---

[1] Hugh Macdonald of Baleshare. *L. M.* i, 327, 372.
[2] O'Neil was taken prisoner shortly after this. *A. P.* ii, p. xlvi.

warm till night. They were soon greatly alarmed by seeing four wherries full of armed men making towards shore, which made them extinguish their fire quickly, and to conceal themselves amongst the heath....

At eight o'clock, June 28th, Saturday, 1746, the Prince, Miss Flora MacDonald, Neil MacKechan, &c. [four boatmen][1], set sail in a very clear evening from Benbecula to the Isle of Sky....

They had not rowed from the shore above a league till the sea became rough, and at last tempestuous, and to entertain the company, the Prince sung several songs and seemed to be in good spirits.

In the passage Miss MacDonald fell asleep, and then the Prince carefully guarded her, lest in the darkness any of the men should chance to step upon her. She awaked in a surprize with some little bustle in the boat, and wondered what was the matter, &c.

Next morning, Sunday, June 29th, the boatmen knew not where they were, having no compass, and the wind varying several times, it being then again calm. However, at last they made to the point of Waternish, in the west corner of Sky, where they thought to have landed, but found the place possessed by a body of forces, who had three boats or yawls near the shore. One on board one of the boats fired at them to make them bring-to; but they rowed away as fast as they could, being all the chance they had to escape, because there were several ships of war within sight. They got into a creek, or rather clift of a rock, and there remained some short time to rest the men, who had been all night at.work, and to get their dinners of what provisions they had along with them. As soon as they could they set forwards again, because, as the militia could not bring them to, they had sent up to alarm a little town not far off. It was very lucky for them that it was a calm then, for otherwise they must inevitably have perished or have been taken.

From hence they rowed on and landed at Kilbride, in Troternish, in the Isle of Sky, about twelve miles north from the above-

[1] Their names are given in *L. M.* iii, 22.

mentioned point. There were also several parties of militia in the neighbourhood of Kilbride. Miss left the Prince in the boat and went with her servant, Neil MacKechan, to Mougstot [Monkstat], Sir Alexander MacDonald's house, and desired one of the servants to let Lady Margaret MacDonald know she was come to see her ladyship in her way to her mother's house. Lady Margaret knew her errand well enough by one Mrs MacDonald[1], who had gone a little before to apprize her of it.

As Mr Alexander MacDonald of Kingsburgh was accidentally there, Lady Margaret desired him to conduct the Prince to his house; for it is to be remarked that Lady Margaret did not see the Prince in any shape. Kingsburgh sent a boy down to the boat with instructions whither to conduct the Prince about a mile, and he (Kingsburgh) would be there ready to conduct him. Then Kingsburgh took some wine, &c., to refresh the Prince with, and set forwards for the place of rendezvous, leaving Miss MacDonald with Lady Margaret at Mougstot, where the commanding officer of the parties in search of the Prince was, and who asked Miss whence she came, whither she was going, what news? &c., all which Miss answered as she thought most proper, and so as to prevent any discovery of what she had been engaged in.

Lady Margaret pressed Miss very much in presence of the officer to stay, telling her that she had promised to make some stay the first time she should happen to come there. But Miss desired to be excused at that time, because she wanted to see her mother, and to be at home in these troublesome times. Lady Margaret at last let her go, and she and Mrs MacDonald above mentioned set forwards with Neil MacKechan and said Mrs MacDonald's maid and her man-servant. They overtook the Prince and Kingsburgh. Mrs MacDonald was very desirous to see the Prince's countenance; but as he went along he always turned away his face from Mrs MacDonald to the opposite side whenever he perceived her endeavouring to stare him in the countenance. But she got several opportunities of seeing his face,

[1] Mrs John Macdonald of Kirkibost. Cf. *L. M.* ii, 13, 17. Lady Macdonald already had sent Hugh Macdonald of Baleshare to relieve the Prince in South Uist. *L. M.* ii, 95.

though in disguise, which the maid could not help taking notice of, and said she had never seen such an impudent-looked woman, and durst say she was either an Irish woman or else a man in a woman's dress. Miss MacDonald replied she was an Irish woman, for she had seen her before. The maid also took notice of the Prince's awkward way of managing the petticoats, and what long strides he took in walking along, &c., which obliged Miss Mac-Donald to desire Mrs MacDonald (they being both on horse-back) to step a little faster and leave those on foot, because, as there were many parties of militia in the great roads, it was necessary for the Prince to cross the country, and it was not proper to let Mrs MacDonald's man or maid servant see it. So on they went, and the Prince and Kingsburgh went over the hills and travelled south-south-east till they arrived at Kings-burgh's house, which was about twelve o'clock at night, and they were very wet. But Miss MacDonald, who had parted with her companions and her man-servant on the road, arrived some short time before the Prince.

When[1] the Prince came to Kingsburgh's house (Sunday, June 29th)...Mrs MacDonald, not expecting to see her husband that night, was making ready to go to bed. One of her servant maids came and told her that Kingsburgh was come home and had brought some company with him. 'What company?' says Mrs MacDonald. 'Milton's daughter, I believe,' says the maid, 'and some company with her.' 'Milton's daughter,' replies Mrs MacDonald, 'is very welcome to come here with any company she pleases to bring. But you'll give my service to her, and tell her to make free with anything in the house; for I am very sleepy, and cannot see her this night.' In a little, her own daughter came and told her in a surprize, 'O mother, my father had brought in a very odd, muckle, ill-shaken-up wife as ever I saw! I never saw the like of her, and he has gone into the hall with her.' She had scarce done with telling her tale when Kings-burgh came and desired his lady to fasten on her bucklings again, and to get some supper for him and the company he had brought

[1] L. M. i, 117. From a collection of 'Remarks, etc., and particular sayings of some who were concerned in the Prince's preservation,' made by Bishop Forbes, and dated July 20, 1747.

with him. 'Pray, goodman,' says she, 'what company is this you have brought with you?' 'Why, goodwife,' said he, 'you shall know that in due time; only make haste and get some supper in the meantime.' Mrs MacDonald desired her daughter to go and fetch her the keys she had left in the hall. When the daughter came to the door of the hall, she started back, ran to her mother and told her she could not go in for the keys, for the muckle woman was walking up and down in the hall, and she was so frighted at seeing her that she could not have the courage to enter. Mrs MacDonald went herself to get the keys, and I [Bishop Forbes] heard her more than once declare that upon looking in at the door she had not the courage to go forward. 'For,' said she, 'I saw such an odd muckle trallup of a carlin making lang wide steps through the hall, that I could not like her appearance at all.' Mrs MacDonald called Kingsburgh, and very seriously begged to know what a lang, odd hussie was this he had brought to the house....'Did you never see a woman before,' said he, 'good-wife? What frights you at seeing a woman? Pray, make haste, and get us some supper.' Kingsburgh would not go for the keys, and therefore his lady behov'd to go for them. When she entered the hall, the Prince happen'd to be sitting; but immediately he arose, went forward and saluted Mrs MacDonald, who, feeling a long stiff beard, trembled to think that this behoved to be some distressed nobleman or gentleman in disguise, for she never dream'd it to be the Prince....She very soon made out of the hall with her keys, never saying one word. Immediately she importun'd Kingsburgh to tell her who the person was, for that she was sure by the salute that it was some distressed gentleman. Kingsburgh smiled at the mention of the bearded kiss, and said, 'Why, my dear, it is the Prince. You have the honour to have him in your house.' 'The Prince,' cried she. 'O Lord, we are a' ruin'd and undone for ever! We will a' be hang'd now!' 'Hout, goodwife,' says the honest stout soul, 'we will die but ance; and if we are hanged for this, I am sure we die in a good cause. Pray, make no delay; go, get some supper. Fetch what is readiest. You have eggs and butter and cheese in the house, get them as quickly as possible.' 'Eggs and butter and cheese!' says Mrs MacDonald, 'what a supper is that for a

Prince?' 'O goodwife,' said he, 'little do you know how this good Prince has been living for some time past. These, I can assure you, will be a feast to him....Make haste, and see that you come to supper.' 'I come to supper!' says Mrs MacDonald; 'how can I come to supper? I know not how to behave before Majesty.' 'You must come,' says Kingsburgh, 'for he will not eat a bit till he see you at the table; and you will find it no difficult matter to behave before him, so obliging and easy is he in his conversation.'

The Prince ate of our roasted eggs, some collops, plenty of bread and butter, &c., and (to use the words of Mrs MacDonald) 'the deel a drap did he want in's weam of twa bottles of sma' beer. God do him good o't; for, well I wat, he had my blessing to gae down wi't.' After he had made a plentiful supper, he called for a dram; and when the bottle of brandy was brought, he said he would fill the glass for himself; 'for,' said he, 'I have learn'd in my skulking to take a hearty dram.' He filled up a bumper and drank it off to the happiness and prosperity of his landlord and landlady. Then, taking a crack'd and broken pipe out of his poutch, wrapt about with thread, he asked Kingsburgh if he could furnish him with some tobacco; for that he had learn'd likewise to smoke in his wanderings. Kingsburgh took from him the broken pipe and laid it carefully up with the brogs, and gave him a new, clean pipe and plenty of tobacco....

After Miss Flora had got up [Monday, June 30], Mrs Mac-Donald told her that she wanted much to have a lock of the Prince's hair, and that she behoved to go into his room and get it for her. Miss Flora refused to do as she desired, because the Prince was not yet out of bed. 'What then,' said Mrs Mac-Donald, 'no harm will happen to you. He is too good to harm you or any person. You must instantly go in and get me the lock.' Mrs MacDonald, taking hold of Miss with one hand, knocked at the door of the room with the other. The Prince called, 'Who is there?' Mrs MacDonald, opening the door, said, 'Sir, it is I, and I am importuneing Miss Flora to come in and get a lock of your hair to me, and she refuses to do it.' 'Pray,' said the Prince, 'desire Miss MacDonald to come in. What should make her afraid to come where I am?' When Miss came in, he begged her to sit down on a chair at the bedside, then laying his arms about her waist, and his head upon her lap, he desired her to cut out the lock with her own hands in token of future and more substantial favours. The one half of the lock Miss gave to Mrs MacDonald, and the other she kept to herself.

Though[1] the Prince was determined (from the observations and persuasion of Kingsburgh[2]) to cast off his disguise, yet it was necessary he should leave the house in the female dress he came in...and therefore in Kingsburgh's house Miss put on his cap for him.

The day [June 30] was far advanced before he set out, and when he arrived at a wood side (as the affair had been concerted), not far from Kingsburgh, he changed his apparel once more and put on the Highland dress Kingsburgh had furnished him with[3]. Then Kingsburgh sent a guide[4] with him to Portree, thro' all byways, while Miss MacDonald went thither on horseback by another road, thereby the better to gain intelligence and at the same time to prevent a discovery. They were very wet, it having rained very much. Here he only dried his clothes, took some little refreshment, and staid about two hours.

Hither Kingsburgh[5] had sent to prepare a boat, and to have it ready to convey the Prince to the place where he wanted to be at....Young [John] MacLeod of Raaza came with [Captain] Malcolm MacLeod to conduct the Prince over to the Isle of Raaza. The Prince was very uneasy he had not a MacDonald to conduct him still.

The[6] Prince no sooner entred [the inn at Portree] than he asked if a dram could be got there, the rain pouring down his

1 *L. M.* i, 302. From Flora Macdonald's narrative.

2 Cf. *Ibid.* 75. Kingsburgh objected that the Prince's feminine airs were 'all so man-like.'

3 Cf. *Ibid.* 76.

4 A boy named Macqueen. Neil Maceachain was also with the Prince. *Ibid.* ii, 21.

5 Shortly after Charles's visit, Kingsburgh was made prisoner. *Ibid.* i, 123, 126.

6 *L. M.* ii, 21. From Captain Roy Macdonald's narrative. He was Baleshare's brother.

cloaths, he having on a plaid without breeches, trews, or even philibeg. Before he sat down he got his dram, and then the company desired him to shift and put on a dry shirt, Captain Roy MacDonald giving him his philabeg. The Prince refused to shift, as Miss Flora MacDonald was in the room; but the Captain and Neil MacKechan told him it was not a time to stand upon ceremonies, and prevailed upon him to put on a dry shirt....

Before the Prince got on his coats, just in his shirt, he fell heartily to the meat, and made good use of his time, having travelled on foot from Kingsburgh to Portree, being seven good Highland miles. He brought along with him four shirts, a cold hen, a bottle of brandy, and a lump of sugar, in one of his pockets; all which small stock of provisions (adding to them a bottle of whiskie he bought from the landlord of Portree)[1] he took along with him to the Island of Rasay....

The Prince called for some tobacco that he might smoke a pipe before he should go off....The Captain ordered the landlord to fetch a quarter of a pound, which he did in the scales, at fourpence halfpenny. The Prince gave a sixpence, but the landlord was desired by the Captain to bring in the change. The Prince smiled at the Captain's exactness, and would not be at the pain to take the three halfpence. The Captain insisted he should take them...opend the purse, and finding an empty partition, put the bawbees into it....

The Prince now began to bid farewell to Miss MacDonald and Neil MacKechan (the Captain being always begging him to depart), and turning to Miss, he said, 'I believe, Madam, I owe you a crown of borrowed money.' She told him it was only half-a-crown, which accordingly he paid her with thanks. He then saluted her, and expressed himself in these or the like words, 'For all that has happened I hope, Madam, we shall meet in St James's yet.' He then bad farewel to honest MacKechan, who stayed that night with Miss MacDonald at Portree, and attended her next day to the place she intended to go to[2]. This MacKechan found the way afterwards to get off to France with the Prince.

[1] Charles Macnab. *L. M.* ii, 21.

[2] Flora Macdonald was taken prisoner a week or ten days later. *Ibid.* i, 303.

When the Prince was about going off from Portree, he tied the bottle of whiskie to his belt at one side, and the bottle of brandy, the shirts, and the cold hen in a napkin at the other side....In their way to the boat the Prince...taking the lump of sugar out of his pocket gave it to the Captain, and said, 'Pray, MacDonald, give this piece of sugar to *our lady* [Flora], for I am afraid she will get no sugar where she is going.' The Captain refused to take it, begging the Prince to keep it for his own use, for that he would stand in need of it yet. The Prince would not take it again. Upon which the Captain slipt it privately into Malcolm MacLeod's hands, desiring him to preserve it for the Prince's use. The Prince enjoined the Captain a strict silence in these or the like words, 'Tell nobody, no, not *our lady*, which way I am gone, for it is right that my course should not be known.'

The Prince then took leave of the Captain (about the dawning of the day, Tuesday, July 1st), the boat steering away for Rasay.

Early[1] in the morning, July 1st, they[2] arrived at Glam, in Raaza, where they remained two days in a mean, low hut; and young Raaza [John MacLeod] was the person that brought provisions to them, viz., a lamb and a kid in the nook of his plaid....

The Prince began to be anxious to be out of Raaza, alleging the island to be too narrow and confin'd in its bounds for his purpose, and proposed setting out for Troternish in Sky...pretending he had a tryst there with a gentleman which he would not break for any thing, that his friends yielded to his importunity.

July 2d. About 7 o'clock at night he went on board [a] small boat, attended by the young Laird of Raaza...and his brother Murdoch, Captain [Malcolm] MacLeod and the two boatmen, John MacKenzie and Donald MacFrier, who had been both out in his service, the one a sergeant and the other a private man. They had not well left the shore till the wind blew a hard gale....

[1] *L. M.* i, 131. From Captain Malcolm Macleod's narrative.

[2] On the voyage to Raasay the Prince was accompanied by Captain Malcolm Macleod, Murdoch Macleod, and Young Raasay. *Ibid.* 130, 302.

The Prince would by no means hear of returning, and to divert the men from thinking on the danger, he sung them a merry Highland song. About nine or ten o'clock the same night they landed at a place in Sky called Nicolson's Rock, near Scorobreck, in Troternish....They went forwards to a cow-byre on the rock, about two miles from Scorobreck, a gentleman's house. In this byre the Prince took up his quarters, the whole company still attending him. Here they took some little refreshment of bread and cheese they had along with them, the cakes being mouldered down into very small crumbles.

Captain MacLeod intreated the Prince to put on a dry shirt and to take some sleep; but he continued sitting in his wet cloaths, and did not then incline to sleep. However, at last he began to nap a little, and would frequently start in his sleep, look briskly up, and stare boldly in the face of every one of them as if he had been to fight them....

About six or seven o'clock at night [July 3] the Prince, taking the little baggage in his hand, stept out of the byre, and desired the Captain [Malcolm Macleod] to follow him....

The Prince proposed to pass for the Captain's servant, the better to conceal him, which was agreed to, and that he should be named Lewie Caw, there being of that name a young surgeon lad (who had been in the Prince's service) skulking at that time in Sky, where he had some relations....

As they were marching along and talking of the fatigues the Prince was obliged to undergoe, he said: 'MacLeod...I have had this philibeg on now for some days, and I find I do as well with it as any the best breeches I ever put on. I hope in God, MacLeod, to walk the streets of London with it yet.'...The Captain remarked it was proper they should pass the road that leads to the Laird of MacLeod's country in the night time for fear of parties spying them; which accordingly they did by break of day. And the Prince looking about him, and seeing nothing but hills all around them, said, 'I am sure, the Devil cannot find us out now.'

As they were coming near Strath, MacKinnon's country, the Captain suggested to the Prince that now he was coming to a country where he would be known, and consequently liable to be discovered in every corner of it, as MacKinnon and his men had been out in his service, some shift behoved to be faln upon to disguise him more and more still. The Prince proposed blacking his face with some one thing or another. But the Captain was against that proposal as what would serve rather to discover him all at once than to conceal him. The Prince then pulling off the periwig and putting it into his pocket, took out a dirty white napkin and desired the Captain to tye that about his head, and to bring it down upon his eyes and nose. He put the bonnet on above the napkin....MacLeod told him—this would not do yet, for that those who had ever seen him before would still discover his face for all the disguise he was in. The Prince said, 'This is an odd remarkable face I have got that nothing can disguise it.'

When [July 4] they were near the place the Captain designed to set up at, he told the Prince that he had a sister that dwelt there, who was married to John MacKinnon, a captain, lately under the Laird of MacKinnon, and that he judged it advisable to go to his sister's house, advising the Prince in the meantime to sit at a little distance from the house....Mr MacLeod accordingly went to the house, where he found his sister, but her husband was not at home. After the usual compliments he told his sister that he had come there perhaps to pass some little time there, provided that no party was near them....He told her that he had no body along with him but one Lewie Caw (son of Mr Caw, surgeon in Crief) who had been out in the late affair, and consequently in the same condemnation with himself; and that he was with him as his servant. Upon this Lewie Caw was called upon to come into the house, the place being called Ellagol, or Ellighuil, near Kilvory or Kilmaree...in Strath. When Lewie entered the house with the baggage on his back and the napkin about his head, he took off his bonnet, made a low bow, and sat at a distance from his master. The Captain's sister said there was something about that lad that she liked unco well, and she could not help admiring his looks. When meat and drink, viz. bread and cheese, milk, &c., were set down before the master... sick Lewie made it shy, and refused to eat with his master, and alledged he knew better manners. But the master ordering him to come and take a share, he obeyed, still keeping off the bonnet....

Malcolm importuned the Prince to go to bed and take some rest. The Prince then asked who would keep guard for fear of an alarm? Malcolm said he would do it himself. The Prince at last was prevailed upon to throw himself upon a bed, but would not strip. Malcolm desired his sister to go out, and sit upon the top of a knowe near the house and keep watch while he and his servant Lewie should take some sleep, which she accordingly did.

The Captain hearing that the landlord was coming towards home went out to meet him. After saluting him he asked if he saw these ships of war (pointing to them) that were hovering about upon the coast. Mr MacKinnon said he saw them very well. 'What,' said MacLeod, 'if our Prince be on board one of them?' 'God forbid,' replied MacKinnon....'I wish with all my heart we had him here, for he would be safe enough.' 'Well, then,' said MacLeod, 'he is here already. He is just now in your house. But when you go in you must be careful to take no notice of him at all. He passes for one Lewie Caw, my servant.' John faithfully promised to observe the direction, and thought he could perform it well enough. But he was no sooner entred the house than he could not hold his eyes from staring upon Lewie, and very soon he was forced to turn his face away from the Prince and to weep. In this house the Prince diverted himself with a young child, Neil MacKinnon, carrying him in his arms and singing to him, and said, 'I hope this child may be a captain in my service yet.'

The Prince and Malcolm...judged it advisable to desire John MacKinnon to hire a boat under a pretence of Malcolm MacLeod's only sailing to the continent, taking his promise in the meantime that he should not communicate anything of the matter at all to the old Laird [of Mackinnon] if he should chance to see him. Accordingly John went to hire the boat, and meeting with the old chiftain, he could not keep the matter from him. The Laird told John that he should get a right boat and manage that matter well enough, and that he would instantly come to the place where the Prince was. John returned to the

Prince and told him what he had done, and that old MacKinnon was coming to wait upon him. Upon this Malcolm represented to the Prince that...he should leave the Prince altogether to the management of old MacKinnon, who he was persuaded would be very careful of him, and exceedingly true and firm to the trust....With much reluctancy the Prince at last agreed to the proposal, and upon old MacKinnon's coming to them they went directly to the boat, John MacKinnon going with them, who likewise accompanied the Prince and old MacKinnon to the continent [mainland][1].

The[2] Prince and his company arrived next morning [July 5] about 4 on the south side of Loch Nevis, near little Mallack [Mallaig], where they landed and lay three nights in the open air. The Laird [Mackinnon] and one of the men (John M'Guines) having gone the fourth day [July 8] to seek a cave to lie in, the Prince, with John MacKinnon and the other 3 rowers, took to the boat, and rowed up Loch Nevis along the coast. As they turned a point they spied a boat tied to the rock, and five men with red crosses over their bonnets standing on the shore[3]. These immediately called out, demanding whence they came. John MacKinnon's people answered, 'From Slate,' whereupon they were ordered ashore. But not complying with this summons, the five red crosses jumped into their boat, and set 4 oars agoing in pursuit of them....Upon this John [Mackinnon], taking an oar himself, plied it so manfully, and so animated his fellow-tuggers, that they out-rowed their blood-thirsty pursuers, turned quick round a point, and stood in towards the shore, which they had no sooner reached than the Prince sprung out of the boat, and attended by John and another, mounted nimbly to the top of the hill[4]....

On this eminence the Prince slept three hours, and then

1 Captain Malcolm Macleod left the Prince here and was made prisoner a few days later in Raasay. *L. M.* i, 143.

2 *L. M.* ii, 251. From materials collected by Mr John Walkinshaw of London, put together by Mr James Elphinstone of Edinburgh, and by him communicated to Bishop Forbes.

3 The militia were quartered at Earnsaig, on Loch Nevis. *B. I.* 55.

4 Traditionally Aonach. *Ibid.* 55.

returning down the hill, he re-imbarked and crossed the loch to a little island[1] about a mile from Scotus's [Donald Macdonald's] house, where Clanranald, to whom he sent a message by John MacKinnon, then was. Upon John's return they repassed the loch and landed at Mallack, where having refreshed themselves, and met with Old M'Kinnon and servant, they set out for [Allan] M'Donald of Moran's [Morar's] seat, which was about 7 or 8 miles distant....A little before day [July 9] they arrived at Moran's borthe or hut, his house having been burned by Captain Fergusson. M'Kinnon went in alone, and Moran immediately getting out of bed, they both hasted to the door to introduce the strangers. This done, Moran's first care was to dismiss all the children and servants, keeping only his lady, who is Lochiel's daughter. She knowing the Prince at first sight, he saluted her, and the meeting was extremely tender, the lady bursting into a flood of tears. After having some refreshment of cold salmon warmed again, but no bread, the travellers left the borthe, and were conducted by Moran to a cave, where they slept ten hours, Moran being in the meantime dispatched in quest of young Clanranald. About noon Moran returned with accounts that Clanranald was not to be found[2]. So it was resolved to part with old M'Kinnon and Moran, and in the evening to set out with a boy for the house of Aneas or Angus M'Donald of Burghdale [Borradale], in Arisaig, which was the first house the Prince was in when he came to the continent. Here they arrived before day [July 10], found the house burned by Captain Fergusson, and Mr M'Donald himself with two men at a borthe hard by. John M'Kinnon went in abruptly, desiring that unfortunate gentleman to rise....Then John asked him if he had heard anything of the Prince. Aneas answered, 'No....Time was that I would have given a hearty bottle to see him safe, but since I see you I expect to hear some news of him.' 'Well, then,' replies John, 'I have brought him here and will commit him to your

[1] Eilean na Glaschoille, or Prince's Isle. *B. I.* 56. Besides Campbell's militia and Loudoun's irregulars a chain of sentries had been placed between Inverness and Inveraray at the important passes, so that the Prince's escape was believed to be impossible. Cf. *A. P.* i, 11.

[2] Cf. *L. M.* iii, 184.

charge.'...'I am glad of it,' said Angus, 'and shall not fail to take care of him[1].'

Angus[2] MacDonald, having his houses burnt and effects destroyed by the troops under General Campbell's command, was obliged to remove with his royal highness to a hut in a neighbouring wood, where he refreshed him the best way he could for three days [July 11–13].

Upon the [13th] of July his royal highness wrote a private letter...to Alexander MacDonald of Glenaladale, major to Clanranald in his royal highness's service, and who was well known to his royal highness before, commanding his attendance at the foresaid place to concert measures for his royal highness's safety....

Immediately after sending off the above-mentioned express, his royal highness got an account of MacKinnon's being taken, which made it, he judged, proper for his royal highness to remove, upon the [13th], four miles to the eastward, to an inaccessible cave (known to very few of the country people) accompanied by the said Angus MacDonald of Boradale and his son (Ranald, formerly lieutenant to Clanranald's own company), where he was to stay till Glenaladale should join him.

On the [15th] of July at night, Glenaladale met with the foresaid Angus MacDonald at the place they had formerly agreed upon, from whence he was conducted to his royal highness. On the [16th] Angus MacDonald got a letter from a son-in-law...representing how dangerous it was for them to stay any longer there, and making an offer of a place he had prepared. Accordingly Ranald MacDonald was sent to reconnoitre the place.

Upon the [17th] of July...his royal highness judged it proper[3] to remove...to the place prepared for him in the Glen of Moror ...and sent Angus MacDonald to provide some necessaries. Upon his royal highness's arrival at his quarters, an information was

[1] Old Mackinnon and John Mackinnon were shortly after made prisoners. L. M. ii, 253.

[2] L. M. i, 333. From Captain Alexander Macdonald of Glenaladale's Journal, in young Clanranald's handwriting. I have emended his dates. Cf. B. I. 56.

[3] Cf. L. M. iii, 377.

brought that General Campbell, with six men-of-war, well furnished with troops, had anchored at Loch Naives [Nevis]... whereupon two men were sent off by Loch Moror to Loch Naives to observe General Campbell's motions. But before they had time to return, Angus MacDonald came back upon the [18th] early...and brought intelligence that Captain [Carolina] Scott[1] had come to the lower part of Arisaig from Glengary's Moror.

His royal highness, and the small company that was with him, finding upon this information that Clanranald's country was surrounded[2],...sets out [July 18] accompanied only by Major MacDonald of Glenaladale and his brother (Lieutenant John MacDonald), and the other Lieutenant John MacDonald, junior, Boradale's son, being obliged to part with Angus Mac-Donald[3] of Boradale, and his son-in-law (Angus MacEachine) ...and by twelve o'clock they came to the top of a hill in the outmost bounds of Arisaig called Scoorvuy [Sgur Mhuide], where having taken some refreshment it was thought proper to send Lieutenant John MacDonald (Glenaladale's brother) to Glenfinnin [Glenfinnan]...as well for intelligence as to bring two men Glenaladale kept still on guard there, and appointed them to meet him about ten o'clock at night on the top of a hill above Locharkaig in Lochiel's country, called Scoorwick Corrichan [Sgor nan Coireachan].

Lieutenant MacDonald being sent off, his royal highness set out, and by two o'clock came to the top of a neighbouring hill called Fruighvein [Fraochbheinn], where, observing some cattle in motion...Major MacDonald of Glenaladale went to examine what that might mean; who upon examination found this to be some of his own tenants removing with their cattle from the troops, who by this time, to the number of five or seven hundred, had come to the head of Locharkaig, in order to inclose his royal highness in Clanranald's country....This being the route they were resolved to hold, pretty much disconcerted their measures. Major

[1] See *A. P.* i, 11.
[2] The troops were placed in twenty-seven camps, from the head of Loch Eil to the head of Loch Hourn. *L. M.* ii, 364.
[3] He had served as a surgeon in the Glengarry regiment. *B. O.* 229.

MacDonald of Glenaladale bringing back word to his royal highness of what he had heard, they resolved to alter their course, and accordingly the Major sent...to call back Lieutenant MacDonald...and sent...for one Donald Cameron of Glenpean...in order to learn...if he would undertake to guide his royal highness by their guards if possible....

Soon after, the express sent to Glenfinnan...brought word that a hundred of the Argyle-shire militia had come to the very foot of the hill where his royal highness stayed; whereupon...as there was no time to wait for Donald Cameron...his royal highness...set out about sun-setting with his small retinue, and travelled pretty hard till about eleven o'clock at night, when, passing thro' a hollow between two hills, they observed a man coming down one of the hills...and as Providence would have it, found him to be their intended guide, Donald Cameron....Upon this they pursued their way through roads almost impassable even in day light, and travelling all night they came at four o'clock in the morning upon the [19th] of July to the top of a hill in the Brae of Locharkaig, called Mamnynleallum (Mamnyn Callum], from whence they could (without the help of a prospective glass) discern their enemy's camp, being not above a mile distant. But being informed by the guide that that hill was searched the day before by the troops, they supposed there would not be a second search that day, and therefore they resolved to pass the day there[1]....

His royal highness continued in the top of the said hill all that day, and about nine o'clock at night set out with his retinue to the northward, and by one o'clock in the morning of July [20th] came to a place called Corrinangaull [Coire-nan-gall] in the confines betwixt that part of Glengary's country called Knoydart, and that part of Lochiel's country called Locharkaig....

Being pinched in provisions...they chused a fast place in the face of a hill at the head of Lochqhuaigh [Loch Quoich], to which fastness they came about two o'clock in the morning, having only about a mile in walking to it. After taking an hour's rest there, the guide and Lieutenant MacDonald (Glenaladale's

[1] John Macdonald, Glenaladale's brother, rejoined the party here.

brother) were sent off to the hill above them to furnish some provisions...who came back to them about 3 o'clock, having got only two small cheeses, that would not be a morsel to the piece of them; and brought intelligence that about one hundred of the red-coats were marching up the other side of the hill his royal highness lodged in....Notwithstanding this alarm (the search for his royal highness being general and very narrow all round) they stayed in the same place till about eight o'clock at night, when ...climbing a steep hill called Drimachosi [Druim Cosaidh] to the top, they observed the fires of a camp directly in their front, which they could scarcely shun, at Glenqhosy [Glen Cosaidh]. However, being resolved to pass at any rate, they came so near without being observed as to hear them talk distinctly; and ascending the next hill...spied the fires of another camp at the very foot where they were to descend. But turning a little westward, they passed between two of their guards betwixt one and two o'clock in the morning of July [21st]. After travelling two miles, as they judged, beyond them, they came, betwixt two and three o'clock in the morning, to a place on the Glenealg side of the head of [Loch Hourn] called Corriscorridill [Coire-Sgoir-adail], where, having chosen a fast place[1], they took such refreshment as the exigency of the time afforded them, his royal highness covering a slice of cheese with oatmeal...and drank of the cold stream along with it.

His royal highness passed the whole day in the above place till about eight o'clock at night...and by three o'clock in the morning of July [22nd] they came to Glenshiel in Seaforth's country. As they had run out entirely of their last supply of provisions, the Major and Lieutenant John MacDonald (Boradale's son) were sent off as well to furnish some as to provide a guide to conduct them to Pollieu [Poolewe] in Seaforth's country, where his royal highness had heard some French vessels to have been; and coming to the place where the inhabitants were, the Major bought some provisions, and made application to one of the inhabitants for a guide, which he undertook to provide. In the meantime that the Major was taking about the guide, a Glengary

---

[1] Cf. *L. M.* iii, 378.

man [Donald Macdonell][1] appears coming towards them, who that morning had been chased by the troops...from Glengary to Glensheil. Upon seeing this man the Major knew him...and conceiving him to be a trusty fellow, resolved to make use of him....

About seven o'clock at night, the man who undertook to furnish the guide was seen coming to...the Major, who...after some conversation found that the only French ship that had been [at Poolewe] was gone off, and that no guide could be procured....

Immediately Glenaladale returned to the Prince and told him what had passed; whereupon it was resolved to change their course, and accordingly the Glengary man was introduced to his royal highness, and most chearfully undertook to guide him And, preparing to pursue their journey, they set out late at night, and going on about a quarter of a mile, they stopt a little, which was occasioned by the Major's clapping his hand to his side and missing his purse, wherein he had another purse of gold he had got the charge of from his royal highness in order to defray his charges, and which he had forgot when they had been preparing for their journey....In the midst of his surprize, he reflected it might have been taken away by a little boy sent by their landlord [at Glenshiel], Gilchrist MacCrath, with a compliment of milk....Accordingly the Major and Lieutenant Mac-Donald went all the way to MacCrath's house, which was more than a mile off...to oblige the boy to restore the purse, which he did to a trifle. They returned by a different road from what they had gone before, and came to the Prince, who was in great pain for them, fearing they might have been intercepted by an officer and two private men that pass'd under arms by the place where his royal highness was in their absence....

Having once more got together, his royal highness and his small retinue set out, and travelling all the remainder of the night, came early in the morning of July [23rd] to a hill-side above Strathcluaine [Strathclunie], and chusing a fast place, took some rest till towards three o'clock afternoon, when they set out, and travelling by a hill-side about a mile from the place they

[1] *L. M.* iii, 378.

rested in, they heard the firing of small arms in the hill above them, which they judged to be some of the troops chasing people that had fled with their effects. They steered their course northward, and mounting up a high hill betwixt the Braes of Glenmoriston and Strathglass, came late at night to the very top of it...the only shelter his royal highness could have being an open cave, where he could neither lean nor sleep, being wet to the skin with the heavy rain that had fallen the day before, and having no fuel to make a fire, the only method he had of warming himself was smoking a pipe.

About three o'clock in the morning of July [24th] the Lieutenant (Glenaladale's brother) and the guide (the providential Glengary man) were sent in quest of some trusty people they intended to find out in order to conduct his royal highness to Pollieu, and were appointed to return to the top of a neighbouring hill, where his royal highness and the remainder of his retinue were to meet them. Accordingly, about five o'clock in the morning his royal highness set out, and by seven came to the top of that hill, where meeting with the guide on his return, he told he had found out his intended trustees, who had given him directions...to repair into a cave in the Brae of Glenmoriston called Coiraghoth [Coiredhogha], where they promised to come at an appointed hour with a refreshment. Accordingly his royal highness set out, and by the time appointed came to the place, and meeting with these few friends (who upon sight knew his royal highness, having formerly served in his army), they conducted him to the grotto, where he was refreshed with such chear as the exigency of the time afforded; and making a bed for him, his royal highness was lulled asleep with the sweet murmurs of the finest purling stream that could be, running by his bedside, within the grotto, in which romantic habitation[1] his royal highness pass'd three days, at the end of which he was so well refreshed that he thought himself able to encounter any hardships.

Having time in that space to provide some necessaries and to gather intelligence about the enemy's motions, they removed, on the [28th] of [July], into a place within two miles of them,

---

[1] A picture and ground-plan of the cave are in *B. I.* 60, 61.

called Coirmheadhain [Coire Mheadhoin], where they took up their habitation in a grotto no less romantic than the former.... In this place he resided four days; but, being informed that one Campbell (factor to Seaforth in Kintale, and captain at that time of a company of militia) had...pitched his camp within four miles of them, it was then resolved his royal highness should remove his quarters. Accordingly, upon the [1st] of August, he set out to the northward, and by break of day upon the [2nd], came in upon the Brae of the Chisholm's country, called Strathglass, having left one of their party behind in the Brae of Glenmoriston to wait Campbell's motions. That friend...brought word that they needed not be afraid for that night. Upon this his royal highness repaired to a neighbouring sheally hut....They remained in this place two days, and in that time the prince sent off an express to Pollieu to know the certainty about some French vessels being there.

Early in the morning of August [4th], his royal highness set out to the northward so far on his way to Pollieu in case of any encouragement from that quarter, and travelling a muir road unfrequented, came that night into another sheally hut, about the distance of five or six miles from where they had set out. There they remained all night, and set out about two o'clock in the morning of August [5th], and came about twelve o'clock into a place called Glencanna [Glencannich], where, passing the remainder of the day in a wood, they repaired late at night to a neighbouring village, where they stayed only the dead of night.

About two o'clock in the morning of August [6th] they set out and climbed a hill [Beinn Acharain] on the northmost side of Glencanna, where they pass'd the day and sent off two of their party to furnish a fresh supply of provisions. At night they repaired into a neighbouring sheally hut, where they remained two days, expecting the return of the express sent off to Pollieu [on August 4th], who...brought back word that the only French ship that had come there had sailed off again, and that a couple of gentlemen[1] who had come on board of her had actually landed, and were making...for Lochiel's country in search of the Prince.

[1] French officers.

12—2

He, becoming anxious to know if they had dispatches for him, resolved to return towards the place from whence he had come, in order to meet with them.

August [8th], at night, they set out cross the water of Canna [Cannich] back again, and boldly by young Chisholm's house, came by two o'clock in the morning [August 9th] to a place called Fassanacoill [Fasnakyle] in Strathglass; and, consulting what was best and fittest to be done, it was resolved (before his royal highness should venture any further) to send some spies to the Braes of Glengary and Lochiel's country, in order to get sure information whether or not the search for him in those bounds was over....

They waited the return of the spies, who brought notice that the forces had returned to their camp[1]. Whereupon his royal highness set out by six o'clock in the morning of August [12th] ...and came by ten o'clock to the Braes of Glenmoriston, and, passing the day on the top of a hill, they set out at night, and had not travelled above a mile when they learned that a strong party had been detached to the Braes of Glengary in quest of the Prince. Upon this it was resolved to proceed no further untill the motion of the enemy should be farther known; and then they repaired into a neighbouring shealy hut, where they passed the remainder of the night.

Upon August [13th], in the morning, three expresses were sent off—two to Lochiel's country, Locharkaig, who were to seek out Cluns Cameron, and to tell him from Major Mac-Donald of Glenaladale that he wanted to meet with him in a convenient place; and the third express was to return at the Brae of Glengary, and to bring back word if the party they were informed of the night before had returned to their camp or not....

Accordingly the expresses were sent off, and, upon the [14th], the one that was to return brought word that the road was clear. Whereupon the Prince and his small party, being then ten in number, set out under the advantage of a foggy afternoon, and, passing through Glenmoriston and Glenl[o]yne, came late at

---

[1] The camp at Fort Augustus was broken up on August 13, and the Argyleshire militia were disbanded at Inveraray about August 17. *S. M.* 1746, p. 393.

night to the Brae of Glengary...[and] the night being very dark, they were obliged to pass it on the side of a hill, without any cover, though it rained excessively.

In the morning of August [15th] the Prince set out, the rain still continuing very heavy, and, travelling six miles cross hills and muirs, came about ten o'clock to the Brae of a place called Achnas[ua]l....There they pass'd the day in a most inconvenient habitation, it raining as heavy within as without it. Towards the afternoon...the expresses came to them, and brought word to the Major that Cameron of Cluns...would come to them next morning....Lochgary joined them that night, after which they took their rest.

About ten o'clock in the morning of August [16th], Cluns Cameron joined them, and, remaining there till towards the afternoon, conducted them into a wood at the foot of Locharkaig, where they lodged all night.

Timeous in the morning of August [17th], an express was sent off to Lochiel to command his attendance...who brought word that Lochiel, not being recovered of his wounds, and being at too great a distance, could not come, but he sent his brother, Dr Cameron, to make his apology, who came to his royal highness upon August [20th].

August [21st]. The Prince set out with his attendants, and travelling about a mile, came to a wood opposite to Achnacary called Torramhuilt or Torvauilt; Dr Cameron and Lochgary having parted with his royal highness about three or four o'clock in the afternoon to avoid suspicion, as did also Cluns Cameron, how soon he had conducted his royal highness into this last habitation[1].

We[2] continued in this wood and that over against Achnacarie (having three hutts in different places to which we removed by turns)....Clun's son and I went to the Strath of Cluns for intelligence. We were [August 23?] not half an hour in the hut, which Cluns had built for his family (after his house was burnt),

[1] While at Torvault, the Prince received the two French officers who had landed at Poolewe. Cf. L. M. i, 98, 349; iii, 102.

[2] L. M. i, 99. From the Rev. John Cameron's Journal. He had joined the Prince with Dr Cameron on August 20 at Loch Arkaig.

when a child of six years old went out and returned in haste to tell that she saw a great body of soldiers....We left the hut and marched to a small hill above the wood, from whence we could see a great way up Glenkingie and not be discovered. We got there unobserved, which was owing to the cover of the wood. The Prince examined all our guns, which were in pretty good order, and...sent Cluns and me to take a narrow view of the party, and resolved that night to goe to the top of Mullantagart [Meall-an-Tagraidh], a very high mountain in the Braes of Glenkengie, and to send one to us to know what we discover'd or were informed of. When we came to the Strath of Cluns, the women told us that the party was of Lord Loudon's regiment, consisting of about 200 men, commanded by one Captain Grant, son to Grant of Knockando in Strathspey[1]....In the evening Cluns's son came to us from the Prince, with whom we returned, told him as we were informed, and brought some whiskie, bread, and cheese. This was about 12 at night. He was on the side of the mountain, without fire or any covering. We persuaded him to take a hearty dram and made a fire, which we durst not keep above half an hour lest it should be seen by the people in the neighbourhood. By daylight [August 24?] we went to the top of the mountain, where we continued till eight in the evening without the least cover, and durst not rise out of our seats. The Prince slept all the forenoon in his plaid and wet hose, altho' it was an excessive cold day, made more so by several showers of hail. From thence we went that night to the Strath of Glen-kengie, killed a cow, and lived merrily for some days. From that we went [August 26?] to the Braes of Achnacarie. The Water of Arkeg in crossing came up to our haunches. The Prince in that condition lay that night and next day in open air, and though his cloaths were wet, he did not suffer the least in his health.

In a day or two after, Lochgary and Dr Cameron return'd [August 27] from Lochiel (to whom they had been sent) and told it was Lochiel's opinion and theirs, that the Prince would be safe where he (Lochiel) was skulking. This pleased him much,

[1] After the camp at Fort Augustus was broken up, Lord Loudon was left there with his regiment and some Independent Companies. *S. M.* 1746, p. 394.

and the next night [August 28] he set out with Lochgary, the Doctor and Sandy (Cluns's son), myself and three servants[1]. We travell'd in the night and slept all day, till we came to Lochiel, who was then in the hills betwixt the Braes of Badenoch and Athol.

The[2] Prince lay the first night [August 29] at Corineuir [Coire an Iubhair Mór] at the foot of Benalder after his coming to Badenoch, from which he was conducted next day [August 30] to Mellanmuir [Meal an Odhar?] in Benalder, a sheiling of a very narrow compass where Locheil with M'Pherson of Breakachie, Allan Cameron, his (*i.e.* Lochiel's) principal servant, and two servants of Cluny were at the time....Locheil, tho' lame, made the best of his way to meet his Royal Highness without, who, it may be believed, received him very graciously. The joy at this meeting was certainly very great and much easier to be conceived than express'd. However, such was his Royal Highness circumspection that when the other would have kneeld at his coming up to him, he sad, 'Oh! no, my dear Locheil,' claping him on the shoulder, 'you don't know who may be looking from the tops of yonder hills....' Locheil then ushered him into his habitation, which was indeed but a very poor one as to the accomodation and make....

There was plenty of mutton newly killed, and an anker of whiskie of twenty Scotch pints, with some good beef sassers made the year before, and plenty of butter and cheese, and besides, a large well cured bacon ham....Upon his entry he took a hearty dram, which he pretty often called for thereafter to drink his friends healths; and when there were some minch'd collops dress'd with butter for him in a large sawce pan that Locheil and Cluny carried always about with 'em, which was all the fire vessels they had; he eat heartily, and said with a very chearful and lively countenance, 'Now, gentlemen, I leive like a Prince.'...Two days after...Cluny came [September 1] to 'em there from Achnicarry, and upon his coming into the hut, when he wou'd have kneeled, his Royal Highness took and prevented him, and kissed him, as if he had been an equal, and soon after

[1] Cf. *L. M.* iii, 101.

[2] *L. M.* iii, 39. From information given by Donald Macpherson, Cluny's brother.

said, 'I'm sorry, Cluny, you and your regiment were not at Culloden. I did not hear till of very late that you was so near to have come up with us that day.'

Upon the next day [September 2] after Cluny's coming, he thought it was time to move the quarters, and brought the Prince about two miles further into Benalder, to a little sheill called Uiskchilra [Allt a Chaoil Reidhe], where the hut or bothie was superlatively bad and smockie. Yet his Royal Highness took with everything. Here he remained for two or three nights, and then from thence removed [September 5] to a very romantic comical habitation made out for him by Cluny, at two miles farther distance into Benalder, called the Cage. It was really a curiosity, and can scarcely be described to perfection. 'Twas situate in the face of a very rough, high, rockie mountain called Letternilichk [Litir-na-lic], which is still a part of Benalder, full of great stones and crevices and some scattered wood interspersed. The habitation called the *Cage*, in the face of that mountain, was within a small thick bush of wood. There were first some rows of trees laid down in order to level a floor for the habitation; and as the place was steep, this rais'd the lower side to equall height with the other; and these trees, in the way of jests or planks, were entirely well levelled with earth and gravel. There were betwixt the trees, growing naturally on their own roots, some stakes fixed in the earth, which with the trees were interwoven with ropes made of heath and birch twigs all to the top of the Cage, it being of a round or rather oval shape, and the whole thatched and covered over with foge. This whole fabrick hung as it were by a large tree, which reclined from the one end all along the roof to the other, and which gave it the name of the Cage; and by chance there happen'd to be two stones at a small distance from other in the side next the precipice, resembling the pillars of a bosom chimney, and here was the fire placed. The smock had its vent out there, all along a very stonny plat of the rock, which and the smock were all together so much of a colour that any one coud make no difference in the clearest day, the smock and stones by and through which it pass'd being of such true and real resemblance. The Cage was no larger than to contain six or seven persons, four of which number were frequently employed in playing at cards, one idle looking on, one becking, and another firing bread and cooking[1].

Here his Royal Highness remained till he was acquainted that the shiping for receiving and transporting him to France was arrived[2]....Alexander M'Pherson...brought the express directly to the Cage...about one in the morning the thirteenth of September, on which minute his Royal Highness began his journey for the shipping, and against daylight arrived at his old quarters in Uiskchilra[3]...where he remain'd till near night, and then set off, and was by daylight the 14th at Corvoy [Coir-a-Mhaighe], where he sleep'd some time. Upon his being refresh'd with sleep, he being at a sufficient distance from any country, did spend the day by diverting himself and his company with throwing up of bonnets in the air, and shuting at 'em...in which diversion his Royal Highness by far exceeded; and in the evening of the fourteenth he set forward and went on as far as Uiskni-fichit [Uisge-nam-Fichead], on the confines of Glenroy, which marches with a part of the Braes of Badenoch, in which last place he refresh'd himself some hours with sleep; and before it was daylight got over Glenroy the fifteenth, and kept themselves private all day....

After the morning of the 16th, the Prince arrived in Achni-carry, Locheil's seat, where he was as ill off as anywhere else for accommodation, as the enemy had brunt and demolished all there. All the sixteenth he stayed there, and set out at night and arrived the seventeenth at a place called Glencamger [Cam-gharaidh], in the head of Locharkaig, where he found Cluny and Doctor Cameron, who had prepared for him, expecting him....When he and his company arrived, there was a cow kill'd, on which bannock and beef his royal highnes with his whole retinue were regalled and feasted plentifully that night. On the eighteenth he set out from Glencamger with daylight, and upon the nineteenth arrived at the shipping, what was extant of the Glencamger bonnacks and beef having been all the provisions till then.

[1] Cf. a description of the Cage, quoted in *B. I.* 69.
[2] Two French ships arrived at Loch-na-nuagh on September 6. *A. P.* ii, p. liv. [3] Breakachie here brought John Roy Stewart to the Prince.

The[1] P[rince] being now informed that the French ships were in Lochnanuagh waiting for him, set out immediatly, accompanied by Lochiel, Lochgarie, John Roy Stewart, &c., and going on board the *Happy* [*Heureux*][2], privateer of St Maloes, she immediately set sail the twentieth of September, and escaping all the Government's warships, and being in her way happily favoured by a fog, he arrived safely in France; an unparalell'd instance, upon a review of all the circumstances of this escape, of a very particular Providence interesting itself in his behalf. For what wise end Heaven has thus dissapointed and yet preserved this noble prince, and what future scenes the history of his life may display, time only can tell; yet something very remarkable still seems waiting him and this poor country also. May God grant a happy issue.

Intelligence[3] was no sooner brought to Versailles that the young Chevalier de St George was landed at Roscott near Morlaix in Brittany on the twenty ninth of September [Oct. 10 N.S.] 1746, than the Castle of St Antoine was ordered to be prepared for his reception, and his brother[4], accompanied by several young noblemen, went to meet him, and conducted him directly [October 12] to Versailles, he not chusing to stop at Paris for any refreshment[5]. The King of France, Louis the fifteenth, immediately quitting the Council, which was sitting on affairs of moment, went to receive him, and as he advanced, took him in his arms with every mark of tender affection, and said, '*Mon très cher Prince, je rends grace au Ciel qui me donne le plaisir extrême de vous voir arrivé en bonne santé après tant de fatigues et de dangers. Vous avez fait voir que toutes les grandes qualités des Héros et des Philosophes se trouvent unies en vous; et*

[1] *L. P.* ii, 562. From an account of the Prince's escape by a Highland officer.

[2] Cf. *A. P.* i, 280.

[3] *L. P.* ii, 565. From a letter published in 1749.

[4] A letter from Charles to his brother, announcing his arrival, is in Mahon, *The Forty-Five*, 156.

[5] A week intervened between Charles's arrival at Paris on October 12 (N.S.) and his public reception by Louis XV at Versailles on October 19. Cf. *E. J.* 444.

j'espere qu'un de ces jours vous recevrez la recompense d'un merite si extraordinaire.'

After a quarter of an hour's conversation with the King, the young Chevalier passed to the apartments of the Queen, who welcomed him with every demonstration of good will and satisfaction; and as he quitted the palace, the whole Court crowded about him to pay their compliments, and testified as much joy as if the Dauphin himself had been engaged in the same dangerous expedition and returned in safety....

The little visit he had made at Versailles being as it were *incog.*, it was necessary he should pay his compliments in form and in the character his father had conferred upon him, which was that of Prince-Regent of England, Scotland, and Ireland; accordingly about ten days after [October 19], he set out from the Castle of St Antoine in the following manner. In the first coach were the Lords Ogilvy and Elcho[1], the venerable Glenbucket, and Mr Kelly, the young Chevalier's secretary. In the second were the young Chevalier himself, Lord Lewis Gordon, and the eldest Locheil [John Cameron] as master of the horse; two pages richly dressed lolled on the boot, and ten footmen, in the livery of the character assumed by the young Chevalier, walked on each side. In the third coach were four gentlemen of his bed chamber, one of whom, called Captain Stafford, had some time since been a prisoner in Newgate. The young Locheil with several gentlemen followed on horseback, making a grand appearance altogether, but the young Chevalier himself took off my attention from every thing besides. I shall say nothing of his person, and only tell you that he did not entirely trust to the graces it received from nature for attracting admiration, for his dress had in it, I thought, somewhat of uncommon elegance. His coat was rose-coloured velvet embroidered with silver and lined with silver tissue; his waistcoat was a rich gold brocade, with a spangled fringe set on in scollops. The cockade in his hat, and the buckles of his shoes were diamonds; the George which he wore at his bosom, and the order of St Andrew which he wore also, tied by a piece of green ribbon to one of the buttons of his waistcoat, were prodigiously illustrated with large brilliants;

---

[1] Elcho was not present. Cf. *E. J.* 110.

in short, he glittered all over like the star which they tell you appeared at his nativity. He supped with the King, Queen, and Royal family; and all who attended him were magnificently entertained at the several tables appointed for them, according to the rank they held under him.

But[1] the Prince's reception at Court and at Paris are no part of the expedition I undertook to relate, and have now finished. I only mentioned them as a contrast to the situation he was so long and so lately in. The narrow bounds I prescribed to myself in this work made me omit several little escapes he had during the last two or three months, and likewise abundance of names of the common people that some way or other contributed to his safety. But I must do justice to the several clans, by letting the world know that each of them had some share of the merit. The Prince was at different times in the hands of McDonalds, Camerons, McKenzies, Chisholms, Grants, Frazers, Macphersons, Stuarts, MacLeods, and even Campbells, tho' that clan was in arms against him; nor were those that had him in their power always chosen or recommended to him as honest, discreet men, whom he might trust. Necessity frequently drove him to employ people he knew nothing about, but all gave him convincing proofs of the most zealous attachment and the most inviolable fidelity; while thirty thousand pounds (an immense sum to a poor Highlander) was offered as a reward to any body that delivered him up, and utter destruction was denounced against all those that harboured, or in any shape assisted him. I leave the reader to judge if I [have] reason to say, that whatever may hereafter be the fate of this Prince, he has been early trained up in the school of adversity, and knows, by his own experience, the greatest vicissitudes of fortune.

FINIS

☞ The[2] Reader is desir'd to excuse any Errors that have escaped the Corrector, or Press; the Author's principal Aim throughout the Whole being to set forth Matters of Fact, tho' not flourish'd with that Illustration and Embellishment of Stile, as might be expected from a more abler Pen.

[1] *M. K.* 190. [2] *R.* 440.

TABLE OF PERSONS

An asterisk denotes an article in the *Dictionary of National Biography*

*AGNEW, Sir ANDREW (1687–1771), fought under Marlborough and at Dettingen; held Blair Castle against Lord George Murray in 1746.

*ALBEMARLE, WILLIAM ANNE KEPPEL, 2nd Earl of (1702–54), served at Dettingen and Fontenoy, present at Culloden and succeeded Cumberland as commander-in-chief.

*ATHOLL, WILLIAM MURRAY, Marquess of Tullibardine, titular Duke of (d. 1746), took part in the Risings of 1715 and 1719, one of the 'Seven Men of Moidart,' surrendered after Culloden, and died in the Tower.

BAGOT, Colonel JOHN, an Irishman in French service, commanded troop of Hussars raised by Murray of Broughton.

*BALMERINO, ARTHUR ELPHINSTONE, sixth Baron (1688–1746), fought at Sheriffmuir, colonel of Charles' second troop of Life Guards in 1745–6, surrendered after Culloden, executed in 1746.

BANNERMAN, Sir ALEXANDER, 3rd Baronet, of Elsick, raised a regiment and commanded it at Culloden, escaped to France, died at Paris 1747.

*BELFORD, Colonel WILLIAM (1709–80), entered Royal Artillery on its formation 1726, served in Flanders 1742–5, commanded artillery at Culloden, general 1777.

*BLAKENEY, WILLIAM, Baron (1672–1761), served under Marlborough, lieutenant-governor of Stirling Castle 1744, defended it against Prince Charles 1746, surrendered Minorca after gallant defence 1756.

*BLAND, General HUMPHREY (1686?–1763), served under Marlborough, major-general in Culloden campaign, commander-in-chief in Scotland 1753.

BROWN, Colonel, of Lally's regiment, aide-de-camp to Prince Charles, escaped from Carlisle after surrender 1745, carried news of Falkirk to France 1746.

BURKE, EDWARD, a native of North Uist and a chairman in Edinburgh, presumably joined Prince Charles there, guided him to Borradale after his defeat at Culloden, died at Edinburgh Nov. 13, 1751.

*Cameron, Archibald, brother of Donald C. of Lochiel, practised as a doctor in Lochaber, executed in connection with the Elibank plot 1753.

*Cameron, Donald, of Lochiel (1695–1748), son of John C. of Lochiel (attainted for share in the '15), succeeded to chiefship of his clan on his grandfather's, Sir Ewen C., death 1719, wounded at Falkirk and Culloden, escaped with Charles to France, received a regiment in French service, attainted.

Cameron, Duncan, native of Barra, servant to Old Lochiel at Boulogne, accompanied Charles to Scotland, wrote a journal of his embarkation and arrival, made prisoner while Charles was in England, released and escaped to Holland 1747.

Cameron, John, of Lochiel, chief of clan 1696, out in '15 and '19 and attainted, joined Prince Charles at Perth 1745, d. in France 1747.

Cameron, Ludovick, of Torcastle, brother of John C. of Lochiel, raised 300 of the clan, evaded capture after Culloden, agent for Cluny in distribution of the Loch Arkaig treasure.

Campbell, General John, of Mamore (1693?–1770), commander of troops and garrisons in west of Scotland 1745, 4th Duke of Argyll 1761.

*Charles Edward Stewart, Prince (1720–88), eldest son of titular James III and VIII, born and educated at Rome, served at Gaeta under Don Carlos 1734, escaped to France after the '45, expelled from France 1748, titular Charles III 1766, alienated Jacobites by his disreputable habits, died at Rome 1788.

*Cope, General Sir John, commander-in-chief in Scotland 1745, court-martialed and exonerated, stationed in Ireland 1751, died 1760.

*Crawford, John Lindsay, 20th Earl of (1702–49), accompanied Hessian troops to Scotland 1746.

*Cromarty, George Mackenzie, 3rd Earl of (1702?–66), taken prisoner at Dunrobin 1746, sentenced to death and pardoned 1749, died 1766.

*Cumberland, William Augustus, Duke of (1721–65), third son of George II, commander-in-chief in Netherlands 1744, received thanks of Parliament and £25,000 a year for services in Scotland 1746, resumed command in Netherlands 1747–57, buried in Westminster Abbey 1765.

*Drummond, Lord John, 4th Duke of Perth and brother to titular Duke of P. of the '45, raised Royal Scots regiment in France, at Falkirk and Culloden 1746, died 1747.

DRUMMOND, Lord LEWIS, son of second Earl of Melfort, lieutenant-colonel of the French Royal Scots, lost a leg at Culloden 1746, died at Paris 1792.

DURAND, Colonel, a Frenchman, court-martialled and acquitted (1746) for surrendering Carlisle 1745.

EGUILLES, ALEXANDRE DE BOYER, Marquis d', titular ambassador for Louis XV to Prince Charles, arrived at Holyrood October 14, 1745.

*ELCHO, DAVID WEMYSS, Lord. See *supra*, p. x.

FARQUHARSON, FRANCIS, of Monaltrie, the 'Baron Ban' of the '45, raised regiment and joined Charles at Edinburgh, made prisoner at Culloden, condemned to death and reprieved 1746, liberated 1766, died 1791.

FARQUHARSON, JAMES, of Balmoral, kinsman of Monaltrie, raised 200 of his name and joined Charles after his retreat from England, badly wounded at Falkirk 1746.

FERGUSSON, Captain JOHN, of H.M.S. *Furnace* (or *Furness*), was active in the search for Prince Charles and his partisans.

*FORBES, DUNCAN, of Culloden (1685–1747), President of Court of Session 1737, first to suggest formation of Highland regiments, the most efficient agent on the government side in Scotland during the Rising, but received no recognition.

FRASER, CHARLES, younger, of Inverallochy, lieutenant-colonel of the Fraser regiment, wounded at Culloden and shot, perhaps at Hawley's order, 1746.

*GARDINER, Colonel JAMES (1688–1745), fought at Preston 1715, colonel of 13th Hussars 1743–45, killed at Prestonpans.

GLASCOE, Major NICOLAS, a Frenchman and lieutenant in Dillon's regiment, raised the battery at Montrose and captured the *Hazard* sloop 1745, major and military instructor of Lord Ogilvie's regiment, made prisoner at Culloden, released as a rebel but detained as prisoner of war.

GLENCAIRN, WILLIAM CUNNINGHAM, Earl of, commanded Glasgow militia 1746, d. 1775.

GORDON, CHARLES, of Blelack, joined Lord Lewis G. and took part in Inverurie skirmish 1746.

GORDON, JOHN, of Avochy, nephew of Glenbucket, commanded regiment of Gordons under Lord Lewis G., took part in Inverurie skirmish 1746, joined Charles before Culloden.

GORDON, JOHN, of Glenbucket, factor or chamberlain to the Duke of Gordon, commanded regiment of Gordons in '15, visited Chevalier at Rome and received Major-General's commission 1738, member of Prince Charles' Council 1745.

*GORDON, Lord LEWIS, third son of 2nd Duke of Gordon, lieutenant R.N., joined Charles at Edinburgh, defeated Macleod at Inverurie 1745, attainted 1746, died at Montreuil 1754.

GORDON, MIRABEL DE, engineer, arrived with Lord John Drummond from France 1745, conducted unsuccessful sieges of Stirling Castle and Fort William 1746.

GRANT, Sir JAMES, of Grant, Whig M.P. for Elgin burghs in 1745, withdrew to London during Rising, leaving his eldest son Ludovick to pursue a passive policy; the clan came out in spite of his orders.

GRANT, JAMES ALEXANDER, member of staff of French Royal Observatory, accompanied d'Eguilles to Scotland, master of ordnance to Charles at sieges of Carlisle (1745), Stirling and Fort Augustus (1746), prepared an elaborate map of the campaign 1749[1].

GRANT, Captain, of Rothiemurchus, captain of an Independent Company of Grants, surrendered Inverness Castle to Charles 1746.

*GUEST, General JOSHUA (1660–1747), enlisted 1685, served in Ireland, Flanders, and Spain, lieutenant-general 1745, held Edinburgh Castle 1745–6.

HAMILTON, JOHN, factor to Duke of Gordon, surrendered Carlisle to the Duke of Cumberland 1745, executed 1746.

HANDASYDE, General ROGER, commander-in-chief in Scotland Nov. 14–Dec. 5, 1745.

*HAWLEY, General HENRY (1679?–1759), served under Argyll in the '15, at Dettingen (1743) and Fontenoy (1745), defeated at Falkirk 1746, commanded cavalry at Culloden 1746.

HAY, JOHN, of Restalrig, during Broughton's illness acted as Charles' Secretary, escaped to France after Culloden, knighted at Rome by the Chevalier de St George, served Charles till dismissed 1767.

*HENRY BENEDICT STEWART, Cardinal York (1725–1807), younger brother of Prince Charles, followed him to France, on return to Italy created Cardinal 1747, assumed title Henry IX 1788, residence at Frascati sacked by French 1799, relieved by George III, died 1807.

HEPBURN, JAMES, of Keith, 'out' in '15, one of the members of the Buck Club who promised to join Charles in any event, escorted him to his apartments in Holyrood on his entry into Edinburgh 1745.

[1] See *supra* between pp. 20–21.

*Home, William, 8th Earl, served under Cope and commanded Glasgow volunteers 1745, died 1761.

*James Francis Edward Stewart (1688–1766), only son of James II and VII by Mary of Modena, recognized as King of England by Louis XIV 1701, retired to Lorraine 1713, in Scotland 1715–16, settled at Rome after failure of Spanish plot in 1719, died 1766.

*Kelly, George, an Irishman, imprisoned in Tower 1723–36 for suspected complicity in Atterbury Plot, one of the seven who sailed with Charles to Scotland 1745, carried despatches to French Court in Oct. 1745, subsequently served and was dismissed by Charles.

Ker, Colonel Henry, of Graden (1702–51), in Spanish service 1722–38, aide-de-camp to Charles and Lord George Murray in the '45, captured 1746, released 1748, died in Spanish service 1751.

*Kilmarnock, William Boyd, 4th Earl of (1704–46), raised a troop of horse for Charles after Prestonpans 1745, captured at Culloden and executed 1746.

*Kingston, Sir Evelyn Pierrepont, 2nd Duke of (1711–73), raised a cavalry regiment to oppose Charles 1745, disbanded at close of campaign.

Kinloch, Sir James, 3rd Baronet, commanded 2nd Battalion of Lord Ogilvy's regiment, made prisoner, but reprieved.

*Ligonier, Jean Louis (John), 1st Earl (1680–1770), served under Marlborough, commanded foot at Fontenoy 1745, commanded troops sent from Flanders to Scotland 1745.

*Loudoun, John Campbell, 4th Earl of (1705–82), accompanied Cope to Stirling in August 1745, received command of Independent Companies in the autumn of 1745, failed to surprise Charles at Moy 1746, after fall of Inverness withdrew to Skye, joined General Campbell in sweeping the Highlands after Culloden.

*Lovat, Simon Fraser, 12th Baron (1667?–1747), rallied his clan for the government 1715, in hope of a dukedom joined Association inviting Charles to Scotland, by his instructions the Frasers joined the Prince under his eldest son Simon, Master of Lovat (1726–82), held by Lord Loudoun as hostage for fidelity of clan, executed 1747.

Macdonald, Æneas, son of Ranald Macdonald of Kinlochmoidart and brother of Donald Macdonald of K., a Paris banker, accompanied Prince Charles to Scotland, surrendered 1746, condemned to death and pardoned, killed in Paris during the Revolution.

MACDONALD (or MACDONELL), ALASTAIR (1725–60), eldest son of John M. of Glengarry, identified by Mr A. Lang with Pickle the Spy, member of Charles' Council 1745.

MACDONALD, ALEXANDER, of Boisdale (1698–1768), step-brother to Clanranald, discouraged Charles at the outset, but befriended him after Culloden, was made prisoner 1746, released 1747.

MACDONALD, ALEXANDER, of Glenaladale, among the first to join Charles, and among the last to serve him during his Highland wanderings.

MACDONALD, ALEXANDER, of Glencoe, was 'out' in '15, member of Charles' Council 1745, surrendered after Culloden, in prison as late as 1750.

MACDONALD (or MACDONELL), ALEXANDER, of Keppoch, was 'out' in '15, among earliest to join Charles 1745, killed at Culloden.

MACDONALD, ALEXANDER, of Kingsburgh, factor of Sir Alexander M. of Sleat 1746, made prisoner for befriending Prince Charles, released from Edinburgh Castle 1747, died 1772.

MACDONALD, Sir ALEXANDER, of Sleat (Skye), 7th Baronet, restrained from joining Charles by Duncan Forbes' influence.

MACDONALD, ALLAN, of Morar, lieutenant-colonel of the Clanranald regiment, entertained Charles in July 1746.

MACDONALD, ALLAN, brother of Donald M. of Kinlochmoidart, escaped to France and perished in the Revolution.

MACDONALD, ANGUS, of Borradale, a son of John M., 5th laird of Glenaladale, Charles' host 1745–6, first cousin of Flora Macdonald. His son John provided the eight-oared boat that carried Princes Charles to the Isles.

MACDONALD (or MACDONELL), ANGUS, youngest son of John M. of Glengarry (*infra*), accidentally shot at Falkirk 1746.

MACDONALD (or MACDONELL), ANGUS, of Scotus, brother of Glengarry (Alexander M.) and Barrisdale (Archibald M.).

MACDONALD (or MACDONELL), ARCHIBALD, of Barrisdale, brother of Scotus and Glengarry, took no active part in Rising, but was made prisoner and released, died 1752.

MACDONALD (or MACDONELL), ARCHIBALD, grandson of Archibald M. of B. (*supra*), and son of Coll M. of B. (*infra*), major of the Glengarry regiment 1745, attainted 1746, arrested in connection with the Elibank plot 1753, released 1762, died 1787.

MACDONALD (or MACDONELL), COLL, son of Archibald M. of Barrisdale (*supra*), joined Charles at head of the Glengarry regiment and later raised regiment of his own, fought at Prestonpans and Falkirk, absent from Culloden, excluded from Act of Indemnity 1747, died 1750.

MACDONALD (or MACDONELL), DONALD, eldest son of John M. of Lochgarry, member of Charles' Council 1745, commanded Glengarry regiment, escaped to France with Charles, concerned in the abortive plot of 1752, died in Paris.

MACDONALD, DONALD, of Kinlochmoidart, nephew of Donald Cameron of Lochiel, brother of Æneas M. the Paris banker, made prisoner at Lesmahagow and hanged at Carlisle 1746.

MACDONALD (or MACDONELL), DONALD, eldest son of Angus M. of Scotus (d. 1746), joined Prince Charles with Glengarry 1745, wounded (? killed) at Culloden. His younger sons John and Allan were captains in Glengarry's regiment; his eldest son Ranald fought on the government side in Loudoun's regiment.

MACDONALD (or MACDONELL), DONALD, of Tiendrish (or Tirnadrish), cousin of Keppoch, was the first to draw blood in the Jacobite cause August 16, 1745, only Jacobite officer made prisoner at Falkirk, executed at Carlisle 1746.

MACDONALD, FLORA (1722–90), daughter of Ranald M., farmer at Milton, South Uist, imprisoned in Tower of London for abetting the Prince's escape, released by Act of Indemnity 1747, emigrated to North Carolina 1774, returned to Scotland 1779, died 1790.

MACDONALD, HUGH, step-brother of Allan M. of Morar, educated in France and consecrated Bishop of Diana in partibus 1731, Vicar-Apostolic of the Highlands, visited Charles on his arrival and implored him to return, but blessed the Standard at Glenfinnan, escaped to France with Charles 1746, died 1773.

MACDONALD, HUGH, of Baleshare, of the Sleat family, was sent in June 1746 to South Uist by Sir Alexander M. of Sleat's wife with money and comforts for the Prince. His sister was the wife of Donald Campbell, Charles' host in Scalpa.

MACDONALD, Captain JOHN, officer in French service (Carbineers), one of 'Seven Men of Moidart,' surrendered at Culloden.

MACDONALD (or MACDONELL), JOHN, of Glengarry, did not join Charles, imprisoned (1746) on an accusation of having ordered out his clan.

MACDONALD, RANALD, of Clanranald, assured Charles of his readiness to come 'out' 1744, but remained inactive.

MACDONALD, RANALD, younger, of Clanranald, one of Charles' Council 1745, escaped to France after Culloden, returned to England and imprisoned 1752, released 1754, died 1777.

MACGILLIVRAY, ALEXANDER, of Dunmaglass, commanded the Mackintoshes 1745, killed at Culloden.

MACGREGOR, GREGOR, of Glengyle (1689–1777), participated in
capture of Fort of Inversnaid 1745, not present at Culloden.

MACGREGOR (or DRUMMOND), WILLIAM, of Balhaldie, son of Sir
Alexander M. of B., grandson of Sir Ewen Cameron of Lochiel,
fought at Sheriffmuir 1715, agent to Chevalier de St George 1740.
See R. L. Stevenson's *Catriona*.

MACKINNON, JOHN, of Mackinnon, joined Prince Charles at Edinburgh
1745, absent at Culloden, conducted Charles from Skye to mainland 1746, arrested and released 1747, died in 1756.

MACKINTOSH, ANNE, of Mackintosh, daughter of James Farquharson,
9th of Invercauld (1723–87), m. Æneas M., 22nd of Mackintosh
(a captain in Loudoun's regiment), raised her clan for Prince
Charles and foiled Loudoun's attempt to capture him at Moy
1746, arrested and released after Culloden.

MACLACHLAN, LACHLAN, of Maclachlan, Commissary-General in
Charles' army, sent from Carlyle to order clans in Scotland to
follow Charles into England, killed at Culloden, where he commanded united regiment of Maclachlans and Macleans.

MACLEAN, CHARLES, of Drimnin, lieutenant-colonel of united regiment
of Maclachlans and Macleans, joined Charles after Falkirk, killed
at Culloden.

MACLEAN, Sir HECTOR, of Duart, 5th Baronet (1704–50), major in
Lord John Drummond's French regiment of Royal Scots, sent to
Scotland to announce Charles' coming 1745, captured and ulti-
mately treated as prisoner of war, died at Rome 1750.

MACLEOD, ALEXANDER, son of John Macleod of Muiravonside, Stirling,
aide-de-camp to Lord George Murray at Culloden.

MACLEOD, DONALD, of Gualtergil, on Dunvegan Loch, Skye, through
his wife related to Borradale and Flora Macdonald, Charles' guide
April-June 1746, captured (1746) and released 1747, died 1749,
aged 72.

MACLEOD, Lord, eldest son of George Mackenzie, 3rd Earl of
Cromarty, made prisoner with his father at Golspie on April 15,
1746.

MACLEOD, MALCOLM, joined Charles after Prestonpans, conveyed him
from Skye to Raasay, made prisoner July 1746, released 1747.

MACLEOD, NORMAN, 19th of Macleod (1706–72), engaged to join
Charles, but broke his word, sided with the government.

MACPHERSON, EVAN, younger, of Cluny, eldest son of Lachlan M. of

C., held a commission in George II's service but joined Prince Charles, entertained him in Cluny's Cage in Ben Alder 1746, entrusted with distribution of the Loch Arkaig treasure, died at Dunkirk 1756.

*Marischal, George Keith, 10th Earl (1693?–1778), engaged in the '15 and '19, corresponded with Charles but took no part in the '45.

Menzies, ——, of Shian, led his clan at Prestonpans.

*Milton, Andrew Fletcher, Lord (1692–1766), Lord Justice Clerk 1735–48.

Moir, James, 3rd of Stonywood (1712–86), commanded regiment raised by Lord Lewis Gordon, engaged at Inverurie, escaped to Continent, permitted to return 1762.

Monro, Captain George, of Culcairn (1685–1746), brother of Sir Robert M. of Foulis, joined Cope at Inverness, shot on the roadside August 1746.

*Mordaunt, General Sir John (1697–1780), brigadier-general at Falkirk and Culloden.

*Murray, Lord George (1700?–60), son of 1st Duke of Atholl, 'out' in '15 and '19, joined Prince Charles at Perth 1745, retired to France after Culloden, died in Holland 1760.

*Murray, Lord John (1711–87), son of 1st Duke of Atholl and brother of Lord George M., colonel of the 42nd Foot (Black Watch) 1745–87.

Murray, John, of Broughton. See *supra*, p. xi.

*Nairne, John, 3rd Baron, son of 2nd Baron, made prisoner at Preston 1715, marched into England 1745, escaped after Culloden, died in France 1770.

*Norris, Admiral Sir John (1660?–1749), commanded Channel fleet 1739–44.

*Ogilvy, David, Lord, titular Earl of Airlie (1725–1803), commanded Jacobite cavalry during retreat from Derby, at Falkirk and Culloden 1746, escaped to France, restored to full rights 1782.

*Oglethorpe, James Edward (1696–1785), brigadier-general 1743, served in Lancashire against the Jacobites 1745.

O'Neil, Captain Felix, captain in Lally's French-Irish regiment, sent to Scotland with despatches from France 1746, shared Charles' discomforts after Culloden, captured in Benbecula and released on parole from Edinburgh Castle 1747.

*Ormonde, James Butler, 2nd Duke of (1665–1745), recognised leader of English Jacobites, attainted 1715, commanded Spanish fleet for Stewart restoration 1719, visited Madrid to suggest invasion of England 1740, proposed to take part in French expedition from Dunkirk 1744.

*O'Sullivan, Colonel John William, born 1700, an Irishman educated in France, in French service, entered Charles' household 1744, accompanied the Prince on his Highland wanderings 1746, escaped to France, created a baronet of Ireland 1753.

*Perth, James Drummond, 3rd titular Duke of (1713–46), son of James D., 2nd titular Duke, educated at Douay, lieutenant-general of Jacobite army, died on voyage to France 1746.

*Pitsligo, Alexander Forbes, 4th and last Baron (1678–1762), took part in the '15, escaped to France, returned to Scotland 1720, raised a regiment 1745.

Reay, George Mackay, 3rd Baron (1678–1748), consistently supported the established dynasty in 1715, 1719 and 1745.

Rutledge, Walter, Irish merchant at Dunkirk, joined Anthony Walsh in advancing money carried by Charles in the *Du Teillay*.

Scot, Captain John, afterwards general, of Balcomie, captured in first skirmish of the campaign 1745, released on parole.

Scott, Captain Carolina Frederick, of Guises regiment, active in search for Prince Charles 1746.

Sempill, Francis, son and heir of Robert S. (created a peer of Scotland (*circ.* 1723) by the Chevalier de St George, d. at Paris 1737), Jacobite agent at French Court, died 1748.

Sheridan, Sir Thomas, son of Thomas S. (Fellow of Trinity College, Dublin), engaged in the '15, tutor to Prince Charles 1724 or 1725, created a baronet 1726, accompanied Charles to Scotland 1745, escaped to France and died at Rome 1746.

*Stair, John Dalrymple, 2nd Earl of (1673–1747), commander-in-chief in England 1744.

Stapleton, Walter, lieutenant-colonel in French service (Berwick's regiment), died of wounds received at Culloden 1746.

Stewart, Alexander, of Invernahyle, 'out' in 1715, brought up the Appin men after Prestonpans, in hiding after Culloden.

Stewart, Archibald, Provost of Edinburgh, tried (1747) and acquitted for surrendering Edinburgh to Charles 1745.

Stewart, Charles, 5th of Ardshiel, led the Stewarts of Appin in Appin's place 1745, escaped to France 1746, died 1757.

Stewart, Dugald, 8th of Appin, titular Lord Appin 1743, did not join Charles, sold Appin 1765, died 1769.

Stewart (or Steuart), Sir James, 2nd Baronet of Goodtrees, born

1712, joined Charles at Holyrood 1745, excepted from Indemnity Act 1747, pardoned 1771, died 1780.

STEWART, JOHN ROY, formerly quartermaster of Scots Greys, later in French service, sent to France with report of Culloden, rejoined Charles September 1746 and returned with him to France.

*STRATHALLAN, WILLIAM DRUMMOND, 4th Viscount (1690–1746), made prisoner at Sheriffmuir 1715, released 1717, killed at Culloden.

STRICKLAND, FRANCIS, companion to Charles in Italy, accompanied him to Scotland, died at Carlisle 1746.

*TOWNELEY, FRANCIS (1709–46), commissioned by Louis XV to raise English forces to support Charles, joined him at Manchester and accompanied him to Carlisle, captured there and executed 1746.

TRAQUAIR, CHARLES STUART, 5th Earl of, opposed Charles' landing without French aid, took no part in the '45, imprisoned in Tower and released, died 1764.

*TWEEDDALE, JOHN HAY, 4th Marquess of, Secretary of State for Scotland 1742–46, died 1762.

*WADE, Field-Marshal GEORGE (1673–1748), made military roads in Scotland 1726–33, field-marshal 1743, commander-in-chief in England 1745, superseded for failing to stop Charles' advance.

*WALSH, ANTOINE VINCENT (1702–63), of Irish extraction, born at St Malo, shipowner at Nantes, accompanied Charles to Scotland, created an Irish Earl by Chevalier de St George, ennobled by Louis XV 1755, died in St Domingo.

WEIR, or VERE, a government spy, principal witness against prisoners taken at Carlisle.

*WHITEFOORD, Captain CHARLES, fought under Cope as volunteer at Prestonpans, died 1753.

WHITNEY, Lieutenant-Colonel, commanded a squadron of 14th Hussars at Prestonpans, killed at Falkirk 1746.

*YORKE, JOSEPH, Baron Dover (1724–92), aide-de-camp to Cumberland in Scotland 1745–6.

INDEX

For EU product safety concerns, contact us at Calle de José Abascal, 56–1°, 28003 Madrid, Spain or eugpsr@cambridge.org.

www.ingramcontent.com/pod-product-compliance
Ingram Content Group UK Ltd.
Pitfield, Milton Keynes, MK11 3LW, UK
UKHW012335130625
459647UK00009B/294